LGBT
Families

Contemporary Family Perspectives

Series Editor
Susan J. Ferguson
Grinnell College

Volumes in the Series

LGBT

Families

CONTEMPORARY
FAMILY
PERSPECTIVES

NANCY J. MEZEY

Monmouth University

SUSAN J. FERGUSON, SERIES EDITOR

$SAGE

Los Angeles | London | New Delhi
Singapore | Washington DC

Los Angeles | London | New Delhi
Singapore | Washington DC

FOR INFORMATION:

SAGE Publications, Inc.
2455 Teller Road
Thousand Oaks, California 91320
E-mail: order@sagepub.com

SAGE Publications Ltd.
1 Oliver's Yard
55 City Road
London EC1Y 1SP
United Kingdom

SAGE Publications India Pvt. Ltd.
B 1/I 1 Mohan Cooperative Industrial Area
Mathura Road, New Delhi 110 044
India

SAGE Publications Asia-Pacific Pte. Ltd.
3 Church Street
#10-04 Samsung Hub
Singapore 049483

Acquisitions Editor: Jeff Lasser
Editorial Assistant: Nick Pachelli
Production Editor: Melanie Birdsall
Copy Editor: Patrice Sutton
Typesetter: C&M Digitals (P) Ltd.
Proofreader: Victoria Reed-Castro
Indexer: Maria Sosnowski
Cover Designer: Candice Harman
Marketing Manager: Erica DeLuca

Copyright © 2015 by SAGE Publications, Inc.

Printed in the United States of America

Library of Congress Cataloging-in-Publication Data

Mezey, Nancy J.

LGBT families / Nancy J. Mezey, Monmouth University.

pages cm. — (Contemporary family perspectives)

Includes bibliographical references and index.

ISBN 978-1-4522-1738-3 (pbk. : alk. paper)

1. Gay parents—United States. 2. Gay couples—United States. 3. Lesbian couples—United States. 4. Sexual minorities' families—United States. I. Title.

HQ75.28.U6M49 2015

306.874086′6—dc23   2014014478

This book is printed on acid-free paper.

14 15 16 17 18 10 9 8 7 6 5 4 3 2 1

Contents

Series Preface

The family is one of the most private and pervasive social institutions in U.S. society. At the same time, public discussions and debates about the institution of the family persist. Some scholars and public figures claim that the family is declining or dying, or that the contemporary family is morally deficient. Other scholars argue that the family is caught in the larger culture wars currently taking place in the United States. The recent debates on the right of same-sex couples to marry are one example of this larger public discussion about the institution of the family. Regardless of one's perspective that the family is declining or caught in broader political struggles, scholars agree that the institution has undergone dramatic transformations in recent decades. U.S. demographic data reveal that fewer people are married, divorce rates remain high at almost 50%, and more families are living in poverty. In addition, people are creating new kinds of families via Internet dating, cohabitation, single-parent adoption, committed couples living apart, donor insemination, and polyamorous relationships. The demographic data and ethnographic research on new family forms require that family scholars pay attention to a variety of family structures, processes, ideologies, and social norms. In particular, scholars need to address important questions about the family, such as, what is the future of marriage? Is divorce harmful to individuals, to the institution of the family, and/or to society? Why are rates of family violence so high? Are we living in a postdating culture? How do poverty and welfare policies affect families? How is childrearing changing now that so many parents work outside the home and children spend time with caretakers other than their parents? Finally, how are families socially constructed in different societies and cultures?

Most sociologists and family scholars agree that the family is a dynamic social institution that is continually changing as other social structures and individuals in society change. The family also is a social construction with complex and shifting age, gender, race, and social class meanings. Many excellent studies are currently investigating the changing structures of the institution of the family and the lived experiences and meanings of families. Contemporary Family Perspectives is a series of short texts and research monographs that provides a forum for the best of this burgeoning scholarship. The series aims to recognize the diversity of families that exist in the United States and globally. A second goal is for the series to better inform pedagogy and future family scholarship about this diversity of families. The series also seeks to connect family scholarship to a broader audience beyond the classroom by informing the public and by ensuring that family studies remain central to contemporary policy debates and to social action. Each short text contains the most outstanding current scholarship on the family from a variety of disciplines, including sociology, demography, policy studies, social work, human development, and psychology. Moreover, each short text is authored by a leading family scholar or scholars who bring their unique disciplinary perspective to an understanding of contemporary families.

Contemporary Family Perspectives provides the most advanced scholarship and up-to-date findings on the family. Each volume provides a brief overview of significant scholarship on that family topic, including critical current debates or areas of scholarly disagreement. In addition to providing an assessment of the latest findings related to their family topic, authors also examine the family, utilizing an intersectional framework of race-ethnicity, social class, gender, and sexuality. Much of the research is inter-disciplinary, with a number of theoretical frameworks and methodological approaches presented. Several of the family scholars use a historical lens as well to ground their contemporary research. A particular strength of the series is that the short texts appeal to undergraduate students as well as to family scholars, but they are written in a way that makes them accessible to a larger public.

About This Volume

In June 2013, the U.S. Supreme Court ruled against the Defense of Marriage Act (DOMA), clearing the way for gay and lesbian couples to obtain access to federal marriage benefits in the United States. At the same time, the Supreme Court declined to hear a case from California that would deny marriage to same-sex couples. As of March 2014, 17 states plus the District of Columbia now allow same-sex couples to marry. These recent landmark legal decisions cannot be fully understood without first studying the history of LGBT families. *LGBT Families* is a comprehensive research volume that examines how LGBT families are shaped by history, and how these changes in marriage laws have come about. The author, Nancy J. Mezey (Monmouth University), has studied LGBT families for more than ten years and has published articles and a book, *New Choices, New Families: How Lesbians Decide about Motherhood* (The Johns Hopkins Press, 2008). This timely volume expands on Mezey's earlier ethnographic research to examine more broadly the diversity of LGBT families in the United States.

Mezey argues that LGBT families are socially constructed and therefore defined by history, economics, and other social factors. Mezey also states that most of the problems LGBT families face are the result of homophobia, heterosexism, and gender discrimination. As such, scholars and students alike need to appreciate the sources of this discrimination and the fear many people have of sexual difference. Mezey believes that if we can learn more about LGBT families, we can become stronger advocates for social change, including making better policies for LGBT families.

Mezey begins in the first chapter by defining what LGBT families are, providing a brief history and explaining how she will examine these families using a sociological lens. After laying this groundwork, Mezey turns her attention to marriage equality and why LGBT activists have focused on this issue. The next two chapters focus in turn on adult and parenting relationships and then on LGBT children and youth. Understanding how LGBT people decide to become parents or not and the different challenges facing them is central to appreciating this family form. Mezey also examines the work-family balance, the division of household labor, and other family and work issues. The chapter on LGBT youth explores identity and the struggles many LGBT children face. Sadly, due to discrimination, many LGBT youth encounter bullying, familial rejection, or experience mental health issues. These factors encourage all of us to demand changes to support children and youth growing up LGBT-identified. The last substantive chapter turns our attention to intimate partner violence and what we know about its prevalence and nature within LGBT relationships and families. Mezey concludes this volume with an emphasis on what we can learn from LGBT families. Simply put, to understand the institution of the family in the 21st century, we need to understand how LGBT families form and their diversity across the United States. Mezey also argues that LGBT families benefit society. Mezey ends by providing suggestions for strengthening LGBT families.

A unique feature of this book is Mezey's use of Global Boxes that examine policies and issues related to LGBT and families from around the globe. While most of Mezey's analysis is on LGBT families in the United States, this added feature, written by Morganne Firmstone, enables readers to understand better some of the different issues faced by LGBT people in other countries.

LGBT Families is appropriate for use in any class concerned with family structure, family policy, social inequality, gender and sexuality, and how government affects which families are legally recognized. This book is a valuable resource to teachers and students in beginning and advanced courses in sociology, family studies, women's and gender studies, LGBT studies, social work, public policy, and other disciplines. It also finds an audience in any person interested in comparative family studies or among those who work in various human services fields, including human development, social work, education, counseling, health services, and the government. This last statement is particularly true for social service employees who work with lesbian, gay, bisexual, or transgendered populations. This volume can help them to better understand how discrimination and governmental policy can dramatically impact LGBT individuals and their families.

—Susan J. Ferguson
Grinnell College

Preface and Acknowledgments

My purpose in writing this book has been to add to the series on Contemporary Family Perspectives by presenting and analyzing research on lesbian, gay, bisexual, and transgender (LGBT) families. My aim was to be as inclusive as possible, to focus not just on lesbian and gay but also on bisexual and transgender people, and to include a diversity of research across racial, class, and age boundaries. At the suggestion of Susan Ferguson, series editor, I wanted to provide an analysis of the research on LGBT families. Studying and writing about LGBT families is certainly not a neutral endeavor. And while I try to be as objective as possible in my presentation of the research, the main purpose of this book is to highlight four main points:

1. LGBT families, like all families, are socially constructed. This means that how we define family, the experiences that people have within families, and the privileges bestowed upon or denied to certain families are based on historical, economic, social, cultural, and political factors, not on biological mandates.

2. Nearly every problem that LGBT people around the world face as LGBT people—including those in the United States—are due to heterosexism, homophobia, and dominant gender norms that define masculinity and femininity in ways that leave little if any room for variation. In other words, the problems LGBT families and people face are caused by factors external to themselves. However, people around the world are quick to blame LGBT people for problems that are caused by other factors.

3. People's fears of LGBT people, as strong as those fears may be, are unfounded. Such fears are based on beliefs, not on facts. The facts show that LGBT families do not harm society; indeed LGBT families benefit society in a variety of ways.

4. A change in policies, coupled with the continuing change of hearts and minds, will lead to equality for LGBT people and eliminate many of the problems facing LGBT people and their families today.

I address these four points throughout the book.

The literature that I analyze focuses almost exclusively on LGBT families in the United States. However, I recognize that life in the United States does not represent the lives of those around the world. Therefore, through Global Boxes written by Morganne Firmstone, a graduate of Monmouth University's master of public policy program, the book addresses some issues and policies related to LGBT people and families around the world. Morganne's writing of the Global Boxes provides readers a glimpse into some of the issues that LGBT people face in different countries and the ways in which different countries both support and greatly hinder the rights of people of diverse gender and sexual identities. I am particularly grateful to Morganne for her hard work and thank her for the research and writing she did to complete the Global Boxes, as well as the film, DVD, and web resources she provided at the end of Chapters 1 through 5.

In addition to Morganne, I owe thanks to many others who have helped me in a variety of ways through the process of writing this book. First and foremost, I thank Susan Ferguson for encouraging me to submit a prospectus to Sage, and for guiding and supporting my work throughout the research and writing process. I am honored and thrilled to have the opportunity to work with Susan and be part of the Contemporary Family Perspectives series. I also thank my Sage editor, Jeff Lasser, as well as Melanie Birdsall, Patricia Sutton, and the Sage staff for all their help and support. They have helped make the writing and publications process a truly pleasurable one.

Thank you to Maxine Baca Zinn for reading and commenting on my original prospectus. Her suggestions to include elder LGBT people and provide a global focus were very valuable. I also thank Johanna Foster for her support and comments on early drafts of the first several chapters. I owe a special thanks to Monmouth University for granting me a summer sabbatical, thus providing me with concentrated time and funding to work on a significant portion of the book. Thank you also to the faculty and staff in the Department of Political Science and Sociology for covering my administrative duties while I was writing.

In addition to my mentors, colleagues, and friends in academia, my personal friends and family were also instrumental in helping me complete this work. Many thanks to Donel Young who had the wonderful ability to thoughtfully help me focus my work. Donel was particularly instrumental by asking the question, "Why do straight people fear LGBT people so much?" I also thank Donel for helping me shape Chapter 6 and for encouraging me to keep an eye to a broad audience who will hopefully benefit from reading the book.

I thank my parents, sisters, in-laws, and extended family for exemplifying how support can lead people to comfortably and successfully pursue their goals and dreams. Thank you to my children Jack and Sophie for keeping me sane and reminding me that parenthood is the toughest job I will ever love. And most of all, I thank my partner, Karen. Not only is she my rock and keeps me grounded, but she also edits my work.

—Nancy J. Mezey
Monmouth University

Publisher's Acknowledgments

SAGE gratefully acknowledges the contributions of the following reviewers:

Pamela J. Forman, University of Wisconsin–Eau Claire

Sara Raley, McDaniel College

Jill M. Smith, The Ohio State University

About the Author

Dr. Nancy J. Mezey received her PhD in sociology from Michigan State University. She is currently an Associate Professor of Sociology, the Sociology Program Director, and advisor to the Sociology Club at Monmouth University. At Monmouth, Dr. Mezey has also served as the chair of the faculty governance body, was Associate Director and Director of the Institute for Global Understanding, and was the 2011 recipient of the Distinguished Teacher Award. Her areas of specialization are family sociology, gender studies, the sociology of sexualities, race-class-gender studies, and qualitative methods. Her research focuses largely on how historical factors, social inequalities, social activism, and policies shape and affect new family forms. Her first book, *New Choices, New Families: How Lesbians Decide about Motherhood*, is a multiracial feminist study of how lesbians decide to become mothers or remain childfree. Dr. Mezey has also published in a variety of academic journals and books in the areas of LGBT families and intimate partner violence. She is an active member of the Society for the Study of Social Problems (SSSP), where she has held several elected and appointed positions, and is an engaged member of Sociologists for Women in Society (SWS) as well as several other sociological organizations. Dr. Mezey is also a returned Peace Corps Volunteer where she served in Mali, West Africa, from 1988 to 1990.

This book is dedicated to
Ann Stein
and
Dorothy Cerami
Two devoutly religious people who understood that
love really does make a family.

1

LGBT Families

My grandpa majored in biology in college, but he wasn't allowed to teach at a high school because he was black. Not long ago, I spoke on a panel at a high school with my mom. This guy in the audience told my mom that he wouldn't want her to teach his kids because she is a lesbian. It reminded me so much of what happened to my grandpa. I think homophobia is like any other "ism."...Like racism, you learn it from the people you grow up with, from your parents, from television, and from society.

—Rayna White, eleventh grader, daughter
of a lesbian mother (PrideSource, 2013, para. 9)

What we collectively define and accept as family has far-reaching implications. The boundaries that we—and others—make between family and nonfamily play both subtle and not-so-subtle roles in our daily lives.

—Powell et al., 2010, pp. 1–2

Because of cultural, political, and religious debates over the past several decades about how families must be structured and function in order to perform a productive role in society, lesbian, gay, bisexual, and transgender (LGBT) families have captured the interest of politicians, academics, and the general public. Fierce debates persist concerning who should be able to form families through marriage, adoption, and the use of reproductive technologies. Policies and laws concerning families in general are developing out of those debates, thus reacting to a changing family landscape and in turn shaping a new family landscape. Amid the debates and changing laws, members of LGBT communities are negotiating the political, cultural, and social terrain that regulate their material and ideological access to the title of "family." Therefore, if we want to understand how families are changing today, and how those families fit into, are shaped by, and also shape larger society, then we must understand one of the most important growing segments of current families: LGBT families.

In 2010, there were approximately 594,000 same-sex partner households in the United States making up about 1% of all American households (Krivickas & Lofquist, 2011) spread over 99% of all counties in the United States (Gates & Ost, 2004). Of the total 594,000 households, 115,000 (19.3%) reported having children living with them, 84% of whom were children of the householder. In 2008, 13.9% of male-male unmarried households, and 26.5% of female-female unmarried households reported having children (Krivickas & Lofquist, 2011). The numbers of lesbian and gay households with children have increased since 2000 when estimates suggested that only 5% of partnered gay men and 22% of partnered lesbians had children in their households (Black, Gates, Sanders, & Taylor, 2000). While these numbers do not take into account single lesbians and gay men, bisexual women and men, and transgender people who are not living in same-sex households, the data offer some evidence that there is an increasing and substantial number of families in the United States that are headed at minimum by lesbian and gay parents. In addition, in 2010, approximately 78% of LGB people in the United States said they would like the right to marry (Herek, Norton, Allen, & Sims, 2010). In practice, by 2010 government offices within seven states and Washington, D.C. had issued at minimum 41,700 marriage licenses to same-sex couples (Chamie & Mirkin, 2011). The number of states allowing lesbians and gay men to marry has increased from one state (Massachusetts) in 2003 to 19 states plus the District of Columbia by the middle of 2014. Coupled with the U.S. Supreme Court's 2013 verdict that the federal government must honor all legal state marriages regardless of the sexual identity of those married, we can expect to see the number of married lesbians and gay men increase, as well as an increase in visibility of LGBT families within public arenas, because of changing marriage laws.

Social science research strongly suggests that families are socially, not biologically, constructed. This means that the ways in which families are formed—the roles and functions families perform, their structure in terms of who occupies them, and the experiences of their members—are born out of the social, economic, cultural, political, and historical context in which those families exist. There is nothing natural, or normal, or biologically inherent or mandated about any particular family type. We can see how families are socially constructed by studying how families have changed throughout history and how they are structured and function in different geographic locations. Therefore, as a sociologist who understands families to be socially constructed, I wonder about three particular questions: (a) How and why do different family forms develop in particular social and historical contexts, (b) why are new family forms so threatening to certain groups of people in society, and (c) how are new family forms beneficial to the society in which they exist?

Based on the current trends in LGBT families and on my three questions above, the purpose of the book *LGBT Families* is to provide an understanding of what LGBT families are, why they have developed at this historical moment, how they are socially constructed, why conservative thinkers perceive LGBT families to be a threat to society, and how LGBT families are in fact an important and positive addition to the U.S. family landscape. The book draws on cutting-edge scholarship and data concerning LGBT families, focusing specifically on social constructionist and intersectional (i.e., race-class-gender-sexuality) perspectives. In doing so, *LGBT Families* highlights the diversity of such families in the United States, as well as globally. This book not only organizes and presents current research on LGBT families, but it also uses that research to better understand how LGBT families strengthen the institution of family. In addition, although the book focuses primarily on the experiences of people within LGBT families, a major theme of how external forces shape these families runs throughout the book in order to place LGBT families in a sociological context.

To start the conversation of what LGBT families are and how they have formed historically, this initial chapter first deconstructs and defines key terms. Then, to illustrate how LGBT families have been socially constructed out of the culmination of several historical factors, the chapter provides a brief history of the development of LGBT families. The chapter then focuses on current barriers that LGBT families face, and finishes with a discussion of the plan of the remaining book.

Deconstructing and Defining Terms

The connection between an active and effective LGBT rights movement, an equally active and effective conservative movement against LGBT families, and policies and laws concerning issues such as marriage and immigration have led to a public discourse on what constitutes family and where LGBT families fit into the current U.S. family landscape. As the quote by Powell and his colleagues at the beginning of this chapter states, how we define family and who we accept as having legitimate claims to being recognized as a family has both serious implications for the United States and beyond, as well as for the individuals within those families.

Although the term *LGBT families* seems simple enough, the deconstruction of this term illustrates the complexities within LGBT families themselves. While teaching family sociology courses over the past 15 years or so, and through the reading of a variety of sources, I have developed and use the following definition of family: Family is a social institution found in all societies comprising two or more people related by birth, law, or intimate affectionate relationships, who may or may not reside together. I use the above definition because it includes as many configurations of families about which I have read or heard. The more we learn about the diversity of families, the more we can test and stretch our definitions of "family." For example, some of my students argue that the definition should include animal companions (aka "pets") as well. In fact, in their study of who Americans count as family, Powell, Bolzendahl, Geist, and Steelman (2010) found that 51% of those surveyed believe that pets count as family. While that fact is interesting, what is more interesting is that only 30% of Americans count gay and lesbian couples without children to be family. So, as these authors pointedly remark, more Americans believe that pets count as family than do gay and lesbian couples (p. 45).

To be clear, my definition of family is not one accepted by a court of law or upon which politicians base family policy. Legal definitions of family generally include people who are connected only by bloodlines or legal ties (e.g., marriage, adoption, legal guardianship, and foster care), although some judges are beginning to use social definitions of family particularly in determining court cases involving LGBT families (Richman, 2009).

I use an inclusive definition for this book because while "family" is a legal term, it is also an ideological and socially constructed term that means many different things to many different people. Family is an *idea* about how human relationships *should* be organized. How as a society we define family, who we think should be included or not included in our families, the functions of families, and the structure of families, change over time and over geographic location or space. So there is nothing fixed or innate or "natural" about families. In other words, what families look like and how we think about them depends on the social and historical context and moment in which we are thinking about them. The definition of family above works well for this book not only because LGBT families fit into that definition but also because the definition allows us to compare other definitions used throughout judicial and political systems.

Thinking about the definition of family in general also leads to a question that Judith Stacey asked in her 1996 book, *In the Name of the Family*: What is an LGBT family? In trying to answer this question, Stacey asked additional questions:

Should we count only families in which every single member is gay? Clearly there are not very many, if even any, of these. Or does the presence of just one gay member color a family gay? Just as clearly, there are many of these, including those of Ronald Reagan, Colin Powell, Phyllis Schafly and Newt Gingrich. (1996, p. 107)

Stacey's question of what we mean by LGBT families is important. In 1991, Kath Weston published a book called *Families We Choose*, in which she argued that gays and lesbians have been "exiles from kinship" (Weston, 1991). She wrote that "for years, and in an amazing variety of contexts, claiming a lesbian or gay identity has been portrayed as a rejection of 'the family' and a departure from kinship" (p. 22). In other words, until very recently, media and other public portrayals of LGBT people assumed that "LGBT" and "family" could not possibly go together. This portrayal was based on two assumptions: (a) that gays and lesbians cannot or do not have children, and (b) anyone who is LGBT must have been rejected by, and therefore alienated from, their families of origin (e.g., their parents, siblings, grandparents, aunts, uncles, cousins, etc.).

Current data and research provide strong evidence that these two assumptions are no longer (if they ever were) true. So what is an LGBT family? Not only Stacey, but other social scientists have also grappled with this question. As Baca Zinn, Eitzen, and Wells (2011) stated, defining LGBT families is difficult "because individuals—not families—have sexual orientation" (p. 429). These authors point out that typically members of families often have sexual identities that differ from one another. Furthermore, sexual identities can change over a life course such that a family member may embrace a particular sexual or gender identity at one point but then later in life embrace another sexual or gender identity. Therefore, defining an LGBT family can be difficult.

Some scholars define LGBT families by the presence of one or more LGBT adults in the family (Allen & Demo, 1995). Others have included "couples, parents, children, and youth, as well as intentional communities" within the definition of LGBT families (Doherty, 2006, p. xxii). For the purpose of this book, I drew on previous definitions, as well as my own general definition of family, to define LGBT families as two or more people related by birth, law, or intimate affectionate relationships, who may or may not reside together, and where the LGBT identity of at least one family member impacts other family members in some meaningful way. This definition is intentionally broad to be as inclusive as possible.

Built into my definition of LGBT families are a variety of sexual and gender identities. Trying to define sexual and gender categories is not always easy, particularly if we understand such categories to be socially constructed, that is, gaining their purpose and meaning from the social, cultural, political, economic, and historical context in which they are created. In fact, queer theory challenges traditional sexual categories and shows how these categories are "products of particular constellations of power and knowledge" (Epstein, 1994, p. 192). Queer theorists, such as Eve Kosofsky Sedgwick (1993) and Judith Butler (1993), have problematized sexual categories. For example, Sedgwick argues that sexualities have traditionally been couched in false dichotomies. The notions of out versus in, gay versus straight, male versus female all lead to a false view that masks the fluid and mutable nature of human sexuality. Butler also argues that gender and sexual categories are unstable and contestable because they rely on the social and historical moment in which they exist (Butler, 1993). By revealing how unstable categories really are, there is no end to the ways in which queer theorists can deconstruct gender and sexual categories. Sociologists tend to depart from queer theory at the point of endless deconstruction because sociologists are interested in understanding how underlying and unifying factors create similar experiences for different groups of people based on social structural factors, such as sexuality, as well as race, social class, and gender (Epstein, 1994). That is, sociologists want to examine how the categorization of people is "materially experienced across the world" by specific groups of people (Stein & Plummer, 1994, p. 184).

In defining sexual categories, we tend to use terms that identify the gender toward whom our emotional, romantic, or sexual attractions are directed (Stryker, 2008); for example, "'heterosexual' (toward a member of another gender), 'homosexual' (toward a member of the same gender), 'bisexual' (toward a member of any gender)" (Stryker 2008, p. 16). To complicate matters even more, historian Susan Stryker (2008) pointed out that the sexual terms mentioned above "depend on our understanding of our own gender"; that is, the terms homo- and hetero- "make sense only in relation to a gender they are the 'same as' or 'different from'" (p. 16). If people do not have a fixed or clear gender identity (as discussed below) then definitions of sexual categories begin to lose meaning.

Perhaps to avoid confusion about how sexuality and gender relate to one another, the American Psychological Association (APA, 2013) defined sexual categories by referring to attractions based on someone's "sex" rather than "gender." The distinction between the two is that we think of "sex" as being the biological makeup that determines if someone is physically male or female, which is often easier to identify than gender (i.e., "the socially learned behaviors and expectations associated with being men and women") (Andersen & Witham, 2011, p. 418). Yet in her work on people who are intersexual (i.e., who have ambiguous genitalia), biologist Anne Fausto-Sterling (1993, 2000) suggested that there are at least five different varieties of "sex" found in the biological world. Thus, even our desire to construct and maintain the myth of only two biological sexes (female and male) is in fact socially constructed. All this is to say that the definitions of heterosexual, homosexual, and bisexual (referring to the possibility of only desiring two—"bi"—sexes, rather than two *or more* sexes) are based on limited, if not false understandings of the biological, psychological, and sociological world.

Sociologists argue that although we as a society must understand that categories based on sexual and gender identities are problematic and that the lines between and among these categories are in reality blurry and unclear, we must also understand that many of our laws, policies, practices, and beliefs are based on distinct categories. Furthermore, in order to understand how people in sexual and gender categories create and experience family life, we also need to have some understanding of how we as a society define sexual and gender categories. We also need to understand how people and systems use those categories to dole out rewards and resources in unequal ways such that we have developed discrimination based on seemingly real, yet socially constructed, gender and sexual categories. Such discrimination includes homophobia (the fear of gays and lesbians), biphobia (the fear of bisexual people), transphobia (the fear of transgender people), heterosexism (the assumption that being heterosexual is best, and the systematic privileging of heterosexuals over people who are not heterosexual), as well as more commonly understood sexism, racism, classism, ageism, and so on.

So how do we define sexual and gender categories? "Gay" generally refers to men who have emotional, romantic, and sexual attractions to other men, although some women also refer to themselves as gay. "Lesbian" refers almost exclusively to women who have emotional, romantic, and sexual attractions to other women (APA, 2008), although there are some men who refer to themselves as "male lesbians." These are men who either wish that they "had been born a woman, but who (even if he had been a woman) could only make love to another woman and never to a man" (Gilmartin, 1987, p. 125) or who embody the "ideological, ethical, or political posture" of lesbians (Zita, 1992, p. 110). Bisexual refers to people who have emotional, romantic, and sexual attractions to multiple genders (Burleson, 2005; Seidman, 2009). The category of bisexual is complicated because there are many compound bisexual identities as well, such as "lesbian-identified bisexual," "bisexual lesbian," "gay bisexual," and "heterosexual-identified bisexual" (Rust, 2000, p. 39). In addition, attraction does not necessarily imply action. Therefore, although bisexual people may be attracted to more than one gender, they may not act on that attraction (Burleson, 2005) and thus may appear to outsiders as heterosexual or as lesbian or gay if they remain in committed, monogamous relationships.

In addition to sexual categories, definitions of gender categories can be complicated as well. In general, people refer to two main gender categories, based on two main biological sexes: male and female. Male refers to those born with XY chromosomes and female to those born with XX chromosomes. When these sex categories gain social and cultural meaning, they become gender categories, such that people develop masculine and feminine identities. Masculinity is the collection of cultural ideas, beliefs, values, and norms that shape what dominant society considers appropriate social action for those assigned the status of boys and men. Femininity is the same except for girls and women. Not all masculinities and femininities are equally valued and rewarded, however. Gender scholar R. W. Connell (1987) explained that there is a hegemonic masculinity against which all other masculinities are measured. Hegemony refers to dominance; thus, hegemonic masculinity is the most dominant and socially accepted form of masculinity that maintains patriarchy and dominance over women and other men (Connell, 1987). Hegemonic masculinity not only works to keep women subordinate to men but also to humiliate men who stray from dominant definitions of accepted masculinity in any given society, including gay men. Connell also referred to the dominant femininity that we value and reward as "emphasized femininity," and defined such femininity as being "oriented to accommodating the interests and desires of men" (p. 183). Therefore, emphasized femininity also works to keep patriarchal power in place by having women conform to an ideal of womanhood that benefits men.

In relation to the two main gender categories, there are also multiple gender categories or identities important to this book that fall under the umbrella term *transgender*. Transgender indicates "anyone who does not feel comfortable in the gender role they were attributed with at birth, or who has a gender identity at odds with the labels 'man' or 'woman' credited to them by formal authorities" (Whittle, 2006, p. xi).

Many identities fall within the category of transgender. One such identity is transsexual, which refers to people "who feel a strong desire to change their sexual morphology in order to live entirely as permanent, full-time members of the gender other than the one they were assigned to at birth" (Stryker, 2008, p. 18). According to clinical sexologist, Mildred Brown, transsexuals often feel "trapped—destined to live out their lives 'imprisoned in the wrong body' unless they correct the situation with hormones or sex reassignment surgery" (Brown & Rounsley, 1996, p. 6). The terms "transmen," "female-to-male" (FTM), "transgender men," and "transsexual men" all refer to "people who were born with female bodies but consider themselves to be men and live socially as men" (Stryker, 2008, p. 20). Similarly, "transwomen," "male-to-female" (MTF), "transgender women," and "transsexual women" are categories that "refer to people who were born with male bodies but consider themselves to be women and live socially as women" (p. 20).

The category of transgender also includes people who cross-dress, who are drag queens, drag kings, and genderqueers. The term *cross-dresser* is intended to be "a non-judgmental replacement for 'transvestite'" (Stryker, 2008, p. 17) and includes those who like to "wear clothing that is traditionally or stereo-typically worn by another gender in their culture" but who are "usually comfortable with their assigned sex and do not wish to change it" (APA, 2011, p. 1). Drag queens and drag kings generally refer to gay men and les-bians, respectively, who dress as another gender "for the purpose of entertain-ing others at bars, clubs, or other events" (APA, 2013, p. 2). Genderqueers are "people who identify their gender as falling outside the binary constructs of 'male' and 'female.' They may define their gender as falling somewhere on a continuum between male and female, or they may define it as wholly different from these terms" (APA, 2011, p. 2). Genderqueers often use gender-neutral pronouns, that is, pronouns that do not indicate whether a person is either masculine or feminine, such as "ze" (pronounced "zee") or "sie" (pronounced "see"), instead of "he" or "she," or "hir" (pronounced "here") instead of "his" or "her" (Feinberg, 1998; Stryker, 2008). Some genderqueers also use "they" for "him" or "her" to degender language. Important to note is that because sexual and gender categories are different from one another, there are transgender people who are lesbian, gay, and bisexual (Burleson, 2005; Rodriguez Rust, 2000a; Weinberg, Williams, & Pryor, 1995). Understanding categories of people based on gender and sexual identities is significant to understanding LGBT families because we need to understand who is creating and occupying those families.

A Brief History of the Development of LGBT Families

The definitions discussed above have developed out of a historical context. Indeed, prior to the 1980s, the term *LGBT families* was an oxymoron. This section discusses the history of the development of LGBT families to provide evidence of how LGBT families have developed out of a coalescing of particular social, economic, political, and cultural factors over time. Providing this history contributes to our understanding of how LGBT families are socially constructed.

Elsewhere, I have documented a longer history of the development of lesbian and gay families (Mezey, 2008a). Here, I offer a shortened version that incorporates bisexual and transgender history to help explain the historical context out of which LGBT families have developed. LGBT families have emerged out of four key factors: (a) the gay liberation movement, (b) the women's rights movement, (c) the HIV/AIDS epidemic, and (d) the development of reproductive and conceptive technologies. These were not the only factors, but they were perhaps the most influential in helping LGBT people develop their families today.

The gay liberation movement was instrumental in helping people outside of dominant gender and sexual categories develop a positive self-image and group identity. Starting as the homophile movement during the first half of the 20th century, White, middle-class homosexuals began to meet through organizations such as the Mattachine Society (for homosexual men) and the Daughters of Bilitis (for homosexual women). These groups served to connect homosexuals and fight against sexual discrimination (D'Emilio, 1998). Outside of these largely White groups, groups of homosexual racial-ethnic minorities also started to socialize in separate groups, particularly in bars (Kennedy & Davis, 1993).

Concurrently, bisexual and transgender people began to organize as well. The concept of "bisexual" was not identified until the early 20th century. Previously, people held the "common belief that bisexuality didn't exist or was either self-deception or a transition phase" (Dworkin, 2000, p. 118). Because of these perceptions, both heterosexuals and homosexuals ostracized bisexual people. However, coming out of a desire for sexual freedom as well as heterosexual "swinger" communities (Highleyman, 2001), bisexual people began to understand their own sexual desires as real. Alfred Kinsey's 1948 and 1953 publications of his "Kinsey Scale" in which he identified a continuum of sexual desires ranging from "exclusively heterosexual" to "exclusively homosexual" also helped bisexual people make sense of their own sexual desires (Dworkin, 2000; Kinsey, Pomeroy, & Martin, 1948; Kinsey, Pomeroy, Martin, & Gebhard, 1953). Through a burgeoning awareness, bisexual people began to gain self-identity through groups such as the Sexual Freedom League, a group that experimented sexually with both heterosexual and same-sex partners, and the National Sex Forum, a group that educated pastors and therapists about homosexuality, lesbianism, and bisexuality (Dworkin, 2000).

Transgender people also started organizing in the wake of Kinsey's work, as well as through the work of psychiatrists like Karl Bowman who were researching diverse gendered behaviors. Through the work of early transgender activists, such as Louise Lawrence and Virginia Prince in the 1940s and 1950s, social networking and organizing of transgender people around the country began to increase, and organizations such as the Foundation for Personality Expression (FPE) and the Labyrinth were started (Stryker, 2008). Similar to homosexuals, race divisions existed among transgender people as well. As Stryker (2008) wrote, "While white suburban transgender people were sneaking out to clandestine meetings, many transgender people of color were highly visible parts of urban culture" through drag balls held in major urban areas (p. 56).

During the time that LGBT people began to form their own groups, the civil rights movement was developing in ways that provided examples of how to organize politically. Drawing on the strategies of Dr. Martin Luther King Jr., as well as more radical groups, such as the Black Panthers, the Nation of Islam, and the Congress of Racial Equality, LGBT people began to organize their own protests and find new ways of community organizing (D'Emilio, 1983, 2007; Stryker, 2008). The new sense of pride that LGBT people developed out of the early homophile movement developed into the gay liberation movement after a group of LGBT bar-goers revolted against police riots at the Stonewall Bar in New York City on June 28, 1969 (D'Emilio, 1983; Faderman, 1991; Stryker, 2008).

At the same time that the gay liberation movement was picking up momentum, early second-wave feminists were also working toward securing women's rights. Despite homophobia, biphobia, and transphobia among early activists (Rust, 1995; Stryker, 2008), feminism and the women's rights movement were nevertheless instrumental in the development of LGBT families. Through the women's rights movement and the development of a feminist consciousness, women began to interact more specifically with other women, creating spaces in which they could explore lesbian relationships. Because feminists encouraged women to take control of their own bodies and to more freely experiment in sexual ways, bisexual women and men began to explore their sexualities in ways that cultural norms had previously prohibited (Dworkin, 2000).

At this time, White radical feminists began to critique the nuclear family, arguing that housework, motherhood, and catering to husbands oppressed women and limited women's access to higher education and paid labor (Allen, 1983; D'Emilio, 2007; Firestone, 1970; Gimenez, 1983). As feminist theories developed, women of color began examining the relationship between race and gender oppression, drawing on connections they made between the civil rights and the women's liberation movements (Collins, 1990; Moraga & Anzaldúa, 1984). As women in general developed a new feminist way of conceiving gender relations and as men and women increasingly began to have sexual relations with the purpose of pleasure rather than procreation, the differences between heterosexual relationships and same-sex relationships began to diminish (Faderman, 1991).

During this time, particularly in the 1970s and 1980s, bisexual and transgender people found both the gay liberation and women's liberation movements to be hostile spaces. Feminists such as those in the Daughters of Bilitis did not consider transwomen to be "real" women and therefore prevented transwomen from entering women-only spaces and events, a division line that still exists in some feminist circles (Stryker, 2008). Similarly, some gay and lesbian organizations, such as those that organized San Francisco's gay pride events, "opposed drag and expressly forbid transgender people from participating" (Stryker, 2008, p. 102). In addition, gay and lesbian groups often prevented bisexual people from joining. As a result, bisexuals started their own organizations, such as the San Francisco Sexual Information (SFSI), the Bi Center, and BiPOL (a bisexual political action group) in San Francisco (Dworkin, 2000) and the National Bisexual Liberation Group in New York, as well as later groups developing in major cities throughout the United States (Highleyman, 2001). The effect of being excluded from both the women's and gay liberation movements was that bisexual and transgender people began to form their own communities and senses of identity (Dworkin, 2000; Stryker, 2008).

As LGBT people began to develop a stronger identity—albeit often separated by race, social class, sexual, and gender divisions—in the 1980s, gay men, bisexual men, and transgender people in particular were faced with a new challenge in the form of the HIV/AIDS epidemic (Stryker 2008). Regarding the development of LGBT families, the HIV/AIDS epidemic had three important effects. First, the epidemic brought separate sexual and gender communities together. Because people initially associated the AIDS epidemic with gay male sex and because heterosexual people feared that bisexual men would infect heterosexual women, homophobia and biphobia were heightened during this time (Dworkin, 2000; Highleyman, 2001). Therefore, as Stryker (2008) wrote, "To adequately respond to the AIDS epidemic demanded a new kind of alliance politics, in which specific communities came together across the dividing lines of race and gender, social class and nationality, citizenship and sexual orientation" (p. 134).

Under the reclaimed umbrella of "queer," organizations such as Aids Coalition to Unleash Power (ACT-UP) and Queer Nation worked to unify forces and create a "new kind of unabashedly progay, nonseparatist, anti-assimilationist alliance politics to combat AIDS" (Stryker, 2008, p. 134).

By the mid-1990s, many organizations that had formally focused only on gay-lesbian issues, or gay-lesbian-bisexual issues, now included transgender in their causes and efforts (Stryker, 2008).

The second important effect the HIV/AIDS epidemic had on the development of LGBT families is that the epidemic openly displayed the deep disregard society had for LGBT relationships. The illness and death that struck gay and bisexual men forced the dying men, their partners, and their friends to acknowledge how poorly recognized their families were by physicians and courts. Issues relating to "next of kin," such as "hospital visitation rights; decision making about medical care; choices about funeral arrangements and burials; and the access of survivors to homes, possessions, and inheritance" all brought the lack of recognition of their intimate partner relationships into clear focus for LGBT people (D'Emilio, 2007, p. 49).

Third, evidence suggests that one reason lesbians and gay men began to have and adopt children in the 1980s was to counteract the deaths that the LGBT community was experiencing related to HIV/AIDS (Lewin, 1993; Mallon, 2011; Moraga, 1997; Weston, 1991), as well as to care for children who lived with HIV/AIDS (Mallon, 2011). The loss of community members was particularly salient for men of color as they constituted over 41% of the total HIV/AIDS cases at the time (Centers for Disease Control and Prevention [CDC], 1988, as cited in Morales, 1990). Not surprisingly, therefore, Latino and African American LGBT community groups led many of the local battles against the epidemic (D'Emilio, 2007). The irony is that while lesbians began having more children during this time perhaps partially to counterbalance the epidemic, they were also less willing to use the sperm from gay and bisexual men because they feared contracting the disease themselves or passing it on to their offspring (Bernstein & Stephenson, 1995; Stacey, 1996; Sullivan, 2004; Weston, 1991). The result was that more lesbians began using tested sperm from sperm banks, thus, reducing the number of gay and bisexual men as parents (Weston, 1991).

During the 1980s and 1990s, lesbians were able to access tested sperm because of the increased use and access to reproductive and conceptive technologies (Stacey, 1998), the fourth main historical factor in the development of LGBT families today. Reproductive technologies, also known as assisted reproductive technologies (ARTs), refer to "the use of non-coital technologies to conceive a child and initiate pregnancy. Most widely used is artificial insemination, but in vitro fertilization (IVF), egg donation, surrogacy, and genetic screening techniques are also available" (Robertson, 2005, p. 324). ARTs have revolutionized most types of families, not just LGBT families, because they allow people who historically could not have children (e.g., infertile men, older women) to have children through a variety of means that potentially separate genetic, gestational, and social parenting from one another (Gimenez, 1991). Although the use of ARTs are often expensive and not always covered by insurance, they allow LGBT people who can afford the services to have genetically connected children without getting involved in heterosexual sexual relations.

The culmination of the gay liberation movement, the women's rights movement, the HIV/AIDS epidemic, and the development of reproductive and conceptive technologies have combined forces to create the current existence of LGBT families. These four factors supported in positive ways the formation of LGBT identities, communities, and ultimately families. However, as the following section illustrates, forces working against the formation of LGBT families continue to persist.

Remaining Barriers for LGBT Families

Despite the historical landscape in which LGBT people are now forming families, there remain barriers preventing LGBT family formation as well. As suggested through the opening comment of the chapter spoken by an eleventh grader whose mother is a lesbian, these barriers come out of an ideological battle between those who believe that LGBT people are immoral and hurting the fabric of American culture, and those who believe that LGBT people should have the same rights as heterosexual Americans. The debate surrounding LGBT families, and truly families in general, involves asking one main question: Is there one best type of family that creates the best quality of life for those within the family and for larger society? Related to this one main question are two subquestions: (a) Who should be able to get married?, and (b) Who should be able to raise children? These questions are asked by politicians, academics, and the general public in response to the single fact that almost everyone can agree upon: Families in the United States are changing.

In trying to make sense of why families are changing and the consequences of those changes, people have participated in a long-standing discussion about cause and effect called the family values debate. The two main sides of the debate include "conservatives"—or "the decline of the family" lamenters (Powell et al., 2010, p. 8)—and "progressives"—or "diversity defenders" (Cherlin, 2003, as cited in Powell et al., 2010, p. 10). People who identify with conservatives through the family values debate largely consist of certain religious leaders, politicians, and social scientists who argue that families are changing because Americans no longer value the "traditional" nuclear family (i.e., dad at work, mom at home, with direct offspring living in their own home with a white picket fence, suggesting economic security and independence). Such conservatives argue that the move away from the traditional nuclear family is causing a decline in material and economic conditions nationwide (Blankenhorn, 1991; Dill, Baca Zinn, & Patton, 1998; Stacey, 1996; Wilson, 1993).

Family values conservatives also claim "that the traditional nuclear family is the basis of social organization and cohesion in the United States" (Dill et al., 1998, p. 6). According to these conservatives, the breakdown of the nuclear-family structure causes societal ills such as poverty, teen pregnancy, divorce, drug use, crime, and poor education (Dill et al., 1998). Conservatives in the family values debate further argue that biological differences between men and women justify the nuclear-family form because women are biologically disposed caregivers and men are biologically disposed breadwinners (Andersen & Witham, 2011). In addition, in order for a family to function "properly," husbands or fathers must be present (Blankenhorn, 1991; Popenoe, 1999).

For such conservatives, the traditional heterosexual family is not only the glue that keeps society together, but also marriage (between one man and one woman) is the glue that keeps the traditional family together. According to family values conservatives, marriage is necessary for families to maintain social cohesion and strong child welfare. Marriage is so prominent a point that it has taken on the form of the "marriage movement" to promote the benefits of heterosexual marriage to couples and society (Heath, 2012). Conservatives draw on research suggesting that marital arrangements promote longer lives, greater household financial stability, greater physical and mental health for women and men, and more sexual satisfaction than nonmarital arrangements (see for example, research conducted by Waite & Gallagher, 2001). Following this logic, a reduction in marriage and the increase in divorce are main causes of family decline and a majority of social problems (Cahill & Tobias, 2007; National Hispanic Christian Leadership Conference [NHCLC], 2013; Popenoe, 1993; Whitehead, 1993).

Although supporters of the marriage movement agree that marriage benefits individuals and society, there is some disagreement as to whether or not marriage should be extended to lesbians and gays (Waite & Gallagher, 2001, pp. 200–201). Most conservatives within the family values debate feel strongly that both marriage and family remain heterosexual institutions (Stacey, 1996). To ensure the heterosexual nature of marriage and family, Republicans introduced a bill in 1996 called the Defense of Marriage Act (DOMA), which Democratic President Bill Clinton signed into law. DOMA states that marriage is "a legal union between one man and one woman as husband and wife" (Dunlap, as cited in Stacey, 1996, p. 120). As Representative Bob Barr (R-GA), the architect of DOMA, stated, "The flames of hedonism, the flames of narcissism, the flames of self-centered morality are licking at the very foundations of our society: the family unit" (DOMA Debate, as cited in Cahill & Tobias, 2007, p. 3). Therefore, to protect the traditional family and the social, economic, cultural, political, and moral fabric of the nation, DOMA specifically and intentionally left LGBT people out of the legal definition of marriage and family. That is, family values conservatives believe that LGBT families stand in direct opposition to the "traditional" family and therefore will cause major social problems to occur if allowed to develop. This sentiment is exemplified through a statement posted on the website of the conservative National Hispanic Christian Leadership Conference (NHCLC; 2013), in partnership with the Alliance For Marriage, that called

to define marriage in order to strengthen families and reinforce the threads that enable families to thrive and prosper. This is not about being anti-gay or discriminating against anyone. This is about strengthening the family to make sure that the successful historical model which embodies the fundamental fiber of society continues to be strengthened and not undermined by activist judges. The primary deterrent in the Latino community to drug abuse, gang violence, teenage pregnancy, and other social ills is faith in God and a family with both a mother and a father. (NHCLC, 2013, para. 1)

This view expressed by the NHCLC is not isolated to Hispanics or religious groups (see, for example, the Family Research Council and the Heritage Foundation) but rather is a popular sentiment among family values conservatives nationwide and has far-reaching policy implications.

The opinions of conservative lawmakers and judges often shape the outcomes of trials concerning LGBT families and the family laws that policy makers implement in a variety of states. Sociologist and legal studies professor Kimberly Richman (2009) wrote that judges made explicit references to morality and religion in their judicial decisions in 34% of custody and adoption cases between 1952 and 2004 involving an LGBT parent. Similarly, as of May 2014, 28 states had constitutional amendments and 3 states had instituted a state-level DOMA that bans same-sex marriage (Human Rights Campaign [HRC], 2014b). Many of these laws were instituted around the time or in direct effect of the 2004 presidential election of George W. Bush, who pushed a conservative agenda and used the promise of banning marriage for same-sex couples as part of his campaign platform (Olson, Harrison, & College, 2006). Thus, the family values debate "and the public debates surrounding morality it has spurred, have been part and parcel of evolving judicial and public attitudes toward LGBT parents and families" (Richman, 2009, p. 26).

On the other hand, progressives, who consist largely of specific historians and social scientists, have pushed back against the arguments made by conservative scholars, religious leaders, and politicians (Coontz, 1993; Dill et al., 1998; Stacey, 1996). Progressive scholars argue that as society changes, families change. Therefore, in trying to understand why and how families have been changing throughout time, progressives look to factors external to families. These factors are both economic (e.g., shifts in work and the economy) and cultural (e.g., large social movements fueled by structural shifts). Progressives also look to data suggesting that families in the United States have always been changing (Coontz, 1993).

As opposed to conservatives, progressive scholars argue that diverse family structures are not a natural given but rather result from social, cultural, economic, and political changes (Dill et al., 1998). According to progressive scholars, diverse family forms are not the cause of social ills. Rather, diverse family forms have developed historically as survival strategies in response to adverse social, economic, and cultural challenges.

Progressives refute conservative assumptions by drawing on a variety of social science and historical research. First, they argue that the nuclear family form has not been the dominant historical form; nor has the family changed over time simply because of cultural values. Rather, the traditional family is really a modern, White middle-class phenomenon that grew out of structural changes, such as the industrial revolution, the Great Depression, World War II, automated machinery, increased reliance on the computer chip, and globalization. These are the same factors that have also increased social problems in the United States, such as unemployment, decrease of the middle class, and increased poverty (Coontz, 2007; Eitzen, Baca Zinn, & Smith, 2013; Stacey, 1996). According to progressive research, families change in order to survive such structural changes, thus, diverging from the traditional model, not because they are lazy or because they have faulty cultural values but because unstable financial situations deny them access to the resources necessary to maintain (if they want) a traditional family. In other words, changes in family structures serve as survival strategies and positive adjustments to negative social forces, such as economic hardships and social discrimination.

Progressives also challenge conservative assertions that biological ties are necessary in families by pointing to research showing that both motherhood and fatherhood are socially constructed and that fathers can develop nurturing skills when they become primary caregivers to their children (Coltrane, 1989; Glenn, 1994). Furthermore, progressives show how maintaining rigid and traditional family divisions of labor based on gender is not feasible for or beneficial to many working- and lower class families, particularly during economic recessions or for families that have recently emigrated from another country (Coltrane, 2007; Hill, 2012; Hondagneu-Sotelo, 1994).

Progressives also refute marriage as the only legitimate defining characteristic of a family. They point to research showing how female-headed households and children who grow up with divorced parents or in step-families are no worse than children who grow up in two-biological-parent families. Progressives argue that it is not the structure of the family but rather the quality of the relationships between adults and children that determine the welfare of the children (Demo, 1992). They look to research on LGBT families showing that children with LGBT parents are at least as psychologically and socially healthy as children with heterosexual parents (Stacey & Biblarz, 2001).

Progressives argue that the reliance on an ahistorical approach, on cultural and biological determinism, and on marriage, lead conservatives to a reversed sense of cause-and-effect in the relationship between family and society. That is, by ignoring historical and structural factors that prevent individuals from forming "traditional" families, conservatives are able to treat "the family as the cause of social conditions, rather than as a reflection of them" (Dill et al., 1998, p. 11). Thus, rather than discussing how family forms are changing in positive ways to counter negative economic, social, and political forces, conservatives state that economic, social, and political situations are changing because the traditional family is disintegrating.

The dueling sides of the family values debate mean that although there are conservative laws and policies being instituted that undermine LGBT families, there are simultaneously progressive laws and policies being instituted that support LGBT families. Thus, at the same time that states are banning marriage equality, they are also recognizing legal parenthood of LGBT adults by increasing access to ARTs and decreasing barriers to adoption for potential and existing gay and lesbian parents (Richman, 2009). In other words, one result of the family values debate is that the political and social ground upon which LGBT families are forming is constantly shifting. In addition, where LGBT people live within the United States may determine how difficult or easy it is for them to form and maintain their families, as laws differ from state to state, as detailed in Chapter 2.

Plan of the Book

How do we make sense of these opposing viewpoints and their consequences for LGBT people and their potential and existing families? In this book, I take a progressive stance and present data suggesting that LGBT families have not only risen out of social structural factors but are also reacting against discrimination and economic hardship to create a model that strengthens the institution of family and adds positively to the fundamental fiber of our society. I delve deeply and widely into the literature and research and use data to draw conclusions about how such factors shape our current families. I also examine what the consequences for LGBT families and society in general are, and try to help readers understand how the fear of LGBT families conjured up by family values conservatives is indeed unfounded.

Each of the following chapters is designed to present information concerning a different aspect of LGBT families and explain how LGBT families—while certainly not perfect—at times mirror heterosexual families and at times present alternatives from which heterosexuals might learn to strengthen their own families. Although the book focuses primarily on LGBT families in the United States, Chapters 1 through 5 each contain a Global Box authored by Morganne Firmstone with information examining specific issues facing LGBT members within global communities. Those chapters also conclude with suggested films and Internet resources addressing issues raised in that chapter.

Chapter 2 addresses the question of marriage, the legal and socially dominant recognition of what makes a family and a major focus of LGBT activists as well as the general public. This chapter discusses why marriage equality is paramount to many LGBT families philosophically, socially, and economically. The chapter also examines the historical and current struggle for marriage equality, as well as the backlash against marriage equality. In the chapter, I discuss current state and federal legislation regarding marriage equality, and compare marriage, civil unions, and domestic partnerships. The chapter examines how LGBT people who do not have access to marriage, civil unions, or domestic partnerships organize their families; and why some LGBT people believe that marriage is not worth fighting for.

Chapter 3 addresses parenting. Since the late 1970s and early 1980s, lesbians and gay men have been birthing and adopting children in record numbers, starting what many people are calling the "gayby" boom. The gayby boom started with women and men who became parents within heterosexual identities and then later identified as lesbian or gay. More recently, lesbians and gay men within these identities have been choosing parenthood by adopting and birthing children. Because of the fierce cultural debates surrounding LGBT parenthood and what happens to children raised by LGBT parents, the third chapter covers a variety of issues regarding children and parenting, starting with how LGBT people decide to become parents and how LGBT people actually become parents (e.g., through heterosexual relationships, donor insemination, adoption, and surrogacy). The chapter examines co-parents, stepparents, multiple parents, and second-parent adoption; household division of labor and work-family balance; transracial LGBT families; strategies for raising children in homophobic and heterosexist contexts; and divorce and separation. The chapter concludes with a brief discussion of LGBT grandparents.

Chapter 4 examines the lives and experiences of LGBT children and youth in families. The chapter focuses on how and when children come out; family reactions to their coming out; negotiations between families and other social institutions, such as schools and medical professionals; and mental health issues that children face when they come out or transition. The chapter pays particular attention to how LGBT children fare within the context of hegemonic masculinity, emphasized femininity, homo/bi/trans-phobia, and heterosexism.

Chapter 5 takes an in-depth look at intimate partner violence (IPV) within LGBT relationships. Originally labeled wife battering, then referred to as domestic violence, and now recognized as IPV, the field of under-standing how adults commit violence and other forms of abuse against their intimate partners has developed dramatically since the 1980s. Included in the significant body of empirical and theoretical work in the field of IPV is a growing understanding of violence and abuse within LGBT relationships and families. Because of homophobia and heterosexism, violence in LGBT families has been largely hidden; and working to end violence has been poorly supported by community organizations and law enforcement agencies. This chapter examines the following issues: the prevalence and nature of IPV within LGBT families; explanations for why violence and abuse exist within LGBT families; options for, and responses by, LGBT people in abusive relationships; the response of law enforcement to LGBT abusers and victims; and community and other support for LGBT victims and abusers, including shelter options and rehabilitative programs.

Chapter 6 concludes the book by focusing on what we can learn by studying LGBT families and how LGBT families benefit society. LGBT families have developed out of the coalescing and intersections of specific social, political, economic, and cultural factors and are, therefore, a product of their time. Despite the fact—or perhaps because of the fact—that LGBT families are becoming more prevalent and visible in society, they live under political and cultural scrutiny and face serious challenges in forming and maintaining themselves. And yet, because we are living in difficult economic and political times, many of the issues that challenge LGBT families also challenge heterosexual families. The chapter concludes by making recommendations for how policy makers, private and public agencies, communities, and people in general can support LGBT families to ensure that they are as healthy as possible.

GLOBAL BOX

by Morganne Firmstone

The global landscape of LGBT families is a complicated intersection of cultural beliefs and practices, policies, and environment. Violence, discrimination, restricted access, and loss of identity within societal norms are just a few of the vast number of daily challenges facing LGBT families. Not only do LGBT families face a variety of trials in their everyday lives, but they have also the added difficulty of navigating through the winding path of global politics surrounding what it means to be a partner, family, parent, son, daughter, and sibling.

One of the most basic means of forming families is through the institution of marriage. Through marriage, people solidify and document their union with one another in order to receive particular benefits—whether they are legal, social, emotional, political, or financial. In essence, marriage provides access to social legitimacy and material benefits. Not everyone is legally entitled to this access, however. Many countries have strict policies and definitions about who may enter into the institution of marriage and, consequently, who may not. The UN Office of the High Commissioner for Human Rights (2012) noted that 76 countries worldwide have discriminatory policies that ban "private, consensual same-sex relationships" (p. 7). LGBT individuals in these countries are at a higher risk of arrest, prosecution, and imprisonment simply for not being heterosexual (UN High Commissioner for Human Rights [UN High Commissioner], 2012). Based mainly on dominant cultural definitions, values, and norms regarding the meanings of the words "gender" and "sexuality," countries enact policies that affect the ability to marry, or even have a relationship.

While LGBT couples around the world face diminished access to marriage, some couples are not even granted the acknowledgment of existence. For example, most African countries prohibit marriage between same-sex couples. According to Mujuzi (2009), the governing legal documents of most African countries recognize only heterosexual unions. Furthermore, sexual relationships among same-sex partners are banned and, in some cases, punishable. National policies that deny the existence of LGBT relationships have profound consequences when discussing LGBT families because such relationships cannot even exist under law. Not only do LGBT families barely exist in Africa, but even homosexual acts, and as an extension, homosexual identities, are also banned from many African nations.

In fact, in 2009, Ugandan parliamentarian David Bahati introduced the Uganda Anti-Homosexuality Bill. According to the U.S. Department of State (2011), this legislation would "impose punishments ranging from imprisonment

(Continued)

(Continued)

to the death penalty on individuals twice convicted of 'homosexuality' or 'related offenses'" (p. 47). In addition, several administrative-level members of the Ugandan government have openly expressed support for some form of the anti-homosexuality bill. Indeed, in February 2014, the Ugandan President Yoweri Museveni signed the bill into law. The law "toughens penalties against gay people and defines some homosexual acts as crimes punishable by life in prison" (CNN, 2014).

Despite the backlash against LGBT people in Uganda, several African nations have made progress in instituting some form of marriage equality to protect the rights of LGBT people. Shockingly enough, despite being part of one of the most conservative continents, the African nation of South Africa instituted a same-sex marriage policy in 2006. The new law reaches only so far, however, because under the law, religious and civil officials can refuse to perform marriage ceremonies to same-sex couples (Heaton, 2010). Moreover, South Africa is not immune to incidence of violence. According to a UN Human Rights Council report (UN High Commissioner, 2011), lesbians in South Africa have been singled out as victims of hate crimes. In one case, two lesbians were "beaten, stoned, and one stabbed to death" (p. 9). Beliefs surrounding heterosexism and marriage are extremely deep-rooted and inherent within culture; policy advancements alone cannot readily resolve these tensions.

In addition to South Africa, several Asian countries have tried to advance the rights of LGBT people. For example, India has worked toward LGBT policy advancements over the past 5 years, but not without setbacks. In 2009, the Delhi High Court overturned provisions of the Indian Penal Code which prohibited same-sex sexual activity (U.S. Department of State, Bureau of Democracy, 2013). Despite this decision, the U.S. State Department (2013) reported that "the abolished clause continued to be used sporadically to target, harass, and punish lesbian, gay, bisexual, and transgender (LGBT) persons" (p. 54). Although LGBT groups were active throughout India, including involvement in parades, speeches, rallies, and marches, they faced "discrimination and violence throughout society, particularly in rural areas" (U.S. Department of State, Bureau of Democracy, 2013, p. 54).

LGBT people in India still experience difficulty in obtaining medical treatment, as well as job discrimination, physical attacks, rape, and police brutality and coercion (U.S. Department of State, Bureau of Democracy, 2013). In the case of Diya Rai, a transgender person, the level of abuse and discrimination in India was apparent. According to the U.S. State Department (2013), Diya Rai submitted a complaint to the Bengal Human Rights Commission regarding an illegal detainment. Diya Rai was held at a police station in Baguiati for 9 hours while law enforcement officials taunted her about her sexuality. According to the report, Diya Rai was "later released without being charged and [she] alleged that police made her sign a 'personal bond' to never return to the area" (p. 55). Such stories provide evidence that LGBT people face not only exclusion but also active and directed discouragement, and at times even more severe harassment, violence, and in some cases, death.

Despite discouragement, LGBT advocates and nongovernmental organizations (NGOs) around the world have not given up the fight for equality. The issues and concerns of LGBT people and families have reached a global stage on several occasions. The Declaration of Montreal and the Yogyakarta Principles were two of the forefront documents signed in a global context. The Declaration of Montreal was introduced by the participants of the International Conference on LGBT Human Rights held in Canada in 2006. The document is an attempt to summarize the demands of the international LGBT movement in the broadest sense, and it could serve as a basis for political discussion by contextualizing the needs and demands of the LGBT community based on a human rights platform (Outgames Montréal, 2006).

According to O'Flaherty and Fisher (2008), the Yogyakarta Principles on the Application of Human Rights Law in Relation to Sexual Orientation were launched in 2007 by a group of human rights experts who intended to create a document that identified the "obligation of the States to respect, protect, and fulfill the human rights of all persons regardless of their sexual orientation or gender identity" (p. 207). O'Flaherty and Fisher (2008) believe that the principles will play a crucial role in advocacy efforts and in "jurisprudential development" (p. 207).

Perhaps one of the most historic international reports, *Discriminatory Laws and Practices and Acts of Violence Against Individuals Based on Their Sexual Orientation and Gender Identity* was issued in 2011 by the United Nations (UN High Commissioner, 2011). This was the first-ever UN report on human rights, sexual orientation, and gender identity. The report documents global discrimination and violence faced by LGBT people and encourages states to use the human rights legal framework to help end violence and human rights violations committed against LGBT people (UN High Commissioner, 2011). The report makes several recommendations to nations worldwide, including repealing laws that prohibit same-sex relations between consensual adults, thoroughly investigating any crimes or killings committed against those for reasons of real or perceived gender identity or sexual orientation, enacting antidiscrimination legislation, providing sensitivity training to police and other law enforcement personnel, and supporting public information campaigns to reduce homophobia and promote acceptance (UN High Commissioner, 2011).

Framing the experiences of LGBT people as a human rights issue is the first step toward recognizing that if individual LGBT acts and identities are not sanctified by the policies of a nation, there is little hope for LGBT families to form. In other words, nations need to first protect the rights of LGBT people before those individuals can safely and legally form families. Although several policy initiatives have gained momentum in recent years, many nations have a long, rigorous road of legal battles ahead.

ADDITIONAL RESOURCES

Compiled by Morganne Firmstone

Websites

- Center for American Progress
  - http://www.americanprogress.org

- Gay & Lesbian Advocates & Defenders
  - http://www.glad.org

- The Gay & Lesbian Alliance Against Defamation
  - http://www.glaad.org/about

- Human Rights Campaign
  - http://hrc.org

- Human Rights Watch
  - http://www.hrw.org

- International Gay and Lesbian Human Rights Commission
  - http://www.iglhrc.org

- National Center for Lesbian Rights
  - http://www.nclrights.org

- National Gay and Lesbian Task Force
  - http://www.ngltf.org

Films

- *Born This Way (2013 Documentary)*
  - A portrait of the underground gay and lesbian community in Cameroon. It follows Cedric and Gertrude, two young Cameroonians, as they move between a secret, supportive LGBT community and an outside culture that, though intensely homophobic, is in transition toward greater acceptance.

- *Call Me Kuchu (2012 Documentary)*
  - Explores the struggles of the LGBT community in Uganda, focusing in part on the 2011 murder of LGBT activist David Kato.

- *Fish Out of Water (2009 Documentary)*
  - Showcases the seven Bible verses that are most often used to condemn homosexuality and marriage between same-sex couples.

- *For the Bible Tells Me So (2007 Documentary)*
  - An exploration of the intersection between religion and homosexuality in the United States and how the "religious right" has used its interpretation of the Bible to stigmatize the gay community.

- *A Jihad for Love (2007 Documentary)*
  - A documentary on gay, lesbian, and transgender Muslims across the Muslim and Western worlds.

- *Paragraph 175 (2000 Documentary)*
  - Film chronicling the lives of the handful of known survivors of Germany's Paragraph 175, the sodomy provision of the penal code that led to over 100,000 men being arrested and imprisoned or sent to concentration camps between 1933 and 1945.

- *Rape for Who I Am (2006 Documentary)*
  - Insights into the lives of South Africa's Black lesbians.

- *The World's Worst Place to Be Gay (2013 BBC Documentary)*
  - Scott Mills travels to Uganda where the death penalty could soon be introduced for being gay. The gay Radio 1 DJ finds out what it is like to live in a society that persecutes people like him and meets those who are leading the hate campaign.

2

Marriage

It doesn't bother me to tell kids my parents are gay. It does bother me to say they aren't married. It makes me feel that our family is less than their family.

—Kasey Nicholson-McFadden, son of Karen and
Marcye Nicholson-McFadden, plaintiffs in the
legal suit against New Jersey for marriage
equality, testifying in front of New Jersey
lawmakers in Trenton in 2010 (Wildman, 2010)

DOMA seeks to injure the very class New York seeks to protect. By doing so it violates basic due process and equal protection principles applicable to the Federal Government . . . DOMA cannot survive under these principles. . . . DOMA's unusual deviation from the usual tradition of recognizing and accepting state definitions of marriage here operates to deprive same-sex couples of the benefits and responsibilities that come with the federal recognition of their marriages. . . . The avowed purpose and practical effect of the law here in question are to impose a disadvantage, a separate status, and so a stigma upon all who enter into same-sex marriages made lawful by the unquestioned authority of the States.

—Anthony Kennedy, United States Supreme Court
Justice, in the majority opinion of *The United
States v. Windsor* that deemed section three of the
Defense of Marriage Act (DOMA) unconstitutional
(June 26, 2013, pp. 20–21 of the Opinion)

A s the above quotes suggest, the discussion around marriage is deeply personal and heatedly political. Looking throughout history, we also know that marriage as a social institution is ever changing. Our understanding of the changing tides of marriage is based on a number of measures. We know that over the past 50 years, marriage as a social institution has been failing. Since the early 1960s, the United States has seen a decline in marriage rates, a rise in divorce rates, an increase in children being born to unwed parents, an increase in cohabitation as an alternative to marriage, and an increase in LGBT couples with children (Cherlin, 2003, 2004; Goldstein & Kenney, 2001). Since the 1960s, the annual rate of marriage among unmarried women ages 15 to 44 began falling significantly. In the 1960s, the rate of marriage (i.e., the number of marriages that occurred per 1,000 unmarried women aged 18 and older) was 150 per 1,000. In the 1970s, that rate fell to 110 per 1,000; in the 1980s, the marriage rate fell to 100 per 1,000; and in 2010, that number sank to 35 per 1,000 (Goldstein & Kenney, 2001; Payne & Gibbs, 2011). Since the 1980s, there has been a continual drop in the annual rate of marriage as well (Goldstein & Kenney, 2001), such that in 2008 only 52% of all adults in the United States were married, compared to 72% of American adults in 1960 (Pew Research Center, 2010). The drop in marriage has come with a change in attitudes about the importance of marriage. For example, in 1978, 28% of Americans over the age of 18 said that marriage was obsolete compared to 36% of Americans in 2010 (Pew Research Center, 2010).

If a business has been declining over the past 50 years and fails nearly 50% of the time, we would expect the owners of that business to follow any number of paths, including (a) looking for a new market in which to sell its product, (b) redefining and remaking its business so that its product is more attractive to existing and potential clients, or (c) closing down the business. So why has the institution of marriage not closed shop? And why have so many Americans been so resistant to opening the marriage market to a new group of people—LGBT people—who have been banging steadily for the past several decades on doors of "the marriage club" to let them in? The answer is that marriage is not really a "normal" business, although it certainly is a historically economic institution (Coontz, 2005), and is currently embedded in a vast economic industry of weddings, jewelry, fashion, music, travel, greeting cards, and food that surrounds and relies on the success of marriage—or at least the success of weddings and anniversaries. Rather than being a business, marriage is first and foremost a socially constructed institution steeped in a romantic ideology that not only sees marriage as the backbone of "the family" but also as being integral to the moral fabric of human society (Weeks, Heaphy, & Donovan, 2001). We know that marriage is socially constructed because the age at which we decide to get married, how important we think marriage is, who we think should get married, and how we shape our marital arrangements have changed throughout time and are different across geographic locations (Coontz, 2005; Cott, 2002; Mintz & Kellogg, 1988; Yalom, 2002).

Although marriage is socially constructed, the institution has historically been the main way to create families. With the exception of the Na people of China (Coontz, 2005; Hua, 2001), every known group of humans throughout history has created and depended on some form of marriage to organize its families and kin networks. The universality of marriage stops there, however. Marriage as a social institution has taken on countless forms, meanings, and responsibilities throughout history depending on the social, economic, cultural, and political landscape at any given time. In fact, marriage is universal only in the sense that it has served some major function regarding family and kin networks. These functions have included the legitimization of social arrangements regarding sexual relations, the raising of children, living arrangements, economic relationships, the organization of property and inheritance rights, sharing and dividing household responsibilities, establishing cooperative relationships between families and communities, and sharing one's life with a loved one (Coontz, 2005). Even though marriage has at some point or another held all of the above functions, marriage has rarely if ever held all of these functions in any one society at any one historical moment in time. In fact, "almost every single function that marriage fulfills in one society has been filled by some mechanism other than marriage in another" (Coontz, 2005, p. 32).

Understanding the changing and evolving functions of marriage shows us that marriage is a socially constructed institution created to meet society's particular familial and kin-related needs at any given historical moment. There is nothing fixed or natural or universal about the functions of marriage; nor is the structure of marriage fixed, as we know that marriage can be monogamous or polygamous depending on where in time or geography that relationship exists. Moreover, all of the past and present functions of marriage can be, and in many societies throughout history have been, performed outside of marriage. For example, we do not need marriage to have children. We do not need marriage to pass our wealth onto our children. We do not need marriage to commit ourselves to someone we love.

As stated in Chapter 1, the vast majority of LGB people in the United States said they would like the right to marry. State governments have issued tens of thousands of marriage licenses in the United States. These numbers are accompanied by approximately 60,000 same-sex couples in Europe and South Africa who have married, thus, totaling over 100,000 same-sex couples married throughout the world (Chamie & Mirkin, 2011; Herek, Norton,

Allen, & Sims, 2010). If we do not need marriage to fulfill the functions that marriage currently fulfills, then why do we still have the institution of marriage? How and when did marriage become the battle cry for the current LGBT movement? And equally important, why do many LGBT people want the right to marry?

Before answering the above questions, I need to discuss the language used throughout this chapter. Although most popular and scholarly works refer to "same-sex marriage" or "gay marriage" when discussing the right of LGBT people to legally wed, I agree with lawyer and activist Evan Wolfson (2004) that these terms imply that LGBT people want "rights that are something lesser or different than what non-gay couples have" (p. 17). Instead, I use the term "marriage equality" as it implies that LGBT people are not looking for a different system created especially for them (e.g., gay marriage or same-sex marriage), but rather, they want the right to marry through the exact same legal mechanisms as heterosexual people.

The Struggle for Marriage Equality

So how and when did marriage become the battle cry for many LGBT people? Numerous sources have documented in detail the historical struggle for marriage equality in the United States (Cahill, 2004; Cahill & Tobias, 2007; Chonody, Smith, & Litle, 2012; Mello, 2004; NOLO Law for All, 2005; Robinson & Soderstrom, 2011; Sullivan, 2004; Wolfson, 2004, to name a few). Here, I offer a greatly abridged version.

LGBT people have been fighting for marriage equality since the early 1970s, when they challenged marital laws, "claiming that in accordance with common-law tradition, whatever is not prohibited must be allowed" (Mohr, 1994, p. 35). The courts dismissed this challenge, stating that marriage automatically implies gender difference. Lesbians and gays also challenged courts by referring to the anti-miscegenation laws (laws prohibiting mixed-race marriages), arguing that preventing marriage based on sexuality was similar to preventing marriage based on race. Courts dismissed this challenge as well, until the 1993 *Baehr v. Lewin* case in Hawaii, which drew parallels to anti-miscegenation laws (Tong, 1998). The *Baehr v. Lewin* (and later the *Baehr v. Miike*) case brought wide political attention and media coverage to the issue of marriage equality (Mohr, 1994; Tong, 1998). Until the 1996 passing of DOMA, laws did not specifically state that marriage could occur only between a man and a woman.

LGBT pro-marriage equality activists won their first victory in 1997 when Hawaii gained limited domestic partner benefits for workers in the public sector. The next major victory for marriage equality came in 2000, when Vermont instituted its "Civil Union law" that granted same-sex partners in Vermont "all of the state-level rights and responsibilities of marriage" (Vt. Stat. Ann. Tit. 15 §, as cited in Johnson, 2003, p. 285). Three years later, deciding on the *Goodridge et al. v. Department of Public Health* case and handing down the first-of-its-kind ruling in the United States, the Massachusetts Supreme Court ruled that under its state constitution, Massachusetts must grant same-sex couples the same marital rights as heterosexual couples (Johnson, 2003).

Following Massachusetts, there was a fierce backlash against marriage equality. Starting in 2004, 38 states instituted their own DOMAs on the state level to ensure that marriage was between one man and one woman and that their states did not have to recognize marriage between same-sex couples. In addition, conservative Republican politicians made two unsuccessful attempts—in 2004 and 2006—to amend the U.S. Constitution such that marriage would solely be between one woman and one man.

Despite the backlash against marriage equality, as indicated in Table 2.1, since 2004, in addition to Massachusetts, 22 states and the District of Columbia began offering marriages, civil unions, or domestic partner benefits to same-sex couples on a state level. There are additional seven states in which lower courts have deemed a ban on marriage for same-sex couples to be unconstitutional, but the cases are in appeal processes so marriage equality is not fully achieved. Many of the state struggles have been complicated. Although a detailed discussion of each state history is beyond the scope of this book, by way of example of the complexities of such struggles, we can look at New Jersey and California. While other states, such as Maine and Hawaii, could also provide a picture of a tumultuous fight for marriage equality, I selected New Jersey and California as their stories best exemplify the winding and bumpy roads that many states have taken in order to move toward marriage equality.

In New Jersey, in October 2006, 2 years after Governor James McGreevey signed into law domestic partner benefits for same-sex couples through the Domestic Partnership Act, the New Jersey Supreme Court heard the case *Lewis v. Harris*, ruling that same-sex couples in the state have a constitutional right to the benefits and privileges of marriage. The court mandated the state legislature to determine within 180 days following the verdict whether or not the state would institute marriage or some other form of legal union. The legislature opted for civil unions over marriage, which went into effect in 2007 (Robinson & Soderstrom, 2011).

As part of the Civil Union Act, the New Jersey State Legislature created the New Jersey Civil Union Review Commission to study the fairness of civil

Table 2.1 States With Marriage Equality, Civil Unions, or Domestic Partnerships and Year Legalized; Listed Alphabetically With Most Recent Legal Recognition

	Marriage	Civil Unions	Domestic Partnerships	Court Cases Pending
Arkansas				2014
California	2013			
Colorado		2013		
Connecticut	2008			
Delaware	2013			
Hawaii	2013			
Idaho				2014
Illinois	2014			2014
Iowa	2009			
Kentucky				2014
Maine	2012			
Maryland	2013			
Massachusetts	2004			
Michigan				2014
Minnesota	2013			
Nevada			2009	
New Hampshire		2010		
New Jersey	2013			
New Mexico	2013			
New York	2011			
Oklahoma				2014
Oregon	2014			
Pennsylvania	2014			

	Marriage	Civil Unions	Domestic Partnerships	Court Cases Pending
Rhode Island	2013			
Utah				2014
Vermont	2009			
Virginia				2014
Washington	2012			
Washington, DC	2010		2002	

Source: Chonody et al., 2012; Socarides, 2013; HRC 2014b

unions in the state. In 2008, the commission found that "the separate categorization established by the Civil Union Act invites and encourages unequal treatment of same-sex couples and their children" (New Jersey Civil Union Review Commission, 2008, p. 1). After much lobbying from LGBT organizations, such as Garden State Equality, 10 members of the assembly sponsored, and an additional five members co-sponsored, the Marriage Equality and Religious Exemption Act, an act intended to institute full marriage equality in New Jersey. The state legislature passed the act in February 2012, but Governor Chris Christie vetoed the act shortly thereafter.

Simultaneous to moves within New Jersey's legislature, two LGBT rights organizations—Garden State Equality and Lambda Legal—joined forces to assist seven lesbian and gay couples and their children in suing the state of New Jersey for the right to marry. The case sat nearly idle until 2013, when the U.S. Supreme Court struck down DOMA (see below for a longer discussion). Lambda Legal filed a motion for summary judgment with the New Jersey Supreme Court. They argued that because the federal government does not recognize civil unions, and because the federal government now recognizes marriages between same-sex couples in states where such marriages are legal, the lack of marriage equality in New Jersey disadvantaged lesbian and gay citizens (Lambda Legal, 2013; Rizzo & Sherman, 2013). State Superior Court Judge Mary Jacobson heard the case and ruled on September 27, 2013, that same-sex couples should have the right to marry in New Jersey, ordering the state to allow such marriages to begin 21 days later (Rizzo & Sherman, 2013). Governor Christie appealed Judge Jacobson's decision and requested a stay of marriage licenses to same-sex couples until after the State Supreme Court heard the appealed case. In response to Governor Christie's request for a stay, the New Jersey Supreme Court replied, "The state has advanced a number of arguments, but none of them overcome this reality: same-sex couples who cannot marry are not treated equally under the law today. The harm to them is real, not abstract or speculative" (Rizzo & Sherman, 2013, para. 9.). Recognizing the court's strong position, Governor Christie retracted his appeal, making New Jersey the 14th U.S. state to recognize marriage equality, allowing same-sex couples to legally marry starting on October 19, 2013.

Perhaps more tumultuous than New Jersey's history is the struggle for marriage equality in California. In 1999, California became the first state to institute statewide domestic partnership benefits. As a conservative response, in 2002 California voters approved a ballot initiative called Proposition 22 thus writing into the state's Family Code marriage as only between one man and one woman. Later, in 2004, San Francisco Mayor Gavin Newsome asserted that under the California constitution's Equal Protection Clause, he had the authority to perform marriages for lesbians and gay men. By the time the California Supreme Court banned marriages in March of that year, San Francisco had issued nearly 4,000 marriage licenses, which the state later invalidated (Green, 2012).

In response to Proposition 22, proponents of marriage equality waged a legal battle. In May 2008, the California Supreme Court nullified Proposition 22 thus giving same-sex couples the right to marry in the state (Robinson & Soderstrom, 2011). Soon following the court's decision, opponents of marriage equality put forth another ballot initiative, Proposition 8, which would institute a state constitutional amendment and solidify marriage as being between one man and one woman. In support of marriage equality, Governor Arnold Schwarzenegger pledged to uphold the court's ruling and oppose Proposition 8 (Green, 2012).

In November 2008, Proposition 8 passed with about 52% of Californians voting for the measure. Because "the constitution supersedes the state civil code, same-sex marriage in California [was] once again banned" (Green, 2012). In the court case, *Strauss v. Horton*, the California Supreme Court upheld Proposition 8, even though the same court had recently invalidated Proposition 22, which was a similar measure. The court conceded, however, that all of the approximate 18,000 marriage licenses issued to same-sex couples between May 2008 and May 2009 would remain valid (Green, 2012).

Following the California Supreme Court's decision upholding Proposition 8, supporters of marriage equality filed another lawsuit, *Perry v. Schwarzenegger*, challenging Proposition 8, and arguing that the ballot initiative "violated Due Process and Equal Protection Clauses of the United States Constitution. This was the first federal challenge to a state constitutional amendment banning same-sex marriage" (Robinson & Soderstrom, 2011, p. 534). After a 13-day trial, Federal Judge Vaughn Walker decided the case on August 4, 2010, by ruling that Proposition 8 was unconstitutional. However, the Ninth Circuit Court of Appeals allowed supporters of Proposition 8 to file an appeal. On February 7, 2012, because of that appeal, the Ninth U.S. Circuit Court of Appeals also found Proposition 8 to be unconstitutional, opening the door for the case of marriage equality to be heard by the U.S. Supreme Court (Chonody et al., 2012). On March 26, 2013, the U.S. Supreme Court heard the Proposition 8 case in the form of *Hollingsworth v. Perry*. Three months later, on June 26, 2013, the court gave a 5–4 ruling that "declared that the supporters of Proposition 8 who argued in favor of the California ban on same-sex marriage had no legal standing, and negated the decision of the United States Court of Appeals for the Ninth Circuit" (Schwartz, 2012). The result is that the 2010 ruling from the federal court stands, thus allowing same-sex couples to legally marry in California.

The struggle for marriage equality will continue to unfold throughout the foreseeable future both in the courts and among the general public (Seidman, 2009). As the Global Box at the end of this chapter indicates, at a time when 28 nations on four separate continents (Europe, South America, Australia, and Africa) have legalized some form of federal-level marriage, civil unions, or domestic partnerships (Chonody et al., 2012), the United States continues to grapple with the issue of marriage equality.

Examining the history of the struggle for marriage equality shows us that our understanding of how societies have historically structured marriage is not connected to any natural or biological structure. Cultural understandings about how marriage should or could be structured—either around heterosexual or same-sex unions—are just that: cultural understandings. In other words, looking at the historical struggle for marriage equality lends evidence to how marriage, and the larger institution within which marriage exists (i.e., family), is socially constructed. Furthermore, the backlash against the struggle for marriage equality exemplifies how many conservative thinkers fear a change in the structure of marriage because they can see the institution of marriage shifting away from their own beliefs about marriage. However, as the remaining chapter will discuss, allowing same-sex couples to marry can in fact strengthen LGBT families and therefore strengthen American families in general.

The Importance of Marriage to LGBT Families

In 2004, Cherlin wrote about the "deinstitutionalization of marriage" in which there has been a "weakening of the social norms that define people's behavior in a social institution such as marriage" (p. 848). Despite or perhaps because of the weakening of norms around marriage, Cherlin (2004) argued that for many people throughout the United States, the institution of marriage carries heavy symbolic meaning:

> In times of social stability, the taken-for-granted nature of norms allows people to go about their lives without having to question their actions or the actions of others. But when social change produces situations outside the reach of established norms, individuals can no longer rely on shared understandings of how to act. Rather, they must negotiate new ways of acting, a process that is a potential source of conflict and opportunity. On the one hand, the development of new rules is likely to engender disagreement and tension among the relevant actors. On the other hand, the breakdown of the old rules of a gendered institution such as marriage could lead to the creation of a more egalitarian relationship between wives and husbands. (p. 848)

The position I take in this chapter as well as throughout the book, therefore, is one that builds on Cherlin's work. After reading about the struggle for marriage equality discussed above, I draw on Cherlin's analysis to better understand why marriage matters so much to LGBT people and their families. There are four main reasons: (a) Marriage socially legitimates a group of people, (b) marriage comes with many economic benefits, (c) marriage is a civil right, and (d) there are currently no equal alternatives to marriage in the United States.

Marriage Socially Legitimates a Group of People

The first reason—that marriage legitimates groups of people by legitimating their families—has been true throughout history, and as Cherlin (2004) noted, becomes even more important in times of social upheaval and change. As historian Nancy Cott (2002) wrote, "By incriminating some marriages and encouraging others, marital regulations have drawn lines among the citizenry and defined what kinds of sexual relations and which families will be legitimate" (p. 4). Anthropologist Ellen Lewin (2004) added that not only do the entitlements of marriage mark legitimacy and authenticity of a relationship, but also they "mediate the ability to claim a particular identity in the context of one's community, and they intervene in situations where shame may preclude naming one's most important relationships" (p. 1005).

Thus, marriage legitimates people's family lives—and therefore their very personal lives—in a way that no other institution does (Mezey & Boudreaux, 2005). The legitimation of people's family and personal lives is one of the main points of columnist Jonathon Rauch's book on allowing same-sex couples to marry. Rauch (2004) stated that while marriage is a legal contract between two people, it is also "a contract between two people *and their community*" (p. 32). He argued that when two people pledge to marry, take care of each other, and do the best they can for society, society in turn is pledging to help them, as a family unit, to succeed. The legitimation that marriage offers, therefore, is not just in the eyes of the couple or their families but also in larger communities. Simply put, many LGBT people assume that when they hold the right to marry, they hold society's approval of their very existence.

The relationship between social acceptance and marital rights appears to be circular in nature and important to the fight for marriage equality. As social acceptance increases in general for LGBT people, so does social acceptance for marriage equality; and as marriage equality becomes more accepted, attitudes around LGBT people become more accepted as well. Supporters of marriage equality hope, therefore, that the momentum created around marriage equality will ultimately lead to the eradication of homophobic attitudes and heterosexist practices in the United States, thus, creating greater equality in general for LGBT people.

There is little doubt that increasing social acceptance of LGBT people has been important in the fight for marriage equality. Attitudes toward homosexuality have changed dramatically since the early 1970s; and attitudes around marriage equality reached a turning point around 30 years later (Wolfson, 2004). According to findings from the General Social Survey (GSS), a nationally representative survey of several thousand households conducted approximately every 2 years that tracks the opinions of Americans, between 1973 and the mid-1990s, 65% to 75% of respondents stated that "sexual relations between two adults of the same sex" is "always wrong." By 1998, that number decreased to 54% of respondents where it has hovered through 2006, which is the last recorded GSS survey asking that question (Brewer, 2008; Smith, 2011).

What is equally telling is that while only 11.2% of people in 1973 said that homosexual sexual relations were "not wrong at all," in 2006, that number climbed to 32.3%. However, while that climb makes for a 188% increase over a 33-year period, it also means that the remaining 68% of Americans in 2006 still believed that homosexual sexual relations are "always wrong," "almost always wrong," or "sometimes wrong" (Smith, 2011). In other words, while support for LGBT people and their relationships grew dramatically between 1973 and 2006, the vast majority of Americans in 2006 still did not approve of same-sex relationships. Attitudes have continued to shift, however. As noted in Table 2.2, a 2012 Gallup poll

Table 2.2   Attitudes Toward Same-Sex Marriage, May 2012—Gallup

	Gay/lesbian relations should be legal %	Gay/lesbian relations are morally acceptable %	Same-sex marriages should be legal %
National adults	63	54	50
Men	61	49	42
Women	66	59	56
White	65	55	49
Non-White	59	50	50
18–34	76	65	66
35–54	61	55	47
55 and older	56	46	40
East	74	62	56
Midwest	69	60	53
South	49	43	40
West	68	58	55
Protestant	54	41	39
Catholic	68	66	51
Non-Christian	89	84	84
Republican	46	36	22
Independent	69	58	57
Democrat	72	66	65

Source: Saad, 2012. Copyright © 2012 Gallup, Inc. All rights reserved. The content is used with permission; however, Gallup retains all rights of republication.

reported that 54% of Americans said that gay and lesbian relations are morally acceptable. Furthermore, according to a July 2012 poll conducted by the Pew Research Center, 48% of Americans favored marriage equality, while 44% opposed.

Although the aggregate numbers are important, attitudes concerning the morality of same-sex relationships, as well as marriage equality, are not universal; instead, they vary based on a number of factors, including gender, religion, age, geographic location, political affiliation, and race. Examining the disaggregated data is important because the data suggest what groups in the United States are more or less accepting of LGBT people and marriage equality. The indications of such data are that LGBT people within different demographic groups may experience greater or lesser discrimination and hardship. In addition, groups with powerful political voices can greatly affect laws and policies that support or discriminate against LGBT people and their families.

As Table 2.2 indicates, in 2012, women were more accepting than men of same-sex relations and marriage equality. Similarly, the majority (76%) of Americans aged 18 to 34 years old favored marriage equality compared to nearly 50% of 35 to 54-year-olds and 40% of those aged 55 years and older. Regarding geographic location, Americans located in the East, West, and Midwest were more accepting of marriage equality than those in the south. Furthermore, in 2012, non-Christians were more than twice as accepting of marriage for same-sex couples as Protestants, whereas over half of all Catholics (51%) polled said that marriage for same-sex couples should be legal. Additional studies support this latter finding, showing that Catholics are more supportive of marriage equality than are fundamentalist Protestant groups (Ellison, Acevedo, & Ramos-Wada, 2011; Olson, Harrison, & College, 2006; Sherkat, de Vries, & Creek, 2010).

In addition, as of July 2012, 65% of Democrats favored same-sex marriage, compared to 51% of Independents and 24% of Republicans (Pew Research Center, 2012). However, political affiliation does not always predict attitude, particularly when we account for race. An analysis of a Gallup Poll conducted between 2006 and 2008 of over 3,000 respondents showed that only "30% of black Democrats say they would agree that marriages between same-sex couples should be recognized by law as valid, compared to 57% of nonblack Democrats" (Newport, 2008, para. 6). This finding is important given that Democrats in general tend to be more supportive of marriage equality compared to Republicans, and yet Black Democrats are closer to Republicans in their views of marriage equality for LGBT people (Newport, 2008).

As Table 2.2 also indicates, race is indeed an important factor in shaping people's attitudes toward marriage equality. According to Gallup, in 2012, Whites were more likely to favor marriage equality than what researchers call "non-Whites." As the following discussion indicates, however, the category of "non-Whites" is problematic because there are many diverse groups that fit into this category. In addition, the use of the term "non-Whites" places "Whites" as the "main" or "normal" category and places all other racial groups as a category outside of "normal."

The data on racial-ethnic minorities (i.e., "non-Whites") show that Blacks in the United States are more conservative in their thinking about marriage equality than other racial-ethnic groups, and their attitudes have not shifted much over the past 20 years or so (Sherkat et al., 2010). One reason why many Blacks oppose marriage equality is that they tend to belong to religious communities that condemn same-sex relationships in general (Bennett & Battle, 2001). Nearly two thirds of Black Americans are affiliated with Baptist or other sectarian Protestant denominations that tend to be anti-marriage equality, compared to approximately one third of White Americans. In addition, Blacks tend to worship at churches that are racially homogenous and segregated and that do not support LGBT rights. Therefore, the church experience of many Black Americans does not include a variety of differing opinions regarding homosexuality or marriage equality (Sherkat et al., 2010).

In addition, Black Americans in general do not favor marriage equality because many do not view the current gay liberation movement as being analogous to the civil rights movement of the 1960s, a point discussed in greater detail below (Ghavami & Johnson, 2011). Furthermore, previous research suggests that Whites have equated the sexuality of Black people as being abnormal and even criminal in nature (Collins, 1990). Because of the history of Whites demonizing the sexual behavior of Black people and because of connections to religious institutions, many Blacks today separate themselves from "deviant" sexual identities, thus rejecting LGBT sexual relations within their own communities (Greene, 2009).

Latinos show a slightly different picture than Blacks, particularly because approximately 73% of Latinos are Catholic, as opposed to 23% of Latinos who claim mostly conservative sectarian Protestant affiliations (i.e., fundamentalist, evangelical, and charismatic) (Ellison et al., 2011). Conducting a multivariate analysis of data collected through a large nationwide probability sample of Latinos in the United States, Ellison et al. (2011) found that "evangelical Protestant Latinos are much more resistant to same-sex marriage than their Catholic counterparts" (p. 47). In fact, the likelihood of approving of marriage equality is "84 percent lower among evangelicals who attend services regularly . . . compared to devout Catholics from otherwise similar backgrounds" (p. 47). However, secular Latinos, as well as Protestant Latinos who do not attend religious services, are significantly more supportive of marriage equality than are Catholic Latinos in general (Ellison et al., 2011).

Other attitudinal variations among Latinos also exist and mirror attitudes among similar groups within the United States. For example, among the

Latino population in the United States, we see greater approval for marriage equality among women, people aged 30 and younger, urban, higher educated, native born, and recent immigrant Latinos than among their counterparts. In addition, "Puerto Ricans are markedly more tolerant of same-sex marriage than members of other Latino nationality groups . . ." (Ellison et al., 2011, p. 49). These findings remind us that it is difficult to make generalizations about racial categories of people who are homogeneous by name only and in reality contain significant heterogeneity including attitudes concerning marriage equality.

Although there is limited information on attitudes among Asian Americans concerning marriage equality, and while the category of "Asian American" is incredibly diverse (Yep, Lovaas, & Elia, 2003), the limited evidence suggests that many Asian Americans oppose marriage equality (Rhee, 2006; Shore, 2004). For example, journalist Elena Shore (2004) reported that approximately 7,000 Chinese Americans and their church groups rallied against marriage equality in San Francisco in 2004. Former political candidate Rose Tsai explained the cultural and historical reasons as to why the Chinese community in San Francisco was fighting against marriage equality. She stated, "Chinese, in 5,000 years of history, have acknowledged that homosexuality has always existed. But, it is accepted with the understanding that you don't glorify such relationships" (Shore, 2004, p. 1). Because Tsai based her response on anecdotal evidence, we do not know if her statement truly reflects widespread attitudes among Chinese Americans regarding marriage equality. However, Tsai offers some insight given the dearth of research conducted in this area.

In addition, studies have found similar sentiments among members of Korean American communities (Chung, Oswald, & Wiley, 2006; Rhee, 2006). For example, ethnic studies scholar Margaret Rhee (2006) analyzed *KoreAm Journal*, a printed source addressing Korean American same-sex sexuality, which reflects attitudes regarding marriage equality within Korean American communities. Rhee found that not only do many Korean Americans value a heterosexual, patriarchal family, but also value marriage between two people within the Korean community. Part of this attitude is connected to "traditional Confucius values such as filial piety, family lineage, and patriarchy," a belief system held more firmly by older than younger generations within the Korean American community (Rhee, 2006, p. 77). Attitudes also vary by whether or not someone was born in, or immigrated to, the United States, as well as by economic standing (Rhee, 2006). In addition, one study reported in *KoreAm Journal* found that nearly 75% of Korean Americans are Christian and believe that homosexuality is a choice that can be reversed (Rhee, 2006). It was clear through Rhee's analysis that devout Christianity plays a part in spreading homophobia within the Korean American community as it has within other Christian communities.

Marriage Comes With Many Economic Benefits

In addition to the promise of marriage socially legitimatizing the personal and family lives of LGBT people, the second reason many LGBT people want to legally marry is because marriage comes with a multitude of economic benefits. Therefore, in addition to the cultural benefits of marriage, being part of marriage as a legal institution could help LGBT people secure material benefits that can economically support their families. In 1997, the U.S. General Accounting Office (GAO) counted "1,049 federal laws classified to the United States Code in which marital status is a factor" (Shah, 2004). On December 31, 2003, the GAO updated that number by identifying "a total of 1,138 federal statutory provisions classified to the United States Code in which marital status is a factor in determining or receiving benefits, rights, and privileges" (Shah, 2004).

In referring to 1,138 benefits, there are two caveats worth mentioning. First, some of those laws might actually penalize married couples (Cherlin, 2010). For example, one of the statutes listed "limits the amount of certain crop support payments that one person can receive. For this purpose, a married couple is considered to be one person. But an unmarried couple can apparently escape this restriction and each receive the maximum amount" (Cherlin, 2010, p. 13). Second, the count might be incomplete. As Dayna K. Shah, the associate general counsel of the GAO wrote, "Because of the inherent limitations of any global electronic search and the many ways in which the laws of the United States Code may deal with marital status, we cannot guarantee that we have captured every individual law in the United States Code in which marital status figures" (Shah, 2004, p. 1). Despite these caveats, the counts conducted in 1997 and 2003 suggest that marriage bestows at least 1,000 benefits, giving LGBT people ample reason to want the legal right to marry.

The importance of the legal and economic benefits of marriage cannot be understated. Of course, many people today marry based on love, not money. However, throughout history, marriage has been—and continues to be—an economic institution, one used to transfer wealth and property to offspring, connect and maintain the wealth of families, and build empires (Coontz, 2005). That does not mean that love does not matter in marriage; love has mattered for approximately the past 200 years, and continues to do so (Coontz, 2005; Cott, 2002). But in addition to the personal commitment and social recognition that marriage bestows upon those who wed, the material benefits of entering into a legal marital relationship add innumerable layers of economic support that can help bolster the personal commitment married people make to each other and the quality of their familial relationships.

The 1,138 benefits of marriage fall into 13 categories of law, displayed in Table 2.3. All of these categories and laws are important, although some carry more weight for the vast majority of LGBT families. In their 2009 booklet,

Table 2.3 Overview of the Benefits of Legal Marriage

Category	Provisions
Category 1: Social Security and Related Programs, Housing, and Food Stamps	Includes major federal health and welfare programs including Social Security retirement and disability benefits, food stamps, welfare, and Medicare and Medicaid.
Category 2: Veterans' Benefits	Includes pensions, indemnity compensation for service-connected deaths, medical care, nursing home care, right to burial in veterans' cemeteries, educational assistance, and housing. Husbands or wives of veterans have many rights and privileges by virtue of the marital relationship.
Category 3: Taxation	Married taxpayers have the option to file joint or separate income tax returns. There are different tax consequences, depending on whether a taxpayer is married filing jointly, married filing separately, unmarried but the head of a household, or unmarried and not the head of a household.
Category 4: Federal Civilian and Military Service Benefits	Includes statutory provisions dealing with current and retired federal officers and employees, members of the Armed Forces, elected officials, and judges, in which marital status is a factor. Typically, these provisions address the various health, leave, retirement, survivor, and insurance benefits provided by the United States to those in federal service and their families.
Category 5: Employment Benefits and Related Provisions	Includes laws that address the rights of employees under employer-sponsored employee benefit plans, that provide for continuation of employer-sponsored health benefits after events like the death or divorce of the employee, and that give employees the right to unpaid leave in order to care for a seriously ill spouse, as well as special benefits in connection with certain occupations, like mining and public safety.

(Continued)

Table 2.3 (Continued)

Category	Provisions
Category 6: Immigration, Naturalization, and Aliens	Includes the conditions under which noncitizens may enter and remain in the United States, be deported, or become citizens. The law gives special consideration to spouses of immigrant and nonimmigrant aliens, including the granting of asylum to aliens and their spouses.
Category 7: Indians	Various laws set out the rights to tribal property of "White" men marrying "Indian" women, or of "Indian" women marrying "White" men, as well as the descent and distribution rights for Indians' property in general. The law also pertains to health-care eligibility for Indians and spouses and reimbursement of travel expenses of spouses and candidates seeking positions in the Indian Health Service.
Category 8: Trade, Commerce, and Intellectual Property	Concerns foreign or domestic business and commerce regarding bankruptcy, commerce and trade, copyrights, and customs duties. This category also includes the National Housing Act (rights of mortgage borrowers), the Consumer Credit Protection Act (governs wage garnishment), and the Copyright Act (spousal copyright renewal and termination rights).
Category 9: Financial Disclosure and Conflict of Interest	Federal law imposes obligations on members of Congress, employees or officers of the federal government, and members of the boards of directors of some government-related or government chartered entities, to prevent actual or apparent conflicts of interest. These individuals are required to disclose publicly certain gifts, interests, and transactions. Many of these also apply to the individual's spouse.
Category 10: Crimes and Family Violence	Includes laws that implicate marriage in connection with criminal justice or family violence, including laws dealing with spouses as victims of crimes, spouses as perpetrators, or dealing with crime prevention and family violence.
Category 11: Loans, Guarantees, and Payments in Agriculture	Includes laws regulating federal loan programs in which a spouse's income, business interests, or assets are taken into account for purposes of determining a person's eligibility to participate in the program. Also includes factors determining the amount of federal assistance to which a person is entitled or the repayment schedule, including education loan programs, housing loan programs for veterans, and provisions governing agricultural price supports and loan programs that are affected by the spousal relationship.

Category	Provisions
Category 12: Federal Natural Resources and Related Provisions	Federal law gives special rights to spouses in connection with a variety of transactions involving federal lands and other federal property, including the purchase and sale of land by the federal government and the lease by the government of water and mineral rights.
Category 13: Miscellaneous Provisions	Includes federal statutory provisions that do not fit readily in any of the other 12 categories, such as prohibiting discrimination on the basis of marital status, and patriotic societies chartered in federal law, such as the Veterans of Foreign Wars or the Gold Star Wives of America.

Answers to Questions to Marriage Equality, the Human Rights Campaign (HRC), an organization that has long been documenting discrimination against gays and lesbians and lobbies for anti-discriminatory policies, has explained how some of the lack of access to marriage negatively affects LGBT families. The discussion below builds on HRC's work, fills in some of the details about how marriage offers people certain benefits, and explains how a lack of such benefits affects LGBT people from different backgrounds.

Hospital Visitation, Health Care, and Medical Issues. As Category 1 in Table 2.3 indicates, health insurance is a built-in safety net for married people. Marriage protects couples when dealing with a sick or injured spouse in four major ways: through hospital visitation rights, at nursing homes and assisted care facilities, through the Family Medical Leave Act (FMLA), and through health insurance.

Regarding hospital visitation rights, "Married couples have the automatic right to visit each other in the hospital and make medical decisions. Same-sex couples can be denied the right to visit a sick or injured loved one in the hospital" (HRC, 2009, p. 3). The issue of hospital visitation may be particularly problematic for transgender people who face added discrimination from medical professionals and hospital staff. In 2010, the National Gay and Lesbian Task Force and the National Center for Transgender Equality conducted the most comprehensive study of transgender discrimination to date, surveying 6,450 transgender and gender nonconforming people spread over all 50 states, the District of Columbia, Puerto Rico, Guam, and the U.S. Virgin Islands. The study showed that 19% of those sampled "reported being refused medical care due to their transgender or gender non-conforming status, with even higher numbers among people of color in the survey" (Grant, Mottet, & Tanis, 2011, p. 5). In addition, because many physicians are often uninformed about issues concerning transgender people, "50% of the sample reported having to teach their medical providers about transgender care" (Grant et al., 2011, p. 5). Although marriage may not solve the problem of ignorance among some medical professionals, marriage would at minimum allow transgender people to instantly obtain visitation rights in a medical emergency or involving other hospitalization issues without their partner having to face barriers—and greater emotional turmoil—created by misinformed medical staff and physicians because of the lack of a marriage license.

The second medically related protection provided by marriage involves care at nursing homes and assisted care facilities. "Married couples have a legal right to live together in nursing homes. The rights of elderly gay or lesbian couples are an uneven patchwork of state laws" (HRC, 2009, p. 4), and many elderly LGBT people face great discrimination in such facilities to begin with (Cantor, Brennan, & Shippy, 2004; Claasen, 2005). Although Medicare pays for short stays at nursing home facilities, it does not cover expensive long-term coverage. Therefore, many elderly people (LGBT or otherwise) rely on Medicaid to cover the remaining cost, provided certain income and asset rules apply. When a married person enters a nursing home, or even after that person's death, Medicaid allows the surviving spouse to remain in their house instead of forcing sale to help pay for the care (Cianciotto, 2005; Claasen, 2005). It is only after the survivor's death that

> the state may then take the home to recoup the costs of terminal care. Because same-sex couples cannot marry they are not eligible for this protection, and they may be forced to choose between their home and life's savings or medical coverage. (Cianciotto, 2005, p. 6)

The problem of covering expenses is particularly important for elderly LGBT, who may need to use a nursing home or assisted-care facility as they age. One study showed that at least 20% of LGBT people will rely on Medicaid for their long-term care needs (MetLife Mature Market Institute [MetLife], 2010), compared to approximately 16% to 18% of elderly people in the general population (Congressional Budget Office, 2013).

The third medically related protection that marriage provides is through the FMLA, which allows people to maintain job security while taking 12 weeks of work off without pay to care for a family member, for example, at the birth or adoption of a child or because of a serious health condition or illness. However, because under the law "family" refers to people connected by blood or legal ties, LGBT people who are not legally or biologically related may be excluded from the FMLA. Such exclusion prevents LGBT people from "taking care of their families on equal terms with families headed by opposite-sex couples, and exposes them to additional vulnerabilities in the workplace" if they choose to take time off to provide care outside of FMLA (Cianciotto, 2005, p. 23).

The fourth medically related protection that marriage provides is reflected through health insurance. Although many public and private employers provide health insurance coverage to employees and their spouses, this coverage does not always extend to the "life partners of gay and lesbian employees. Gay and lesbian employees who do receive health coverage for their partners must pay federal income taxes on the value of the insurance" (HRC, 2009, p. 3), thus, placing a financial burden on LGBT families.

The financial cost of not having access to the medical benefits provided through marriage is particularly difficult for LGBT people of color. Studies on Black, Latino, and Asian American lesbians and gay men, as well as transgender people of all races, show that these populations earn significantly less than their heterosexual counterparts, thus, exacerbating the financial burden of not being able to legally marry (Cianciotto, 2005; Dang & Frazer, 2005; Grant et al., 2011; Magpantay, 2006; Yan, Peng, Lee, Rickles, & Abbott, 2004). In addition, often both Black and Latino gays and lesbians work in the public sector (Cianciotto, 2005; Dang & Frazer, 2005). In fact, "Black same-sex partners are about 25 percent more likely than white gay partners to hold public sector jobs" (Cahill & Tobias, 2007, p. 28). While private companies are able to create their own protections for their LGBT employees, such as domestic partnership benefits, employees in the public sector are subject to state and local laws that often lack the protections discussed above.

The difference between private and public employment can be particularly important for those who are able to land positions in large companies. In their 2014 assessment of 734 Fortune 500 and Fortune 1000 companies, the largest law firms, and other large corporations, HRC (2014a) found that 99% included sexual orientation in their nondiscrimination policies. In addition, 86% of these companies included gender orientation in their nondiscrimination policies, 90% provided medical and comprehensive health benefits, and 69% had complete equality in spousal and partner access to "soft" benefits such as bereavement leave, employee assistance programs, employee discounts, and relocation assistance. Eighty-four percent extended retiree health-care coverage to domestic partners, and 46% offered transgender-inclusive health-care coverage options through at least one firmwide plan. The numbers of private corporations protecting LGBT people in their nondiscrimination policies and extending benefits to LGBT people and their families compares to the public sector where only 17 states and the District of Columbia include sexual orientation and gender expression, and an additional four states include only sexual orientation, in their nondiscrimination policies. Therefore, "it remains legal in 29 states to discriminate against job applicants and employees because of their sexual orientation, and in 33 states because of their gender identity" (HRC, 2014b, p. 20). Thus, LGBT people who are working for large supportive companies are likely to receive domestic partner benefits that many states refuse to provide their citizens.

If marriage provides and strengthens options for health benefits and if most states deny LGBT people the right to marry, the result is that as a country we are systematically preventing part of the American population access to health care that they may need. By doing so, we weaken not only some of our families, but also we create a system in which some people are unable to be healthy, productive citizens in ways that strengthen our nation. In other words, healthier family members and workers make for a healthier nation. Yet by denying marriage equality to LGBT people, the United States makes a decision to systematically weaken the nation by not allowing certain citizens to gain access to health benefits through the institution of marriage.

Social Security Benefits, Pensions, and Estate/Inheritance Taxes. In addition to health benefits, certain economic benefits of marriage are also an important reason why LGBT people want to get married:

> Married people receive Social Security payments upon the death of a spouse. Despite paying payroll taxes, gay and lesbian partners receive no Social Security survivor benefits—resulting in an average annual income loss of $5,528 upon the death of a partner. (HRC, 2009, p. 3)

In addition, "After the death of a worker, most pension plans pay survivor benefits only to a legal spouse of the participant. Gay and lesbian partners are excluded from such pension benefits" (HRC, 2009, p. 4). For example, if a married person with a 401k plan specifies her or his spouse as the beneficiary, when that person dies, the surviving spouse can roll the total amount of the distribution into an IRA without paying income tax. However, "if the surviving beneficiary is a same-sex partner, the pension distribution is subject to a 20 percent federal withholding tax" (Cahill & Tobias, 2007, p. 35). The lack of such benefits for unmarried couples greatly affects how LGBT people need to plan for their futures and retirements and also affects the quality of life of elderly LGBT people, particularly as at least one in 10 LGBT couples has a member who is over 65 years of age (Gates, 2003, as cited in Chonody et al., 2012, p. 281). For LGBT people of color, who already earn significantly less than White LGBT people (Cahill & Tobias, 2007), the loss of income in later years may be particularly devastating.

A 2006 study of 1,000 LGBT baby boomers between the ages of 40 and 61 conducted by MetLife showed that the most serious concern of the respondents—particularly women—was financial. Nearly one third of all participants stated that their biggest concern was how they will pay for care as they grow old, with lesbians expressing slightly greater concern than gay men about outliving their income. More specifically, lesbians are particularly worried because without access to their widow's Social Security payments and other marriage-related federal benefits, they "are apprehensive about their financial ability to live comfortably in retirement. For gay men, by contrast, concerns about lack of access to such benefits may be somewhat offset by greater confidence in their overall earning capacity" (MetLife, 2010, p. 52).

Furthermore, LGBT people (both women and men) may have heightened financial fears because some tend to care for others at higher rates than those in the general population (Cantor et al., 2004; MetLife, 2010). In fact, many LGBT people care for other elderly LGBT nonlegal or nonbiologically connected family members "of choice" or "fictive kin" (Dill, 1994; Weston, 1991) because of the compromised financial support that LGBT people experience due to a lack of access to their partner's Social Security benefits and pensions. Thus, not having access to economic benefits that marriage affords means that many LGBT people are concerned about how to take care of themselves while also worrying about how they will take care of others as they grow old.

Given the discussion of how financially disadvantaged unmarried people can be due to rules of Medicaid, FMLA, Social Security, pensions, and other policies, the laws surrounding estate taxes add to the potential economic disadvantage. "A married person automatically inherits all the property of his or her deceased spouse without paying estate taxes. A gay or lesbian taxpayer is forced to pay estate taxes on property inherited from a deceased partner" (HRC, 2009, p. 4). The tax burden is particularly high for wealthier LGBT couples with over $2 million in assets (including any jointly owned home). According to one report from the Williams Institute, over 550 LGBT couples were estimated to be affected by owing an average of 1.1 million additional tax dollars per estate (Steinberger, 2009). Indeed, such taxation was the very issue that prompted the *The United States v. Windsor* case (see the section on "No Equal Alternatives to Marriage" below for a longer discussion).

The result of living in a state that does not allow same-sex couples to legally marry is that both on the federal and state level, LGBT couples often spend thousands of dollars to create legal contracts that protect their family relationships (Cianciotto, 2005; Lev, 2004). Sociologist Amy Agigian (2004) listed nearly 20 contracts that the National Center for Lesbian Rights (NCLR) and the Human Rights Campaign Fund's FamilyNet (HRCF) suggest that LGBT people create in order to protect their families, including Autopsy and Disposition of Remains, Directive to Physicians, Durable Power of Attorney for Finances, Durable Power of Attorney for Healthcare, Hospital Visitation Authorization, and Right to Receive Personal Property (p. 96).

Because of the great economic burdens posed by the inability to marry, the financial fears that LGBT people have as they grow older exist across lines of social class, even among those with college or graduate degrees and median annual incomes of $50,000 to $75,000 (MetLife, 2010). Interestingly, even though many Americans do not support marriage equality, many strongly "support treating same-sex couples equally under Social Security policy (68%) and laws governing inheritance (73%)" (Cahill, 2004, p. 59). Perhaps public support for including LGBT people under certain inheritance policies is because of how obvious the economic inequality is that LGBT people face when they do not receive similar benefits as heterosexual couples. In addition, the economics of Social Security and inheritance taxes generally do not carry the same ideological weight as marriage.

Immigration. "Americans in bi-national relationships are not permitted to petition for their same-sex partners to immigrate. As a result, they are often forced to separate or move to another country" (HRC, 2009, p. 3). According to some estimates, there are approximately 80,000 binational same-sex couples living in the United States. Although currently 20 countries offer some form of national legal recognition of LGBT relationships (see this chapter's Global Box for more details), of the group of binational same-sex couples living in the United States, 80% come from countries that do not grant marital recognition to LGBT people (Badgett, 2011). As LGBT rights movements expand throughout the globe, more LGBT people are traveling via cruises, vacations, business, and political efforts, opening the opportunity for them to meet others with similar interests. "When those relationships deepen, binational couples face not the common question of whether it is time to move in together, but of whether it is even possible to live together in one place" (Badgett, 2011, p. 794). Given immigration restrictions, the Gay and Lesbian Advocates and Defenders (GLAD) issued a warning stating that even in states where gay and lesbians can legally marry, "marriages between same-sex binational couples are ineffective in changing the immigration status of the non-citizen partner and could even lead to deportation or other immigrant consequences," particularly if that partner is undocumented or on a temporary visa (Magpantay, 2006, pp. 111–112). The reason for this warning is that currently, marriage equality is on a state level, while immigration laws exist on both state and federal levels.

The issue of immigration through marriage may be particularly salient for Latinos and Asian American LGBT people because they often come out of and belong to large immigrant populations (Cantú, 2009; Dang & Vianney, 2007).

An analysis of 2000 census data examining lesbians and gays in New York, San Francisco, and Los Angeles—cities claiming the greatest Asian same-sex household populations—showed that 73% of gays and lesbians in San Francisco and 83% in Los Angeles were foreign born (Yan et al., 2004). Studies found similar numbers among Asian American same-sex households in New York (Magpantay, 2006). Immigration was the most important issue to the respondents in Dang and Vianney's (2007) study as well.

Furthermore, 51% of Hispanic same-sex couples reported being born outside the United States, as opposed to 5% of White non-Hispanic same-sex couples (Cianciotto, 2005, p. 48). These numbers suggest that both Hispanic-Latino and Asian American LGBT people may face greater relationship barriers than other groups if not able to marry their foreign-born partners. As the above discussion makes clear, the lack of legal marriage presents many challenges to LGBT families. And as Table 2.3 indicates, the challenges presented in this section are only a very short part of the approximate 1,000 benefits that the institution of marriage offers.

Marriage Is a Civil Right

In addition to legitimizing their families and accessing economic and material benefits, the third reason that many LGBT people want to legally marry is because they believe that marriage is a civil right, one that should be granted to all U.S. citizens (Wolfson, 2004). When people refer to "civil rights," they often associate those rights with the struggle for Blacks to gain freedom from slavery as well as full citizenship rights (regarding the 13th and 14th amendments of the U.S. Constitution, respectively). Therefore, civil rights refers to a group of people's rights to be counted and treated as full citizens in the United States, with all the rights and privileges granted by the nation's rule of law.

Many people, both LGBT and heterosexual, equate the lack of rights for LGBT people, particularly pertaining to marriage, as a civil rights issue. Such thinkers span racial categories; in fact, Coretta Scott King, the wife of Dr. Martin Luther King Jr., was an early supporter of marriage equality, as were several other Black civil rights leaders, Holocaust survivors, and people who had experienced discrimination throughout their lifetimes (Wolfson, 2004). The argument of such allies is that without the right to marry, the United States denies LGBT people the same civil rights granted to other groups of people (Sullivan, 2004). Drawing on examples from the Black civil rights movement and arguing that they are a disadvantaged minority similar to other groups before them (Chauncey, 2004; Epstein, 1987), LGBT activists have also taken the stance that marriage is a civil right. As discussed below, in the early 1990s, in attempts to push the marriage equality agenda forward, lawyers drew on the *Loving v. Virginia* case, which led to the end of anti-miscegenation (i.e., anti-mixed race marriage) laws (Tong, 1998). As sociologist Steven Epstein (1987) wrote, equating themselves as having an "ethnic" or minority identity politically serves LGBT people well because such an identity is "particularly suited to the American experience, with its history of civil-rights struggles and ethnic-based, interest-group competition" (p. 20).

The claim that marriage is a civil right has met resistance from groups within the pro-(heterosexual) marriage movement. White conservatives in particular have argued that we cannot equate the Black civil rights movement with LGBT rights (Wolfson, 2004). Conservative groups, such as the Family Research Council, have allied themselves with conservative Black clergy to argue that homosexuality is a lifestyle choice and therefore not equated with race, which they maintain is biologically determined.

In addition, those opposing marriage equality argue that giving LGBT people "rights" is giving them "special rights" beyond what other Americans receive. In fact, White heterosexual groups argue that giving LGBT people special rights would take away from the existing rights of Black people. To make this argument, opponents of marriage equality portray LGBT people as economically privileged White people who are therefore "undeserving of nondiscrimination protections" (Cahill, 2004, p. 71). In truth, most gay men earn about 20% to 25% less than their heterosexual counterparts do, and lesbian couples earn less than heterosexual couples do because they lack a male wage earner (Cahill, 2004). However, media portrayals showing wealthy, White gay people at lavish affairs create a popular belief that counters reality, deepens stereotypes, and perpetuates a false understanding of LGBT people as a homogeneous group.

Furthermore, lawyer Suzanne Goldberg (1995, as cited in Cahill, 2004, p. 71) and political scientist and lawyer Evan Gerstmann (2004) argued that "special rights" and "gay rights" do not exist. Rather, "there are only legal and constitutional rights that must be applied and protected equally for all people" (Gerstmann, 2004, p. 4). Gerstmann asked the question, "Why would same-sex marriage *not* be included under the fundamental right to marry" (p. 85). He stated that people who oppose marriage equality offer three answers to his question:

1. "The right to marry is a predicate of the right to procreate and raise children in a traditional family setting.

2. The ability to have children is at the core of marriage.

3. Marriage is by definition dual-gendered" (p. 85).

Countering these arguments, proponents of marriage equality point out that these three answers are weak and often false. In this century, certainly having children is not a requirement of marriage; nor is marriage a requirement of having children. People certainly are allowed to legally procreate outside of marriage. In addition, many heterosexual people get married without ever intending to, or actually having, children (Scott, 2009). Indeed, the U.S. Supreme Court's "most thorough discussion of the attributes of marriage barely mentions the issue of having or raising children" (Gerstmann, 2004, p. 91). Furthermore, the Court protects people's rights (married or otherwise) to avoid having children all together through abortion or use of contraceptives (Gerstmann, 2004).

If procreation is not a requirement of marriage, then legal scholars who support marriage equality question why marriage must be "dual-gendered." Arguments against marriage equality have stated that two women or two men cannot procreate together. However, we know that lesbians and gay men are becoming parents in increased numbers, particularly through the use of reproductive technologies and adoption (see Chapter 3 for a detailed discussion). We also know that the law allows infertile heterosexuals to marry.

Some opponents of marriage equality argue that the dual-gender designation is necessary not only to procreate but also to raise children with "proper gender roles" (Blankenhorn, 1996; Popenoe, 1999). The argument is that without a mother and a father present, children will grow up with a confused sense of gender. The problem with this argument is that there are no legal prescriptions as to what proper gender roles are. Similarly, there are no laws forbidding single parents from raising their children, so children are legally allowed to be raised by only a mother or father. How parents chose to raise their children in gendered, or nongendered, ways is just that—the parent's or parents' individual choice, married or not. Furthermore, research shows that children raised by single and same-sex couples have no more confusion about gender than children raised in two-parent married heterosexual families (Biblarz & Stacey, 2010). To say, therefore, that marriage equality would be a special right, or that there are any strong data-driven or even legal explanations as to why marriage for LGBT people would *not* be a fundamental civil right, is based on conservative ideology only.

There Are No Equal Alternatives to Marriage in the United States

The fourth reason that LGBT people want to marry is that there are no equal alternatives to marriage in the United States. Opponents of marriage equality argue that if LGBT people want equal rights, they should be satisfied with a separate system with a different name (Wolfson, 2004). A study conducted by the Pew Research Center found that in 2009, 57% of those polled supported civil unions, but only 39% supported marriage for LGBT people (Pew Research Center, 2009).

The problem with civil unions is that "separate but equal" does not work in the United States. As discussed above, the benefits gained through marriage are both cultural and economic. On a cultural level, there is a hierarchy of relationships, with marriage holding by far the highest cultural status (Natale & Miller-Cribbs, 2012). Other types of relationships, including civil unions, domestic partnerships, and designated beneficiaries, lose cultural status respectively as they move down the hierarchy. The hierarchy works on a material level as well. In the United States, although people wed in individual states, their marital relationship is recognized and honored by all other states, the U.S. federal government, and governments around the world (Shah, 2004).

In contrast, civil unions in the United States exist only at the state level without recognition by most other states, the federal government, or other countries. Therefore, although civil unions may offer similar benefits of marriage provided by a particular state, they do not offer any federal benefits, such as Social Security, FMLA, or immigration rights as discussed above. In addition, often civil unions do not contain the same benefits as state marriage, by law (Natale & Miller-Cribbs, 2012). Because civil unions create separate and unequal systems, and because the United States has a history of failing to create separate but equal systems (e.g., Jim Crow laws), advocates for marriage equality argue that marriage by any other name does not work (Wolfson, 2004).

An often weaker option than civil unions is domestic partnerships. Domestic partnerships emerged in the mid-1980s first at the city and county levels, as well as through private companies and organizations, and later at the state level. Some domestic partnerships are identical to civil unions, as was the case in California (Clifford, Hertz, & Doskow, 2007). However, many times the benefits for domestic partnerships are very limited and grant only limited rights and privileges, for example, those "related to inheritance, hospital visitation, and guardianship in the event of death" but not those relating to taxation and joint insurance claims (Natale & Miller-Cribbs, 2012, p. 157).

Some states also offer "designated beneficiaries" in which an LGBT person can designate his or her partner as the beneficiary to certain rights, such as is found in Colorado. The problem with this arrangement is that designated beneficiary agreements offer "a very limited cadre of rights including funeral arrangements and hospital visitation. These arrangements are not portable to other states and are not recognized at the federal level" (Natale & Miller-Cribbs, 2012, p. 157).

Because of the limited nature of the cultural and economic benefits of civil unions, domestic partnerships, and designated beneficiaries, supporters of marriage equality see anything other than marriage as "second-class solutions" (Kendell, 1998, p. 53). Furthermore, because civil unions and domestic partnerships are not nationally available or recognized, the amount of access LGBT people have to these benefits, and thus the amount of legal recognition and protection their families have, is determined by "the happenstance of geography" (Kendell, 1998, p. 54). Because marriage is the most privileged, respected, familiar, and far-reaching system of support for families, many LGBT people argue that anything short of marriage creates an unequal and unjust divide between themselves and their heterosexual counterparts.

On June 26, 2013, the U.S. Supreme Court agreed with supporters of marriage equality by declaring section three (§3) of DOMA to be unconstitutional. Section three defined marriage as "a legal union between one man and one woman as husband and wife, and the word 'spouse' refers only to a person of the opposite sex who is a husband or a wife" (*The United States v. Windsor*, 2013, p. 2). Section 2, which "allows States to refuse to recognize same-sex marriages performed under the laws of other States" (*The United States v. Windsor*, 2013, p. 2) remained unquestioned and intact. The landmark case (*The United States v. Windsor*) was the result of a case filed by New York resident Edith Windsor who married her partner Thea Spyer in Canada in 2007. Spyer died in 2009, leaving Windsor as the heir of her inheritance. Because DOMA did not allow the federal government to recognize their marriage even though the state of New York did, Windsor had to pay $363,053 in estate taxes, taxes that she would not have had to pay had the federal government recognized Windsor and Spyer's marriage (Dudley & Nolan, 2013). Windsor filed a lawsuit that eventually headed to the U.S. Supreme Court. The Court heard the case on March 27, 2013. Three months later, in a 5–4 decision, Justice Anthony Kennedy wrote in the Opinion of the Court,

> DOMA singles out a class of persons deemed by a State entitled to recognition and protection to enhance their own liberty. It imposes a disability on the class by refusing to acknowledge a status the State finds to be dignified and proper. DOMA instructs all federal officials, and indeed all persons with whom same-sex couples interact, including their own children, that their marriage is less worthy than the marriages of others. . . . By seeking to displace this protection and treating those persons as living in marriages less respected than others, the federal statute is in violation of the Fifth Amendment. (*The United States v. Windsor*, 2013, p. 25)

Therefore, the Supreme Court established through *The United States v. Windsor* that same-sex couples legally married and living in a state that recognizes their marriage will receive federal marriage benefits. However, same-sex couples will not receive federal benefits if they have anything less than marriage (e.g., civil unions or domestic partnerships). In addition, if married LGBT people live in states that do not recognize their marriage from other states or countries, they may also not be eligible for some of the 1,138 benefits of marriage because a variety of different federal agencies distribute these benefits. However, some federal agencies, such as the IRS, honor all legal marriages regardless of where the couple resides (Internal Revenue Service, 2013). The details of how to address continued inequality regarding marriage remains largely in the hands of the U.S. Congress and individual states. Thus, as you read this book, there is a good chance that some states have changed their laws and the U.S. Congress has worked on new language to either grant or hinder the granting of equal marriage rights to same-sex couples.

The LGBT Argument Against Marriage for LGBT People

Although many LGBT people want the right to marry, some LGBT people are wary of the fight for marriage equality. They base their argument partially on the fact that marriage is historically an oppressive institution, built on inequalities of gender, race, social class, and sexuality (Card, 1996; Ettelbrick, 2004; Gaboury, 2005). They question why LGBT people would want to become part of an institution that historically oppressed women, people of color, and poor people who either were used as free labor in marriages (e.g., wives) with no rights to land ownership or self-autonomy, as slaves or cheap labor (African slaves, African Americans, Mexicans, Chinese, etc.), or scapegoats for the ills of society (e.g., poor people who could not or cannot afford to get married and have one parent stay at home).

Moreover, LGBT opponents of marriage equality argue that marriage is a dangerous institution because it is the instrument through which the state decides what family is legitimate. As Jennifer Gaboury (2005), a board member for the advocacy group for unmarried people Alternatives to Marriage Project, wrote, "I don't believe that the state should have the power to say who is and who is not a proper family and distribute public benefits accordingly" (p. 29). Similarly, author and journalist Judith Levine (2005) argued that marriage is intrinsically conservative. It does not just normalize; it requires normality as the ticket in . . . [and] pushes the queerer queers of all sexual persuasions—drag queens, club-crawlers, polyamorists, even ordinary single mothers or teenage lovers—further to the margins. (p. 78)

By allowing any given group into marriage and therefore having society accept that group as normal, society and policy makers give "legitimate" backing to view any other group not allowed to marry as "abnormal." Such labeling has a dual effect of helping some LGBT people assimilate into the mainstream while simultaneously pushing others further to the outside. Allowing those in authority to purposefully include some groups and exclude others from the economic and social benefits of the institution of marriage takes power away from LGBT people in general (Ettelbrick, 2004). As legal expert Paula Ettelbrick (2004) wrote, "Marriage runs contrary to two of the primary goals of the lesbian and gay movement: the affirmation of gay identity and culture and the validation of many forms of relationships" (p. 124). As a possible solution to this problem, others suggest that rather than becoming part of an exclusive institution, LGBT people should fight to create a new system in which the rights and protections that marriage affords some people are available to everyone regardless of their family form (Browning, 2004; Card, 2007; Levine, 2005).

In addition to worrying about the conservative and exclusionary nature of the institution of marriage, some groups of LGBT people argue that marriage is not the most important issue to their families and therefore not the issue into which they wish to put their energies. For example, practicing attorney and law professor Glenn Magpantay (2006) wrote about members of Asian Pacific Americans (APA) LGBT communities. He stated that at the Queer Asian Pacific Legacy conference held in New York City in 2004, a common sentiment among the more than 400 participants was that racism within and outside of the LGBT community was a more compelling issue despite the great need for access to marital benefits. Dang and Vianney (2007) found that 98% of the 860 LGBT Asian and Pacific Islander Americans they surveyed experienced both racial and sexual-gender discrimination. Because many of the "LGBT APAs believe that same-sex marriage is a 'white gay issue' and, therefore, does little to combat racism" (Magpantay, 2006, p. 110), they are less likely than their White counterparts to work toward marriage equality.

Furthermore, the fight for marriage equality is occurring at the state level, and the greatest needs of the LGBT APA community (e.g., immigrant rights) work at the federal level. Another important issue for LGBT APA people is their invisibility or, perhaps worse, the stereotyped and ugly portrayal of them in the media (Dang & Vianney, 2007). For example, media often portray gay Asian men as hypersexualized, exotic chattel, or emasculated (Magpantay, 2006). Therefore, LGBT APAs do not want to spend valuable time and energy supporting a fight for marriage equality when that fight does not help them access the benefits they need or fight against defamation and racism (Magpantay, 2006).

A final argument that some LGBT people make against the fight for marriage equality is that marriage equality will ultimately make it more difficult to terminate relationships because once you have marriage, you also have divorce, another relationship regulated by laws (Card, 2007; Herman, 2012). Access to marriage can both help and hinder LGBT couples who want to dissolve a relationship. If the separation is amicable, then not having legal ties prevents the need for a legal dissolution, just as with a heterosexual cohabitating relationship. However, if there are disagreements about how to divide property, finances, or child custody, then not being legally married creates hardships when not legally divorcing. For example, cohabitating partners (LGBT or otherwise) are not eligible for palimony, which would help cover the expenses of a partner who was not working for pay during the relationship. In addition, there may be tax ramifications for nonmarital partners who are dividing property (Herman, 2012). Despite the potential help of divorce laws, many LGBT people see divorce as a hindrance that comes with the right to marry.

The Heterosexual Backlash Against Marriage Equality

Despite some LGBT people's resistance to marriage equality that is now the battle cry of the LGBT liberation movement, the strongest backlash against marriage equality comes from conservative thinkers, politicians, religious leaders, and the general public. There are a burgeoning number of books and articles written about whether or not states should allow LGBT people to marry. Here, I discuss what I deem to be the top four arguments against marriage for LGBT people, as well as the research and arguments that refute these claims.

Allowing Gay Couples to Marry Will Harm the Institution of Marriage

As discussed in Chapter 1, conservatives believe that without stable families, society will fall apart. In addition, conservatives argue that in order to have stable families, we must maintain a particular family structure that includes two heterosexual adults—one male and one female—who raise their children to adhere to dominant and culturally appropriate gender roles. According to the conservative argument, LGBT families, and particularly marriage equality, threaten that family order and therefore the greater social order. While many Americans hold this belief to be true, there is little evidence to support their claim (Cahill, 2004). First, since at least the 1980s, heterosexual couples, not same-sex couples, have been eroding the institution of marriage through increased divorce and cohabitation rates (Cherlin, 2004). Second, Massachusetts, the state in which same-sex couples have been able to marry the longest and in which same-sex couples make up about 7% of all marriages, has the lowest divorce rate in the country (Cahill, 2004). The Massachusetts divorce rate has remained the same (about 2.2 divorces per 1,000 people) since same-sex couples have been allowed to marry (Kurtzleben, 2011).

Allowing Same-Sex Couples to Marry Will Harm Children

Conservatives argue that having LGBT parents is harmful to children for several reasons: Children will not have a balanced view of gender, will risk living with gay male pedophiles, and will be teased by others (Cahill, 2004). The conservative argument is that sanctioning marriage for same-sex couples not only sanctions homosexual relationships, but also sanctions same-sex couples having children because procreation is a main function of marriage (Gallagher, 2005). Indeed, this is the argument that Supreme Court Justice Scalia made on March 26, 2013, when the Court heard the case on Proposition 8. Justice Scalia stated,

> If you redefine marriage to include same-sex couples, you must . . . permit adoption by same-sex couples, and there's—there's considerable disagreement among . . . sociologists as to what the consequences of raising a child in a—in a single-sex family, whether that is harmful to the child or not. (*Hollingsworth v. Perry*, 2013, p. 18)

Despite Justice Scalia's statement, research conducted on the children of LGBT parents is in fact in *considerable agreement* that conservative assumptions about the harm to children are false. The cumulative research focusing on both adopted and birth children of LGBT parents strongly suggests that these children grow up to be as mentally normal and healthy, *if not healthier in some ways*, as children raised in heterosexual families (see, for example, Biblarz & Savci, 2010; Erich, Hall, Kanenberg, & Case, 2009; Erich, Leung, & Kindle, 2005; Farr & Patterson, 2013; Golombok, 2007; Ross, Siegel,

Dobinson, Epstein, & Steele, 2012; Stacey & Biblarz, 2001; Tasker, 2005; Tasker & Patterson, 2007). In fact, in a recent meta-analysis of all related studies published between 1990 and 2010, Biblarz and Stacey (2010) found that "no research supports the widely held conviction that the gender of parents matters for child well-being" (p. 17).

Only one study conducted by sociologist Mark Regnerus in 2012 declared that children fare worse with gay and lesbian parents than with heterosexual parents. Even acknowledging that most studies on LGBT parents and their children do not use large, representational samples (Marks, 2012; Stacey & Biblarz, 2001), the definitions and methods employed by Regnerus were so flawed that one must wonder how a reputable journal published such blatantly unsound research. As several scholars have noted, the problem with Regnerus's study is that he did not compare heterosexual couples to same-sex couples (Frank, 2012; Sherkat, 2013; Umberson, 2013). As Darren Sherkat (2013), a professor of sociology and a member of the editorial board of *Social Science Research* (the journal in which Regnerus's study was published), stated,

> The key measure of gay and lesbian parenting is simply a farce. The study includes a retrospective question asking if people knew if their mother or father had a "romantic" relationship with someone of the same sex when the respondent was under age 18. This measure is problematic on many levels. Regnerus admits that just two of his respondents were actually raised by a same-sex couple. . . . Since only two respondents were actually raised in gay or lesbian households, this study has absolutely nothing to say about gay parenting outcomes. (para. 19)

Therefore, while those who oppose marriage equality regularly cite Regnerus's findings, the findings are invalid and unreliable. Indeed, in his original report of his findings, Regnerus himself stated that people should not use his study to inform policy. Although he went against his own statement by later testifying in cases, in his original study, Regnerus stated that "American courts are finding arguments against gay marriage decreasingly persuasive (Rosenfeld, 2007). This study is intended to neither undermine nor affirm any legal rights concerning such" (Regnerus, 2012, p. 766). The lesson learned here is that as consumers of information, we need to read the fine print (e.g., the methods section) before we use information to support our beliefs. With respect to the U.S. Supreme Court, the justices relied on one very weak study within a sea of much stronger research to make a critical argument against marriage equality.

Second, the accusation that gay men are likely to be pedophiles and therefore are not suitable parents is also false. Studies indicate that "90% of pedophiles are men, and 95% of these individuals are heterosexual" (Cahill, 2004, p. 35). Additional studies that examined the sexual identity of convicted child molesters have shown that less than 1% of child molesters are lesbian or gay (Cahill, 2004). Therefore, the reality is that children who live with gay fathers and/or lesbian mothers are at significantly lower risks of their parents sexually abusing them than if they lived with heterosexual parents, and particularly with their heterosexual fathers.

Marriage Is a Religious Institution

Another main argument against marriage equality is that marriage is a religious institution, and most religions condemn same-sex relationships. Conservatives make this argument based on two reasons. First, religious conservatives argue that "the institution of marriage between a man and a woman was ordained by the Bible" and therefore prohibits marriage among other gendered formations (Limbaugh, 2005, p. 73). Drawing on the Bible to justify a restricted definition of marriage is not historically new. Men made similar arguments for centuries to justify wives' subservience to their husbands. For example, according to the Bible, God told Eve, "Your urge shall be for your husband and he shall rule over you" (cited in Yalom, 2002, p. 3). Racist people have also made similar arguments to prevent interracial marriages. For example, when Richard Loving and Mildred Jeter legally married in Washington, D.C. in 1958, a Virginia circuit court indicted them for breaking state law. Drawing on religious justification, the judge stated, "Almighty God created the races white, black, yellow, Malay, and red, and He placed them on separate continents. . . . The fact that He separated the races shows that he did not intend for the races to mix" (cited in Tong, 1998, p. 117). Second, for many people, a wedding—the ceremony that makes a marriage official—often takes place within a religious context. Frequently, people hold their weddings, and therefore begin their marriages, in a church, synagogue, mosque, or temple, with a religious leader officiating the service.

Supporters of marriage equality level two main responses against both of these arguments. First, although most religions do not condone, and some condemn, same-sex relationships including marriage, most religions also teach acceptance and tolerance (Roste, 2005). Therefore, by denying LGBT people the right to marry, religious conservatives perpetuate hate and bigotry, which are also condemned by their own religions (Fatah & Tapal, 2005).

In addition, while marriage may have religious connotations for some people, in this country, marriage is first and foremost a civil institution, not a religious one. As Wolfson (2004) wrote, the wedding is "a beautiful and significant occasion, and undoubtedly it's an event that everyone in attendance will remember for many years to come. Yet, in the eyes of the government, it doesn't mean a thing" (p. 105). The religious aspect of marriage does not matter to the U.S. government because marriage falls under civil law, not religious law (Cahill, 2004). In the United States, where our rule of law calls for a separation between church and state, the government cannot dictate that our marriages be framed by religious or secular weddings; the choice is up to the individual couple and their extended families, not the state (Wolfson, 2004).

Supporters of marriage equality acknowledge that religious organizations and leaders fear that the state will mandate their congregations to marry same-sex couples. However, the legalization of marriage for same-sex couples in the United States would not force religious organizations to marry people they see as falling outside their religious beliefs and practices (Cahill, 2004). Therefore, although the marriage of LGBT people may be outside the religious beliefs of some groups of people, the first amendment of the U.S. Constitution prevents religious groups from imposing their views on civil law and the government, and the government from forcing religious groups to act outside their beliefs.

Allowing Marriage Equality Opens the Door for Other Harmful Types of Relationships

Marriage equality opponents fear a "slippery slope" in which once the definition of marriage changes to include LGBT relationships, then the door will open for other forms of relationships (e.g., polygamist, incestuous, bestial, or whatever they may be) to enter the marriage club (Cahill & Tobias, 2007; Rauch, 2004; Sheff, 2011). Ironically, this is "other side of the coin" to what LGBT opponents of marriage equality state—that marriage is narrowly focused and once same-sex couples can marry, other family forms will be ostracized.

Because they see the conservative argument as offensive and ridiculous, most LGBT people do not seriously counter the connection between bestiality and same-sex relationships (Rauch, 2004). However, they do refute issues of incest and polygamy. The response to the fear of incestuous relationships (e.g., parents marrying their children, siblings marrying their siblings, etc.), is that unlike homosexuality and bisexuality, incest is illegal in the United States. Therefore, supporters of marriage equality argue that comparing a legal relationship with an illegal one in the context of marriage makes no sense (Rauch, 2004). In fact, advocates of marriage equality make clear that they are not asking for incestuous relationships to be included in the definition of marriage (Cahill, 2004; Rauch, 2004).

Regarding polygamy, supporters of marriage equality also argue that they want to maintain the "couple" relationship between two people. As Rauch (2004) stated, "Gay people are not asking for the legal right to marry anybody they love or everybody they love. . . . Instead, homosexuals are asking for what all heterosexuals possess already: the legal right to marry *somebody* they love" (p. 125). Note that this argument is somewhat conservative because it assumes that only committed monogamous relationships are healthy, and fits into the LGBT critique of the marriage equality movement (Card, 1996; Gaboury, 2005; Levine, 2005). In an extension of this (conservative) argument, Rauch (2004) acknowledged that polygamous relationships have existed throughout time, and continue to do so in certain countries around the world. However, he noted that to his knowledge, "not a single one of those polygamous societies has ever been a liberal democracy. . . . To the contrary, they tend to be authoritarian rather than liberal, hierarchical and male-supremacist rather than egalitarian, closed rather than open" (p. 129). In essence, Rauch (2004) is drawing on the same relationship of cause and effect that conservatives in the family values debate use as well: Marriage and family shape society (the conservative argument), rather than society shapes marriage and family (the progressive argument). In fact, Rauch's argument fuels some LGBT fears that by mainstreaming monogamous same-sex coupled relationships, the marriage equality movement will push other family forms further to the margins.

Sociologist Elisabeth Sheff (2011) takes a more progressive approach to analyzing marriage through a comparison of polyamorous and lesbian, bisexual, and gay (i.e., "lesbigay") families. Polyamorous families are ones in which the adults are "in openly conducted multiple-partner relationships" (p. 487) and in which those who are involved tend to subscribe "to modern, gender-neutral, egalitarian values" (Stacey & Meadow, 2009, p. 193). Sheff sees both lesbigay and polyamorous families as "an adaptive response to shifting social conditions" (2011, p. 492); therefore, the similarities among them "are not accidental, as the same social forces have shaped both groups' strategies for family maintenance and relationships to institutions" (p. 508). Sheff argued that both family forms are here to stay and need to be understood and analyzed using scientific methods. Furthermore, she argued, assuming that all relationships should be monogamous, or are monogamous, obscures the real variances in American families and reinforce monocentrism (p. 510).

What Sheff's argument reveals is that perhaps some of the conservatives' fears of a "slippery slope" are partially founded. Her work also reveals that in an effort to "normalize" LGBT (monogamous) families, marriage equality activists and scholars are willing to ignore and marginalize other family forms. The reasonable response to the slippery-slope fear is that marriage as a social institution has been changing ever since people and societies first created marital relationships (Coontz, 2005; Cott, 2002; Stacey & Meadow, 2009). There is no reason to think that LGBT families will be the last frontier of new family forms. If we have learned anything from history, we have every reason to believe that new family forms will continue to evolve as our society evolves. In fact, there is evidence that those in polygamous relationships in the United States are drawing on the marriage-equality platform from the LGBT movement to argue for legal recognition of their relationships as well. For example, an article in *Time* magazine about polygamous marriages quotes author, activist, and husband of three wives Joe Darger as saying, "If people are open to gay marriage, it impacts on how they look at plural marriage. . . . You can't talk about gay marriage and still criminalize us for who we love and how we organize our families" (Luscombe, 2012, p. 44).

What We Gain From Marriage Equality

As stated at the beginning of the chapter, marriage is socially constructed such that the meaning we give to marriage, the functions of marriage, and the experiences people have within their marriages change with time and across geographic space. As these new families develop, we see that they threaten what many people consider the normal, traditional, and "correct" form of marriage. However, we also see that by denying existing and future families' access to social legitimacy, as well as access to the economic benefits that the legal institution of marriage offers, we are weakening a growing group of families nationwide. By weakening our families, we are not only denying taxpaying citizens access to the benefits that other citizens receive, but we are also forcing families to make decisions that may jeopardize the mental, physical, and financial health of families and their members.

What is noteworthy here, however, is that the very families that our laws are trying to suppress are in fact the very families that are faring well, particularly when children are involved. As discussed above, children with LGBT parents fare better in terms of mental health than children with heterosexual parents, and they are less likely to experience sexual molestation from either their father or mother. In addition, in the case of Massachusetts, divorce rates have held steady; and nationwide marriage rates among lesbians and gay men have increased. If the conservative agenda is to create safe and healthy homes for our nation's children, and to create families in which the parents marry and remain married, then the research suggests that allowing LGBT people to marry should provide great hope—not great fear—for our nation. And if homophobia and heterosexism are encouraging policy makers to create laws that prevent LGBT people from marrying and from fully forming their families as many want, then imagine how strong LGBT families could be and what great role models they could be for all Americans, if family laws, such as marriage, actually supported LGBT relationships.

GLOBAL BOX

by Morganne Firmstone

According to the Pew Forum on Religion and Public Life, there are currently 15 countries that have instituted marriage equality: Argentina, Brazil, The Netherlands, Belgium, Spain, France, Portugal, Iceland, New Zealand, Canada, South Africa, Denmark, Norway, Sweden, and Uruguay. Although not all countries allow same-sex couples to marry, many nations opt to provide some type of civil union or partnership for couples. Some countries go a step further and provide basic same-sex marriage/partnership rights. But a few European countries, including the United Kingdom, Germany, and Switzerland, are among those who offer what they deem a "comparable-to-marriage" institution through same-sex unions and partnerships (Pew Research Center, 2009; see updates at the center's website: Pewforum.org).

A common occurrence in those nations that allow marriage equality is that their central government has great control over the definition of marriage, whereas in countries like the United States and Mexico, substantial discretion over marriage law is provided to individual states or provinces (Gardiner, 2010). For instance, in the United States of America, same-sex couples can marry in some but not all states. According to the Human Rights Campaign, nearly 30% of Americans are now living in states that recognize or are on the cusp of rec-ognizing marriage equality. With newly added states, 17 states, as well as the District of Columbia, now recognize marriage equality. In June 2013, the Supreme Court deferred California's Proposition 8 ruling to the U.S. District Court's 2010 verdict—that Proposition 8 violated the Due Process and Equal Protection Clauses of the Fourteenth Amendment. Starting June 28, 2013, same-sex marriages resumed in California.

The Supreme Court also issued a 5–4 decision on June 26, 2013, that declared Section 3 of the 1996 Defense of Marriage Act (DOMA) unconstitu-tional under the Due Process Clause of the Fifth Amendment. The repeal of DOMA, which defines the terms "marriage" and "spouse" on a federal level as

(Continued)

(Continued)

pertaining only to one woman and one man as husband and wife, means that the U.S. government will now honor federal rights, protections, and obligations to same-sex marriages.

Societal perceptions of same-sex marriages are changing; accordingly, although a slow process, so is the legal framework that governs these relationships. However, many gray areas still exist within the legal system. For instance, Anthony (2012) made note of the importance in legally defining one's sex when talking about transgender people and marriage. After all, if a state deems a marriage to be between one man and one woman, the state must also clearly define the terms of gender. Anthony (2012) noted few nations clarify such definitions. For example, in the United States, court systems have relied on several inconsistent definitions of an individual's "sex" ranging from "birth certificate records, to physical form at birth, to physical form at marriage, to the ability to engage in penetrative sex at marriage, to reasons that are unclear or inconsistent" (p. 174). The result? A piecemeal of contradictory standards where "one's sex is largely reduced to what state she [he] lives in" (p. 174). Essentially, Anthony (2012) noted, "A legal heterosexual marriage in one state will become an illegal homosexual marriage in another" (p. 174). Individual sexual identities do not fit into concise definitions, which is why the courts have interpreted them differently in case law throughout the years. Until nations and states remove sex altogether as a determining factor in granting fundamental rights, such as marriage, the legal framework will remain fickle and unjust.

While some areas around the world remain trapped in the legal web of marriage equality, several countries completely and unequivocally ban same-sex couples from marrying. These countries include Honduras, Latvia, and Uganda (Pew Research Center, 2009), and most recently Nigeria (Rappard & Karikari-apau, 2014). Furthermore, countries like Afghanistan, Iran, and many African nations still outlaw homosexuality in general, let alone marriage by same-sex couples (Pew Research Center, 2009).

Marriage is not only a legally binding agreement, but also it is a vital part of the patchwork of cultural, spiritual, religious, and societal life. Many people perceive marriage to be an institution that gives order to human relationships and provides a strong foundation for the basic functional unit of life—the family. It is easy to see why any person would place so much emphasis on being allowed to enter into this sacred yet practical union. It is also easy to see how societies use marriage as a weapon of discrimination and prejudice. In Poland, for example, the "low level of homosexuality acceptance and a strong traditional family position in the Polish culture causes many lesbians and gays to cover their identities" (Majka-Rostek, 2011, p. 286). Deemed a "homophobic" state by the European Parliament in 2006, Polish culture tends to honor traditional family ties and rituals that place LGBT couples at a disadvantage when trying to fit into customary family molds (Majka-Rostek, 2011). Interviews conducted by Majka-Rostek (2011) with people in permanent same-sex relationships in Poland testify to this sentiment:

> Because we are not a married couple—not a distinct social unit— holidays are something disturbing for me. It's impossible to imagine for our families that we two could spend Christmas together and on our own. It's not possible that our families could spend Christmas Eve together. Even if I can bring E. with me, I can't bring her mother because neither she would like it nor my grandparents would understand this situation. (p. 288)

As described above, culture plays a tremendous role in marriage equality and granting or restricting access to this social institution. Interestingly enough, Spain (a predominantly Catholic society) has legally recognized marriage between LGBT people since 2005, blurring the lines of traditional cultural beliefs and current societal trends. Many scholars attribute the shift in acceptance of marriage equality in Spain to a variety of factors including activism and grass-roots initiatives, which served as the spark to ignite legal change. In fact, Calvo and Trujillo (2011) attributed much of the LGBT marriage equality shift in Spain to LGBT organizations.

> The political associations and groups that advocate lesbian, gay and transsexual rights are treated as a key social and political actor that links the desires and needs of grass-root non-heterosexual peoples with the higher spheres of institutions, politics, and the law. (p. 562)

Calvo and Trujillo (2011) explained that these advocacy organizations successfully transformed the LGBT movement into a human rights and equality issue, thereby, "de-sexualizing" the claims brought before the state and making the argument for human decency instead of what many people may consider "normal" or "deviant" (p. 562).

Similar to Spain, South Africa counts among the few countries in the world that honor marriage equality, despite its fairly conservative social history. South Africa has made progress in enacting policy, such as its Bill of Rights, which says that no one is subject to unfair discrimination on the ground of sexual orientation (Heaton, 2010). In 2006, the South African Parliament installed the Civil Union Act (which extended marriage rights to same-sex couples) in response to narrow interpretations of LGBT equal rights. However, the Civil Union Act of 2006 is not without criticism. Some say that it does not afford true equality to same-sex couples as the act is the only option for same-sex couples to be recognized under law, whereas heterosexual couples have a

(Continued)

(Continued)

choice between civil union and civil marriage (Heaton, 2010). Heaton (2010) noted that because same-sex couples only have one option, an unfair "separate but equal" remedy has emerged (p. 117).

So where do we stand today? In the United States, the striking down of Section 3 of DOMA was a historic institutional shift that now recognizes married same-sex couples under federal law. However, same-sex couples living in states that do not have marriage equality will not necessarily have immediate access to some federal rights and benefits. For instance, according to the Human Rights Campaign, federal agencies sometimes draw on particular state laws in determining marriage validity for federal benefits. Some agencies reference state laws where a couple lives, others look to where a couple gets married, and many do not have a specific approach at all.

One breakthrough in the rejection of DOMA, deemed by Strozdas (2011) as "the largest obstacle in the way of immigration equality for same-sex binational couples," lies in the ability for transnational same-sex unions to occur (p. 1353). Same-sex couples can now marry in a state that allows same-sex marriage and then petition the federal government for the naturalization of the noncitizen partner (Human Rights Campaign [HRC], n.d.). Even if the couple moves to a state that does not recognize a same-sex union, that state must still honor federal immigration status (HRC, n.d.).

Rapidly changing cultural and societal views have opened the door for marriage equality in recent years. Although some countries are still resistant, most industrialized nations (especially the United States) are beginning to adopt policies that allow same-sex couples the benefits and protections of a legally recognized union. However, until states and nations grant same-sex couples equal access to the same—not separate—institutions of marriage and recognize those marriages across territorial lines, the fight for equality will wage on.

ADDITIONAL RESOURCES

Compiled by Morganne Firmstone

Websites

- Freedom to Marry
  - http://www.freedomtomarry.org

- Immigration Equality
  - http://www.immigrationequality.org

- Lambda Legal
  - http://www.lambdalegal.org

- The Pew Forum on Religion & Public Life
  - http://www.pewforum.org/Gay-Marriage-and-Homosexuality/Gay-Marriage-Around-the-World.aspx

Films

- *8: The Mormon Proposition (2010 Documentary)*
  - Examines The Church of Jesus Christ of Latter-day Saints (LDS Church) and its support of California Proposition 8, stating that the church has been actively involved in the denial of LGBT human rights.

- *The Campaign—Christie Herring (2012 Documentary)*
  - The inside story of the fight to stop California's wildly controversial Proposition 8, which banned gay marriage and ignited a movement.

- *Edie & Thea: A Very Long Engagement (2009 Documentary)*
  - After 42 years, lesbian couple Edie and Thea are finally getting married. From the early 60s to the present day, the tireless community activists persevere through many battles, both personal and political.

- *Freeheld (2007 Documentary)*
  - Chronicles the story of Laurel Hester in her fight against the Ocean County, New Jersey, Board of Chosen Freeholders to give her earned pension benefits to her partner, Stacie.

- *I Can't Marry You—Catherine Gray (2003 Documentary)*
  - Explores same-sex marriage issues through the personal experiences of 20 gay and lesbian couples who have been in long-term relationships of 10–55+ years. Gray shot the film in large and small cities across the country, including New York City; Saugatuck, Michigan; Asheville, North Carolina; San Francisco, California; Fort Lauderdale and West Palm Beach, Florida.

- *Les Invisibles—Sébastien Lifshitz (2012 French Documentary)*
  - Several elderly homosexual men and women speak frankly about their pioneering lives, their fearless decision to live openly in France at a time when society rejected them.

- *The New Black—Yoruba Richen (2013 Documentary)*
  - Tells the story of how the African American community is grappling with the gay rights issue in light of the recent gay marriage movement and the fight over civil rights.

- *Outrage (2009 Documentary)*
  - The film presents a narrative discussing the hypocrisy of individuals purported in the documentary to be closeted politicians who promote antigay legislation.

- *Trembling Before G-d (2001 Documentary)*
  - Film about gay and lesbian Orthodox Jews trying to reconcile their sexuality with their faith.

3

LGBT Parents

I think telling my family [that I wanted to have children] was probably one of the harder things when Deana (her partner) got pregnant. I had already come out to them and they like Deana and she came to all our family stuff and everything, but somehow having a child in the relationship was just like a huge step more radical than even . . . Extra radical. And that was kind of hard for me. They're great about it and they, although my mother doesn't really acknowledge our older son as, I mean, she doesn't, when she counts her grandchildren she doesn't count him. Like when she says to somebody, "Yeah, I have, you know four grandchildren, or five now, five grandchildren" because my, our second child I adopted and she definitely counts him as her grandson. But she sends [our first son] birthday presents and she sends him Christmas presents . . . But that was probably the hardest thing. Now my brothers are quite great. They're like they're the uncles and they're fine. They've been quite great about it. My mother's had a little harder time and I think she just can't figure out how to explain it to people.

—Patricia, a middle-class, White lesbian
interviewed in 2000 for the author's
doctoral research on lesbians' decisions to
become mothers or remain childfree

- *More than one in three lesbians has given birth and one in six gay men have fathered or adopted a child.*
- *More than half of gay men and 41 percent of lesbians want to have a child.*

- *An estimated two million GLB people are interested in adopting.*
- *An estimated 65,500 adopted children are living with a lesbian or gay parent.*
- *More than 16,000 adopted children are living with lesbian and gay parents in California, the highest number among the states.*
- *Gay and lesbian parents are raising four percent of all adopted children in the United States.*
- *Same-sex couples raising adopted children are older, more educated, and have more economic resources than other adoptive parents.*
- *Adopted children with same-sex parents are younger and more likely to be foreign born.*
- *An estimated 14,100 foster children are living with lesbian or gay parents.*
- *Gay and lesbian parents are raising three percent of foster children in the United States.*
- *A national ban on GLB foster care could cost from $87 to $130 million.*
- *Costs to individual states could range from $100,000 to $27 million.*

—2007 report by Gary J. Gates, M. V. Lee
Badgett, Jennifer Ehrle Macomber, and
Kate Chambers from The Williams Institute
and The Urban Institute

Over the past 20 to 30 years, lesbians and gay men have been birthing and adopting children in record numbers, starting what many people originally called the "lesbian baby boom" (Lewin, 1993) and then later called the "gayby" boom (Dunne, 2000). The gayby boom started with people who became parents within heterosexual identities and then came out as LGBT. More recently, LGBT people within their current sexual and gender identities are choosing parenthood. As sociologist Mignon Moore (2011) wrote regarding lesbians, the distinction between the two groups of parents is between "mothers becoming lesbians" and "lesbians becoming mothers" (p. 117), or in a broader sense, parents becoming LGBT and LGBT people becoming parents.

The data presented at the opening of this chapter and in Chapter 1 discuss the number of lesbians and gay men who are parents. To reiterate, we know that 13.9% of gay unmarried-couple households and 26.5% of lesbian unmarried-couple households contain children. That means that 115,000 (19.3%) of all same-sex couple households reported having children living with them in 2010 (Krivickas & Lofquist, 2011). In addition to lesbians and gay men, studies suggest that many bisexual and transgender people are parents as well. For example, in a 2007 study that included 2,000 bisexual people, "38% reported actively playing a part in raising children or stepchildren" (Firestein, 2007, as cited in Ross & Dobinson, 2013, p. 94). Similarly, in a 2011 study of 6,450 transgender people, 38% (or 2,451) were parents.

But as the opening quote from Patricia suggests, because of homophobia and heterosexism, becoming a parent and negotiating parenthood provides challenges to LGBT people that differ from challenges that heterosexual people face. To understand LGBT headed families, this chapter examines how LGBT adults create and organize their families with children. The chapter first looks at how existing parents come out as LGBT and then at how LGBT people become parents. The chapter also examines LGBT parenting experiences and issues, including division of household labor and work-family balance. The chapter looks specifically at how homophobia and heterosexism shape LGBT families and how LGBT families positively add to the changing family landscape.

Parents Becoming LGBT

In the 1970s and 1980s, the first group of LGBT parents largely became parents while in heterosexual marriages and then later came out as LGBT (Barret & Robinson, 2000; Bozett, 1987; Brown & Rounsley, 1996; Burnett, 2005; Hequembourg, 2007; Hill, 1987; Hines, 2006; Lees, 2008; Mallon, 2004; Ross, Steele, & Epstein, 2006; Strah & Margolis, 2003; Tornello & Patterson, 2012; Weinberg, Williams, & Pryor, 1995). In a large, national sample of 2,431 lesbians and bisexual women, Morris, Balsam, and Rothblum (2002) examined lesbian mothers who had children before coming out, who had children after coming out, and who did not have children. Their study showed that 76.5% of White, 64.4% of African American, 82.9% of Latina, 71.9% of Native American, and 20% of Asian American lesbians and bisexual women surveyed became mothers through a previous marriage or primary relationship with a man (p. 152). In contrast, a much smaller number of lesbians, regardless of race, used donor insemination. The next largest group of lesbian mothers became parents through raising their lesbian partners' children or through adoption. Moore (2011) found a similar ratio in her study of 100 African American lesbians, in which 46% of those she interviewed became mothers through previous heterosexual relationships, and 13% of the women were parenting their partners' children. Patterns for gay men becoming parents are similar to those of lesbians in that many either became parents through a heterosexual relationship or through parenting their partners' children (Berkowitz, 2013; Goldberg, 2012; Mallon, 2004; Stacey, 2006; Strah & Margolis, 2003).

Parents in heterosexual relationships who later came out as LGBT first came into the public eye when mental health professionals and clinicians began counseling clients struggling with gender and sexual identity issues. Clinicians began to write about this group of people in the 1970s and 1980s (Tasker, 2013). Since that time, research on this early group of LGBT parents has focused largely on the coming out process, how LGBT people integrate their sexual and gender identities with parental identities, dispelling negative myths about LGBT parents, the effects on and experiences of children whose parents came out, and separation and divorce (Benson, Silverstein, & Auerbach, 2005). I address these issues below and throughout this chapter.

For LGBT people who become parents through heterosexual relationships, the coming out process can be particularly difficult. During this process, parents are not only forced to address external homophobia from communities and social institutions (e.g., religious, medical, legal, etc.) but also their own internal homophobia and fears of how coming out will affect their children, spouses, and other familial relationships (Benson et al., 2005; Buxton, 2006). Many times, LGBT parents are surprised that they have new feelings or that their repressed feelings from earlier years have resurfaced. They also often feel ashamed, harbor self-hate, seek therapy, and have extramarital relationships with someone who fits their new gender or sexual identity (Benson et al., 2005; Buxton, 2006). Once they come out, LGBT parents must reveal their identities to their existing spouses and negotiate new family dynamics with their children and extended family members, an experience that can be both challenging and rewarding.

To say that there is one predominant experience or result for those who transition from heterosexual parenting to LGBT parenting would be misleading. Studies show that in most cases there is tension and stress in the coming out process, a period that can last for several years. Some LGBT people lose both their spouse and children because of that process. Others are able to maintain their original family structure, or they create new family structures through divorce, stepparents, or multiple parents (Benson et al., 2005; Buxton, 2006; Epstein, 2009; Erhardt, 2006; Grant, Mottet, & Tanis, 2011; Hines, 2006; Israel, 2008; Lees, 2008; Lev, 2004; Schacher, Auerbach, & Silverstein, 2005; Thompson, 2002; Winkenhofer, 2008; Wright, 1998, 2001; Yager, Brennan, Steele, Epstein, & Ross, 2010). Much of the outcome relies on the same dynamics that exist between heterosexual parents who are experiencing some form of life change: The more mutual respect and open communication a couple has to begin with, the more likely they will be able to weather marital problems and create new healthy family dynamics and relationships (Ahrons, 2007).

In addition to negotiating the coming out process within their families, because of homophobia and heterosexism within the courts, oftentimes when previously heterosexual parents come out, they face court battles in which they may lose custody of their children (Lewin, 1993; Richman, 2009; Thompson, 2002). In determining custody cases, courts use a standard of what is in "the best interest of the child." As Kimberly Richman (2009) wrote,

> In determining what exactly constitutes the "best interest of the child," there is little formal guidance that is recognized across states, the closest being the Uniform Marriage and Divorce Act, which lists a number of considerations including the wishes of the child and parents, the child's adjustment to the home, community, and schools; the mental and physical health of all parties involved; and the occurrence of abuse, among other things. (p. 33)

Because of the lack of formal guidance, a court in one state may rule that denying custody to the LGBT parent is in the best interest of the child, when in a different state, a court may grant custody to a LGBT parent. How a court rules on the best interest of the child depends largely, therefore, not on some objective standard but rather on the views that court officials hold regarding diverse sexual and gender identities (Richman, 2009).

Courts have historically denied child custody to LGBT parents based on four major factors in which courts have (a) assumed that the "lifestyle" that LGBT people live is not conducive to parenting; (b) labeled LGBT parents as criminal, a factor that was particularly prevalent prior to the 2003 *Lawrence v. Texas* case in which sodomy was outlawed in several states; (c) worried that children in LGBT families will face discrimination from people and communities outside of their family and should be protected from such harm; and (d) feared that the child will become LGBT themselves if they have a LGBT parent (Richman, 2009, pp. 28–29). In addition, for gay men, courts have argued at times that having a gay father is not in a child's best interest because of judges' biased beliefs that mothers—not fathers—should maintain custody of their children (Lev & Sennott, 2013).

There is no doubt that many courts' understanding of the intersection of LGBT identities and parenthood is changing such that LGBT parents are more readily maintaining child custody (Richman, 2009). However, discrimination still exists, particularly for those marginalized within LGBT populations, such as poor transgender parents and transgender parents of color (Crozier, 2012). For example, Grant et al. (2011) conducted a study that included a diverse group of 6,450 transgender and gender nonconforming people from all 50 states, the District of Columbia, Puerto Rico, Guam, and the U.S. Virgin Islands. Out of the total, 2,451 were parents. Of those participants, 13% of the transgender parents experienced court interference regarding their parenting. Within this group, 29% of the Black and 20% of the multiracial "respondents were much more vulnerable to court interference, as were respondents earning a household income of $10,000/year or less (29%), those working in the underground economy (27%) and those who had lost jobs due to bias (26%)" (Grant et al., 2011, p. 98). Unfortunately, no such data exist on bisexual parents, leaving us guessing at the discrimination they face in the courts. The extant literature suggests that the path from heterosexual parent to LGBT parent is often a difficult one with many risks, not the least of which is the possibility of losing children through custody battles.

LGBT People Becoming Parents

In addition to parents who start in heterosexual relationships and later come out as LGBT, a second group of LGBT parents is those who first come out as LGBT and later choose to become parents. This section includes a discussion of three main areas of how LGBT people become parents: (a) the parenting decision-making process, (b) the use of assisted reproductive technologies (ART) to become a parent, and (c) the use of adoption and foster care to become a parent.

The Parenting Decision-Making Process

LGBT people's parenting decisions (i.e., their decisions to become parents or remain childfree) are shaped by several factors, including personal issues, support networks, work-related issues, and intimate partner relationships; and these factors are greatly shaped by structures of race, class, gender, and sexuality. In general, the greater one's race and class privilege, the easier it is for LGBT people to become parents if they so choose (Mezey, 2008a, 2013).

Personal issues include a desire to become a parent or remain childfree, internalized homophobia, and the process of coming out (i.e., revealing one's sexual or gender identity) (Goldberg, 2012; Goldberg & Gianino, 2012; Lev, 2004; Mallon, 2004; Mezey, 2013; Schacher et al., 2005). When someone desires to become a parent or remain childfree, they work to obtain that goal (Gianino, 2008; Goldberg, 2012; Mallon, 2004; Moore, 2011; Stacey, 2006). While this may be true for heterosexual people as well (Gerson, 1985),

LGBT people have unique considerations. For example, between 48% and 60% of pregnancies among heterosexual women between the ages of 15 and 44 are unplanned (Henshaw, 1998), as opposed to near zero percent of unplanned pregnancies among lesbians and gay men (Chabot, 1998; Stacey, 1996). Some lesbians and gay men find themselves in an unplanned parent situation if they are in a poly or open relationship and someone gets pregnant, or if a family member cannot take care of a child and therefore asks their gay or lesbian relative to assume parental responsibilities. However, for the most part, if lesbians and gay men want to have children, they have to make a concerted effort often outside the bedroom and in a physician's office, or through a legal adoption process. Therefore, much research on LGBT people who become parents discusses the *intentional* nature of LGBT parenthood (Agigian, 2004; Bergman, Rubio, Green, & Padrón, 2010; Hequembourg, 2007; Mallon, 2004; Mezey, 2008a; Moore, 2011).

Although the desire for children is important in the parenting decision-making process, just because someone desires children does not mean that they will become a parent. A variety of psychological, social, and economic barriers can prevent a desire from becoming a reality. For example, internalized homophobia, lack of access to information, lack of access to medical or legal professionals, reluctant partners, and a lack of financial means or job flexibility can all create barriers to parenthood despite desires to have children (Bergman et al., 2010; Berkowitz & Marsiglio, 2007; Brown, Smalling, Groza, & Ryan, 2009; Gianino, 2008; Goldberg, 2010; Mallon, 2004; Mezey, 2008a, 2013; Stacey, 1996).

In other words, to become parents LGBT people need access to information through other LGBT parents, as well as legal and medical information and services (Brown et al., 2009; Chabot & Ames, 2004; Henehan, Rothblum, Solomon, & Balsam, 2007; Mezey, 2008a; Moore, 2011). The closer LGBT people are to other LGBT parents and the more knowledge they have about other LGBT parents, the easier it is for them to become parents themselves (Berkowitz & Marsiglio, 2007; Brown et al., 2009; Mallon, 2004; Mezey, 2008a; Yager et al., 2010). Not surprisingly, LGBT people who come from areas with large LGBT communities have greater access to such networks and knowledge than those living in less populated areas (Goldberg, 2010). However, while geographic location is important in general, race and class can also shape LGBT people's access to important support networks. For example, in my work on lesbians' mothering decisions, I found that White, middle-class lesbians had greater access to other networks of lesbian mothers than did working-class lesbians and lesbians of color (Mezey, 2008a).

Although having other LGBT parents as role models is important, LGBT people who want to become parents must also be able to access legal and medical advice and services in order to achieve their goal (Agigian, 2004; Chabot & Ames, 2004; Goldberg, 2010; Hequembourg, 2007; Mallon, 2004; Moore, 2011; Murphy, 2010; Strah & Margolis, 2003; Yager et al., 2010). To access donor (aka alternative) insemination (DI), adoption, or surrogacy, LGBT people need to be able to access medical professionals and lawyers who are willing to work with a diverse clientele, a task that can be difficult particularly because LGBT people challenge conservative definitions of family and sexuality (Downing, Richardson, Kinkler, & Goldberg, 2009; Lasker, 1998; Robertson, 2005).

In addition to personal issues, social networks, and access to medical and legal resources, LGBT people make parenting decisions based on their relationship to work (Mezey, 2008a; Rabun & Oswald, 2009). Work is important in part because medical and legal services are expensive and in part because work facilitates the ease or difficulty in which parents-to-be will have in actually raising their children. Therefore, work that does not offer flexible hours, good health-care benefits, or a comfortable salary can dampen LGBT people's desire to choose parenthood. Because of work, middle- and upper-class LGBT people hold an advantage over working- and lower class LGBT people in turning parenting desires into parenting realities (Berkowitz & Marsiglio, 2007; Kerbo, 2009; Mezey, 2008a; Rabun & Oswald, 2009).

Another important factor that shapes LGBT people's parenting decisions involves the presence of and relationship with an intimate partner (Donoghue, 2009; Goldberg, 2010, 2012; Goldberg & Gianino, 2012; Lev, 2004; Mallon, 2004; Mezey, 2008a; Stacey, 2006; Strah & Margolis, 2003). Simply stated, a supportive partner with a similar parenting desire makes the decision-making process easier for people to decide to become parents or remain childfree. When a partner has a differing parenting desire, or if there is no partner at all, then the decision-making process can be more difficult or derailed all together (Donoghue, 2009; Mezey, 2013). Research on lesbians shows that for White, middle-class lesbians, finding a partner at the time when a lesbian wants to become a parent is easier for middle-class lesbians than for working-class lesbians, who could not always find a partner who is financially stable or emotionally ready to have children (Mezey, 2008a). Gay men differ from lesbians in that finding the right partner at the right time does not matter very much, provided that the gay man's desire for parenthood is strong enough to parent regardless of the presence of a partner (Stacey, 2006). Unfortunately, no research to my knowledge exists on how partners shape bisexual and transgender people's parenting decisions.

The Use of ART to Become a Parent

Once LGBT people decide they want to become parents, they have several options for how they can achieve that goal, including through heterosexual intercourse, DI, adoption, foster care, and surrogacy (Agigian, 2004; Chabot & Ames, 2004; Goldberg, 2010; Hequembourg, 2007; Johnson & O'Connor, 2002; Lev, 2004; Mallon, 2004; Sullivan, 2004). The path to parenthood people choose relies on a variety of factors. Some LGBT people engage in heterosexual intercourse in order to become parents, either because they think that is the most normal, natural, effective, or easiest path to take or because they are in heterosexual relationships (Hequembourg, 2007; Lev, 2004; Mezey, 2008a; Stacey, 2006). One study conducted with a national sample of 2,431 lesbians and bisexual women found that even after coming out, 44% of the women "had children in the context of marriage or partnership with a man" (Morris et al., 2002, p. 150). Not surprisingly, bisexual women and men are more likely than lesbians and gay men to engage in heterosexual intercourse in order to become parents. In fact, some bisexual women choose male partners as co-parents specifically because they want to have children (Ross & Dobinson, 2013).

Despite those willing to engage in heterosexual intercourse in order to have children, many other LGBT people who want to have children who are genetically and biologically connected to at least one of the parents do not want to do so through heterosexual intercourse (Agigian, 2004; Goldberg, 2010). These people often chose ART that can allow lesbians to use their own eggs and gay men to use their own sperm in order to have genetically related children. Similarly, transgender men who were born as biological women and are still able to get pregnant once they transition (provided they stop hormone treatment), and transgender women who bank their sperm prior to transitioning, may also be able to conceive children through ART (Lev, 2004; Murphy, 2010; Ware, 2009). This was the case with Thomas Beatie who gave birth to his three children as a transgender man using his own eggs (Advocate.com, 2010).

ART includes many different technologies with varying degrees of medical intervention. An advantage of ART is that some forms, such as DI, allow a partner to participate in the conceptive process by helping to inseminate at home or in the physician's office, as well as make other important decisions throughout the process, such as what sperm donor, egg donor, or surrogate to use (Chabot & Ames, 2004). DI is the form of ART that lesbians access the most and consists of using the sperm from a donor to fertilize a female's egg (Burnett, 2005). People can select a donor with similar physical characteristics to themselves or their partners, thus creating children who may look like both parents. Choosing such a donor can pose a problem for racial-ethnic and religious minorities, however, because of the difficulty that sperm banks have recruiting African American, Hispanic, Asian, and Jewish donors (Almeling, 2007; Moore, 2011).

After choosing a donor, people have several insemination options as there are multiple forms of DI. For example, intercervical insemination (ICI) is when the sperm is placed in the cervix of the woman during ovulation. This is the least invasive form of DI and can be done at home or by a physician. In interuterine insemination (IUI), a physician uses a thin catheter to place the sperm through a woman's cervix into her uterus. A more medically intensive form of ART that can use DI is in vitro fertilization (IVF) in which a physician retrieves a woman's eggs, fertilizes them in a laboratory, and then puts the fertilized eggs into the woman's uterus in hopes that they will implant themselves in the uterine lining (American Society for Reproductive Medicine, 2011).

Using DI generally costs between $500 and $1000 for the first cycle and between $300 and $700 thereafter. These numbers include registration at a sperm bank (approximately $150), health tests when necessary (which can cost up to $600), shipping of sperm ($100–$200), the sperm itself (ranging from $135–$265 per vial), ovulation-predictor kits ($45–$60), and the procedure—IUI ($150–$275) or ICI ($100 or more). If the client choses special services, such as recipient/donor-photo matching, a donor audio interview, a baby photo, or a medical profile, the cost increases (Agigian, 2004, p. 94). The cost also increases dramatically if more technical medical services are required, such as IVF. In fact, IVF can cost between $12,000 and $17,000 per cycle, and it often requires multiple cycles to achieve a pregnancy (Eckstut, 2008).

Unfortunately, for those who use ART, most insurance companies do not cover the procedures or drug treatments, or they offer only partial coverage (Eckstut, 2008). Only 10 states mandate insurance companies to cover infertility services, and only if there is in fact an infertility issue (Agigian, 2004). Many LGBT people who access ART are not infertile; they simply need the help of a physician to have sperm meet egg. But if there is no medical necessity shown through a physician's diagnosis of infertility, then LGBT people often end up covering the cost of the services out-of-pocket, rather than have their insurance pay (Murphy, 2001).

Because of its high cost, the use of ART is stratified by race and class. The higher one's class status and the better their health benefits, the more likely they are to seek and receive ART (Agigian, 2004). Looking at data from the general population, regardless of sexual or gender identity, non-Hispanic Whites are 25% more likely than Hispanics and Blacks to use any infertility services. Whites are also twice as likely as Hispanics and four times as likely as Black people in general to access ART services (Agigian, 2004, p. 92). Although specific information is sketchy, Agigian (2004) extrapolated that data concerning the general population also apply to lesbians such that lesbians who are well above the poverty level, who identify as "non-Hispanic white" or "non-Hispanic other," and who have obtained at least a high school diploma (or GED) are more likely than other groups of lesbians to use ART. But the intersections of race and class are important to keep in mind. For example, among the African American lesbian mothers who Moore (2011) interviewed, several were able to access IVF because their upper-middle-class occupations "afforded them greater health insurance plans, as well as additional saving to help pay for these [IVF] procedures" (p. 143). Therefore, class, as it intersects with race, appears to influence the use of ART.

In addition to cost, when LGBT people decide to use ART in order to become parents, they have several other issues to consider. In couples with two biologically born women who both want to access DI, the women must decide who will try to get pregnant first, provided both women are fertile. Making this decision can be difficult because the partner who is not the biological parent may not be able to establish legal ties to the child (depending on the state) and may feel alienated from the parenting process (Chabot & Ames, 2004).

Lesbians' decisions concerning who tries to get pregnant first are often based on three factors: desire, age, and relationship to paid labor (Chabot & Ames, 2004; Sullivan, 2004). If one woman has a greater desire to get pregnant, she will generally try to inseminate first. There are instances in which both partners desire to get pregnant simultaneously, although a study of nearly 100 lesbians in Belgium suggests that this occurs in only about 14% of couples (Baetens et al., 2002, as cited in Goldberg, 2012, p. 59). In addition, frequently the older woman tries first given that she has fewer fertile years remaining than her partner (Chabot & Ames, 2004).

Regarding paid labor, in their study of 10 lesbian couples, behavioral scientists Jennifer Chabot and Barbara Ames (2004) found that which partner's "insurance plan was best, who was able to take time off of work with the least financial loss, and who had the most flexible work schedule also influenced selection of the biological parent" (p. 353). Social scientist Maureen Sullivan (2004) had similar findings in her study of 34 families headed by lesbians who used DI to become mothers. Thus, a woman's relationship to and experience with paid labor can help determine which member of a lesbian couple will try to get pregnant first.

If using DI, prospective parents (LGBT or otherwise) must also decide whether to use a known or anonymous donor (Lev, 2004). Some people choose a friend as a known donor because that can be a less expensive option (Agigian, 2004; Boggis, 2001). However, DI can still be expensive if the person using this method wants to have the known donor's sperm tested for sexually transmitted diseases (STDs). Because of the costs and the limited options, some low-income women choose not to have the sperm tested for STDs or HIV (Agigian, 2004), which can place them and their potential children at risk.

In addition to cost, some people choose a known donor because they believe that their children will want to contact or get to know the donor at a later date. Others choose a friend who can provide sperm or who will become a joint parent (Agigian, 2004; Goldberg, 2010; Moore, 2011). However, some LGBT people fear choosing a known donor because they worry about future legal disputes in which the donor will try to gain custody of the children, or they do not want to share parenting responsibilities with a third person (Goldberg, 2010; Sullivan, 2004).

If choosing an anonymous donor, LGBT people need to decide what characteristics to look for and whether or not to choose a donor who is willing to be identified when the child grows older (Goldberg, 2010). In a study of pregnant lesbians and their partners, psychologist Abbie Goldberg (2010) "found that 59% of women chose an unknown donor, and the remaining 10% chose an 'ID release' or 'Yes' donor (i.e., a donor who agreed to be contacted when the child reached some specified age, usually 18 years old)" (p. 60).

Similarly, in the largest and longest running study in the United States, that of 84 planned lesbian families with children conceived through DI, the National Longitudinal Lesbian Family Study (NLLFS) found that of the mostly White, educated, and middle- to upper-class lesbians studied, 36% selected known donors, 40% selected unknown donors, and 24% selected donors who could be contacted when the children reached 18 years of age. Those who selected unknown donors did so because they worried about legal ramifications in the future, or they did not know a possible donor who they wanted to use (Gartrell, Peyser, & Bos, 2012). Those who used a known donor stated that they wanted to know information about health and heritage, and they wanted their children to know the man who helped conceive them. Indeed, 2 years after their children's birth, most known donors were active participants in their children's daily lives; and after 5 years, about one third continued to see their children regularly, while the remaining known donors saw their children only occasionally. After 10 years from their children's birth, the mothers remained satisfied with their decisions to use a known donor (Gartrell et al., 2012). For those who had a choice about meeting the donor at age 18, half were sorry they had to wait that long, and the other half were largely uninterested in the prospective meeting. And most children "with an unknown donor expressed no regrets about not having a father" (Gartrell et al., 2012, p. 116).

For couples with two biologically born men, to use their own sperm, the men either need to find a woman willing to carry and share the child or need to hire a surrogate mother. Increasingly, gay men and lesbians are creating families with children by joining their sperm and egg then sharing childrearing responsibilities. Some children are raised, therefore, with a gay father and lesbian mother or with multiple gay fathers and lesbian mothers (Lev, 2004; Strah & Margolis, 2003). However, some gay men prefer surrogacy arrangements that allow them to become fathers without the addition of another parent. Surrogacy is an ART in which the prospective parent(s) creates a contract with a woman who will get pregnant and carry the fetus to term for the contracted prospective parent (Bergman et al., 2010). Surrogacy involves "rigorous procedures such as psychological testing and interviews, genetic histories, and careful matching of donors and surrogates are utilized in the selection of egg donors, surrogates, and intended parents" (Ragone, 1994, as cited in Bergman et al., 2010, p. 117). Because surrogacy can create confusion about who the "real" (i.e., legal) parents are, the contracts and procedures created for surrogacy are well regulated in the United States.

According to the American Society for Reproductive Medicine (2011), surrogacy arrangements come in two forms: genetic and gestational. With genetic surrogacy, the surrogate woman is inseminated with the sperm of the prospective father. The egg, in this case, comes from the surrogate, thus, creating both a genetic and gestational connection between the surrogate and the fetus. With genetic surrogacy, the prospective parents, and therefore potentially the child or children born from this arrangement, will know who the biological mother is (Lev, 2006). With gestational surrogacy, a physician uses IVF to create an embryo outside the woman's uterus, using a donor egg and the sperm of the prospective father. The physician then places the embryos into the surrogate's uterus, thus, creating a gestational connection, but not a genetic connection between the fetus and surrogate (Bergman et al., 2010). In this case, the potential parents can select an anonymous egg donor, but they will still know the identity of the gestational surrogate.

Estimates of the cost of surrogacy range from $30,000 to $150,000 per pregnancy, placing this method of becoming a parent out of reach for many people (Bergman et al., 2010; Goldberg, 2010, 2012; Lev, 2006; Strah & Margolis, 2003). In some states, part of the cost—approximately $20,000—goes to the surrogate mother to pay for her "prenatal care, vitamins, transportation, maternity clothes, medical, legal and psychological counseling" (Lev, 2006, p. 76). Other states greatly limit the payments that potential parents can make to surrogates for their services (Robertson, 2005).

Surrogacy is complicated not only because of its high cost and need for support from medical and legal professionals but also because of state laws that regulate surrogate arrangements. At least 10 states ban surrogacy all together, while other states ban surrogacy that involves compensation to the surrogate mother. Still some states ban surrogacy for LGBT clientele (The Select Surrogate, n.d.; Wald, 2007, as cited in Goldberg, 2010). Drawing on the work of Deborah H. Wald, Esq., Abbie Goldberg (2010) explained how complicated state laws concerning surrogacy and LGBT parenting can become:

> [T]he initial determination of parentage for any baby (e.g., a baby born to a birth mother or surrogate) generally happens in the state in which the baby is born. Thus, if a couple from New York (where surrogacy is illegal) contracts with a surrogacy agency in California, and in turn matches them with a surrogate in Ohio, the initial determination of parentage should occur in Ohio. (p. 71)

While such an arrangement might work for a heterosexual couple, the arrangement would be problematic for a LGBT couple because Ohio does not allow same-sex couples to openly adopt children in its state (Goldberg, 2010). Therefore, when LGBT people enter into surrogate arrangements, they must work with lawyers to ensure that the arrangement they are engaging in will, in fact, lead to them being able to claim the child upon its birth. Thus, how different states regulate surrogacy in different ways makes using surrogacy more or less difficult to access depending on a person's geographic location (Vaughn, 2011).

The limited studies to date that examine gay men's use of surrogacy suggest that many of the men who use this form of ART are privileged along lines of race and class (Johnson & O'Connor, 2002; Mallon, 2004; Schacher et al., 2005). For example, the participants in Bergman et al.'s (2010) study showed race and class inequalities, with 80% of the fathers being White, and the remaining fathers being Asian, Latino, and Middle Eastern. The mean annual household income of the participants was $270,000, with an income range from $100,000 to $1,200,000. The race and class background of participants is not surprising given the high cost of surrogacy.

Although few studies examine LGBT people's experiences throughout the surrogacy process, therapist Arlene Lev's (2006) interviews with gay men provides some insight into such experiences. The gay men she interviewed stated three reasons why they chose surrogacy to become fathers: (a) They wanted a biological connection to their children; (b) they could raise their children from birth instead of adopting an older infant or child; and (c) because at the time of the interviews some states banned adoption by gays and lesbians, the men found the legal issues less complicated using surrogacy than adoption (Lev, 2006). How complicated this last reason became depended on whether or not the potential parent selected a friend or relative as the surrogate and whether the potential father hired a lawyer or worked with an agency. Working with an agency can remove some of the legal complications. In fact, certain surrogacy agencies, such as Growing Generations in Los Angeles, cater to gay clientele (Lev, 2006; Stacey, 2006). Although working with agencies can be more expensive than hiring a private lawyer, gay men report that the added cost is worth the relief from hassles. Agencies will assist potential "fathers in meeting a surrogate mother, educating the couple about the legal and medical processes, screening the surrogate mother medically and psychologically, co-ordinating the surrogacy arrangements, providing counseling for all parties, and mediating areas of conflict" (Lev, 2006, p. 73). Although working with an agency increases the costs involved, that cost buys gay men and the surrogate mothers vital protections and peace of mind worth the extra cost to many gay men.

Although there is limited research on transgender people's use of ART, the extant literature suggests that transgender people have additional concerns to consider from GLB people. Until recently, the availability of reproductive technologies for transgender people was limited. Therefore, transgender people who wanted to transition generally needed to give up parenthood (De Sutter, 2001). However, as discussed above, for those who have the financial means, options are now available to harvest, freeze, and store one's sperm and eggs. Such options mean that transgender people who wish to preserve their sperm and eggs prior to transitioning in order to use them at a later date can do so (De Sutter, 2001; De Sutter, 2009; De Sutter, Kira, Verschoor, & Hotimsky, 2002).

Although ART options are available, anecdotal examples and limited studies suggest that one barrier to ART for transgender people—and to a lesser extent for lesbians and gays—is the refusal of treatment by physicians. There appears to be a general bias among health-care professionals that those seeking ART are or should be heterosexual (Yager et al., 2010). Such a bias was the case with FTM Thomas Beatie in which physicians refused him services before Beatie finally found a physician who would help him inseminate (Beatie, 2008). At least 42 states and the United States federal government permit "conscience clauses" that provide health-care providers the discretion to choose who they will accept as clients and who they will reject based on if the procedure requested opposes the health-care providers' moral or religious beliefs. Some health-care professionals may be particularly apt to deny services to transgender people because until May 2013, the American Psychiatric Association labeled transgender identities as a "gender identity disorder" (Murphy, 2010). Because of conscious clauses and labeling, LGBT people—and particularly transgender people—who wish to receive ART may not have any legal recourse if a physician refuses them services (Eckstut, 2008).

Despite barriers, there is evidence that many transsexual people want to become parents both before and after they transition (Cook-Daniels, 2008; Sausa, 2008; Wierckx et al., 2012). For example, in a study of 50 transsexual men in the Netherlands, 11 of the men already had children. Eight of these men had become fathers through their female partners using DI. The remaining three had given birth before they started hormone replacement therapy or had sex reassignment surgery (SRS). In addition, over a third of the participants stated that prior to transitioning they would have considered freezing their eggs for future use had this option been available. And most of the participants without children expressed a great desire to become parents in the future (Wierckx et al., 2012).

While Wierckx et al.'s study took place in the Netherlands, becoming a parent using ART is a greater option for those in the United States because unlike most European nations, the United States does not require transgender men to have their ovaries or uterus removed in order to have a legal sex reassignment (Wierckx et al., 2012). Remaining biologically intact allows transgender men in the United States to possibly become pregnant (as in the case of Thomas Beatie), or to use a gestational surrogate using their own eggs through IVF. Transgender people who do not want to use their own sperm or eggs can opt to use ART in the same manner as any other people, provided they can find a trans-friendly physician. Given the various factors and barriers involved with using ART to conceive and birth children, the mental stress is great, both for heterosexual and LGBT people (Spector, 2009). Although some of these stress-related factors overlap between LGBT and heterosexual people (e.g., addressing issues of infertility), additional stress-related factors exist for LGBT people as discussed above.

The Use of Adoption and Foster Care to Become a Parent

In addition to having children through heterosexual relations and the use of ART, many LGBT people become parents through adoption and foster care. Adoption, whether by LGBT people or heterosexuals, is a common way to become a parent in the United States. In fact, one in six Americans have had a "personal experience" with adoption, either through adopting a child themselves or knowing someone with an adopted child (Lev, 2004, p. 58). "Adoption is the legal establishment of a parent/child relationship between individuals who are usually not, with the exception of kinship adoption, related by birth" (Ryan & Whitlock, 2007, as cited in Brown et al., 2009, p. 232). According to the Child Welfare Information Gateway (2011), approximately 136,000 children were adopted in the United States in 2007 and 2008. There are three main types of adoption: Public domestic, private domestic, and international adoption (Downing et al., 2009; Lev, 2004).

In 2008, public agency adoptions accounted for 41% (55,303) of all adoptions (Child Welfare Information Gateway, 2011). Public adoption involves adopting a child through the child welfare system (Downing et al., 2009). These adoptions are financially feasible for most families, with the cost ranging from $0 to $2,500 (Goldberg, 2010; Lev, 2004). To encourage public adoption, some states will also pay a stipend to the adoptive family to help support the child. Public adoption can be a faster process than other forms of adoption, unless the potential parents wish to wait for an infant. However, disruptions to the adoption process can occur in public adoptions, particularly in the case of foster-to-adopt programs in which there are issues involving reunification of the birth family, the rehabilitation of the birth mother, or custody disputes (Lev, 2004).

Private domestic adoption involves using a private agency or lawyer to handle the adoption, and it accounted for 46% (63,094) of all adoptions in 2008 (Child Welfare Information Gateway, 2011). Some private adoptions are "open" in which there is some ongoing relationship with the birth parents; others are "closed" (Downing et al., 2009). Private adoption can also include adopting children of relatives. Regardless of being open or closed, private adoptions are more expensive than public adoptions, ranging in cost from $5,000 to $40,000 per adoption (Goldberg, 2010; Lev, 2004). International adoption involves adopting a child from a country outside the

United States, costs between $7,000 and $30,000 per adoption (Golberg, 2010), and accounted for 13% (17,416) of all adoptions in 2008 (Child Welfare Information Gateway, 2011).

Estimates of how many LGBT adoptive parents there are in the United States or how many children are adopted by LGBT parents is hard to pinpoint. Some estimates suggest that at least one million children, or around 4% of adopted children in the United States, have at least one gay or lesbian parent (Ausbrooks & Russell, 2011; Brown et al., 2009). Other estimates suggest that there are approximately 14,000 children currently fostered by gay or lesbian parents, and over 65,000 children have been adopted by a LGBT parent or couple (Pertman and Howard, 2012). In addition, studies estimate that between one and two million gay men have adopted children in the United States (Mallon, 2004).

Whatever the exact numbers may be, we know that LGBT people's interest in adopting and fostering children is certainly strong and growing. Research suggests that lesbians and gay men are more willing to become parents through adoption and fostering than are heterosexuals (Downs & James, 2006; Mallon, 2011). Whereas most heterosexuals see adoption as a second choice that they use after facing infertility, lesbians and gay men often look to adoption as a first choice means of becoming parents (Lev, 2004). For example, Pertman and Howard (2012) found that while 46.2% of lesbians were favorable toward adoption, only 32.1% of heterosexual women were favorable toward adoption. And 5.7% of lesbians actually do try to adopt, as opposed to 3.3% of heterosexual women (p. 27).

Although data concerning adoption in general are readily available, data on the number and racial-ethnic breakdown of LGBT parents who adopt children are scarce. Most studies on adoptive LGBT families suggest that many parents are White and middle-class (see, for example, Goldberg, 2012; Panozzo, 2010; Schacher et al., 2005). However, other studies suggest that adoption among gays and lesbians of color who become parents is also common, but they tend to occur in more urban areas than in more suburban or rural areas (Moore, 2011; Stacey, 2006). There is also some scant evidence that lesbians of color and working-class White lesbians are more likely than White or middle-class lesbians to adopt a relative's child (Mezey, 2008a; Moore, 2011). For example, in Moore's (2011) study, a Black lesbian adopted one of her nephews because her sister, who had a history of drug abuse and mental health problems, was unable to parent the child. Similarly, I (Mezey, 2008a) interviewed two working-class White lesbians who became adoptive mothers after a social service agency called to say that relatives were no longer able to keep the children. The question about how many people adopt their relatives' children, and whether or not this practice varies by race and class, is one that requires further research before drawing conclusions about this path to parenthood.

While we do not fully know the racial breakdown of LGBT parents who adopt children, we do know from studies that many are White. We also know that many children available for foster care and adoption are children of color in the United States and foreign-born children from Asia, Africa, and to a lesser extent Latin America (Lev, 2004). For example, estimates suggest that over 125,000 children in foster care are eligible for adoption (Mallon, 2004). In 2008, 39% of the children waiting for families in the foster care system were White, 30% were Black, and 21% were Hispanic (U.S. Department of Health and Human Services Administration for Children & Families, 2012). The combination of White parents and children of color means that the number of interracial families created through adoption is commonplace among LGBT families (Ausbrooks & Russell, 2011).

Regardless of the sexual identity of the adoptive parents, transracial adoption is a controversial issue. Some people are concerned that adoptive children will lose their cultural heritage when placed with parents who are unfamiliar with the culture associated with their racial-ethnic or national background of origin. With the passage of the 1994 Multiethnic Placement Act (MEPA), agencies and social workers can no longer legally factor in race and ethnicity when determining foster and adoption placement (Lev, 2004). This means that many agencies are placing children of color with White parents. While organizations such as the National Association of Black Social Workers remain concerned about the creation of transracial families through adoption and foster care, many academics and researchers support such families (Ausbrooks & Russell, 2011; Lev, 2004). Research findings suggest that White LGBT adoptive parents may be better equipped than their heterosexual counterparts to handle the multiple identity and cultural issues that their adoptive children of color may face. This is because LGBT people often experience discrimination and struggle with identity issues that White heterosexual people have not. Such experiences and struggles may help White LGBT parents better address issues of discrimination and identity that their adoptive children may experience as well (Ausbrooks & Russell, 2011).

In addition to the standard adoption procedures discussed above, LGBT people often need to perform "second-parent adoptions." Married heterosexual couples can adopt together. Similarly, when a married heterosexual woman gives birth, her husband automatically becomes the legal father of their child. However, because most LGBT people cannot legally marry, the partner who does not give birth cannot make legal claims to the child; and LGBT couples often cannot adopt a child together. In order to create a legally connected, two-parent family, LGBT couples seek a second-parent adoption, a process through which both parents become legally recognized. Through this process, the existing adoptive or biological parent retains their legal status, while the state simultaneously designates the social parent as an equally legal parent (Hequembourg, 2007).

There are limitations to second-parent adoptions, however. First, all states do not perform this form of adoption. As of 2004, judges in 20 states had performed second-parent adoptions (Mallon, 2004). These adoptions were often on a case-by-case basis in which a handful of judges throughout the state would accept joint adoption cases. On a statewide level, as of 2014, 22 states and the District of Columbia allowed second-parent adoption (Human Rights Campaign [HRC], 2014d), and 21 states and the District of Columbia allowed same-sex joint adoption (HRC, 2014c). This number is up by 11 states since 2011, so the trend of joint adoption is certainly moving in favor of LGBT families. However, for biological or adoptive parents who have had children with another biological or legal parent (e.g., through a known donor or previous relationship), second-parent adoption can become difficult because the biological or legal parent may have to rescind their parental rights before a judge will allow a second-parent adoption to occur (Hequembourg, 2007).

An additional limitation is that similar to other forms of adoption, second-parent adoptions require a home study, even though the two parents may have raised their child together since the child's birth. Home studies are both insulting to the existing parents and costly. Although the emotional and financial costs may prevent some LGBT people from pursuing second-parent adoptions (Hequembourg, 2007), research suggests that those who can pursue second-parent adoption often do (Goldberg, 2012).

As the discussion on second-parent adoption suggests, LGBT people face specific structural, cultural, and personal barriers regarding adoption. Structural barriers exist at the institutional level in the form of state laws and agency policies that prevent LGBT people from adopting children. To date, there have not been any changes to adoption laws, although these might start changing as marriage laws change. Presently, 21 states and the District of Columbia explicitly permit same-sex couples to adopt children, whereas two states (Mississippi and Utah) explicitly ban LGBT people from adopting. Until September 2010, Florida was among those states that banned adoption by LGBT adults; however, since that time the state supreme court deemed the ban unconstitutional. Several other states allow only married couples (regardless of sexual or gender identity) to adopt children. Because marriage equality does not exist in those states, the marriage laws systematically prevent LGBT couples from adopting. Even in states in which there are no laws explicitly banning LGBT people from adopting, evidence suggests that biases among judges can make adoption difficult (Richman, 2009). For example, a case in Arizona indicated a heightened level of scrutiny regarding a bisexual man who wanted to adopt a child. The courts had multiple concerns regarding the petitioner, including his employment and mental health history; however, his bisexual identity was of greatest concern to the court (Appell, 2012).

Not only do state laws create structural barriers, but adoption and foster care agencies can also create roadblocks if those agencies are unwilling to work with LGBT clientele (Downs & James, 2006; Goldberg, 2012; Richman, 2009). This is true despite that fact that nearly every "major professional organization in the legal, child-welfare and health-care fields in the United States have issued [a] statement supporting gay and lesbian parenting and adoption" (Brodzinsky, 2012, p. 65). With these endorsements, and the increased understanding that LGBT people make at least as good parents as heterosexual people (Biblarz & Stacey, 2010; Golombok, 2007; Stacey & Biblarz, 2001), adoption agencies are becoming more willing to work with LGBT clientele.

Despite such changes in understanding and practice, some adoption agencies still refuse to work with LGBT clientele. For example, a study of 30 public and 277 private adoption agencies funded by the Donaldson Institute found that while 60% of adoption agencies were willing to accept applications from lesbian and gay individuals and same-sex couples, 40% were not. In addition, between 1999 and 2000, 39% of agencies surveyed had made at least one placement to lesbian and gay people (Brodzinsky, 2012). However, the study also revealed that 20% of the agencies had rejected gay and lesbian applicants due to two main categories: problems with the applicants themselves and violation of laws, policies, or practices. Rejecting agencies stated the following reasons regarding the applicant: unrealistic expectations regarding adoption (31.8%), psychological problems (31.8%), questionable motives for adopting (24.6%), relationship problems (24.6%), financial problems (8.7%), lack of adequate social support (11.6%), and medical problems (2.9%). Although some of these reasons may in fact be legitimate, agencies' rejections of LGBT applicants may also be due to what "Brooks and Goldberg (2001) refer to . . . as an 'informal or quiet policy' (p. 153) that deters the placement of children with [lesbian and gay] parents" (Brown et al., 2009, p. 232).

The issue of placing children in LGBT families is important to those who desire to become parents through adoption or foster care and those children who could benefit from being in stable loving homes. In addition, as the quote at the top of this chapter indicates, researchers at The Williams

Institute and The Urban Institute estimate that a national ban on LGBT adoption could cost the nation between $87 and $130 million—with an individual cost to states ranging from $100,000 to $27 million (Gates, Badgett, Macomber, & Chambers, 2007). These costs are due to two main reasons. First, if the state removes children from LGBT-headed homes, then the state may need to place those children in institutional settings that are more costly for the state than family foster care. Second, when removed from an LGBT home, the state then needs to recruit and train new heterosexual foster parents. Because recruiting foster parents can be difficult, the state will have the extra financial burden of having to search for qualified foster parents (Gates et al., 2007). Therefore, at minimum, states and the federal government have an economic incentive to allow LGBT adults to become adoptive and foster parents.

Agencies face their own issues, however, even if they are willing to work with LGBT clientele. For those agencies located in conservative states with restrictive laws, social workers and other adoption agency employees often work with LGBT clientele without ever asking about the clients' sexual identity. That is, some agencies and social workers hide the gender and sexual identities of LGBT applicants because of concerns that coming out would jeopardize chances for a successful adoption (Downing et al., 2009; Goldberg, Downing, & Sauck, 2007; Matthews & Cramer, 2006). However, as sexual and gender identities are increasingly less problematic to courts, recent recommendations from social workers, such as professor of social work Gerald P. Mallon (2011), are changing. Mallon (2011) suggested that while there is no one correct way to conduct home studies or interact with potential parents, in general, social workers should not ignore sexual identity "in the assessment process because an individual's sexuality is an aspect of who he or she is as a total person and will impact on his or her life as a parent" (p. 11).

Whereas Mallon's suggestion may be helpful to lesbian and gay applicants, his advice may be less helpful for bisexual applicants who continue to struggle in the adoption process. Similar to gays and lesbians, bisexual people have to choose whether or not to disclose their sexual identities during the adoption process. If they choose not to, then depending on their current relationship status, they may appear to be either heterosexual or lesbian or gay, when in fact they are neither (Eady, Ross, Epstein, & Anderson, 2009). In their qualitative study of 40 single and partnered LGBT people in Ontario between 2006 and 2008, Eady and her colleagues (2009) found the issue of identity disclosure was central to bisexual respondents during the adoption process. On the one hand, bisexual people sometimes have an advantage if the adoption agency thinks they are heterosexual. However, bisexual people can also face a disadvantage if the adoption agency is biphobic and draws on myths and stereotypes about bisexual people (e.g., being non-monogamous or hypersexualized), which may reduce their chances to adopt. In fact, some adoption agencies may be more comfortable with lesbian and gay identities than with bisexual identities (Eady et al., 2009).

In addition to having to decide whether to come out during the adoption process, another barrier that LGBT couples face develops out of laws prohibiting LGBT people from adopting as a couple (i.e., joint adoption). Therefore, agencies do not always know how to address the nonadoptive parent. On the one hand, the agency may ignore or leave out the nonadoptive or nonfoster parent (Brown et al., 2009; Downs & James, 2006). Similarly, some agencies fully include the partner of the person who is adopting when couples cannot adopt together (Brown et al., 2009; Goldberg, 2006). LGBT people discuss the importance of inclusion of both potential parents as being paramount during this early stage of the parenting process, as well as throughout the stages of raising children. In fact, lesbians who have reported positive interactions with adoption agencies have stressed the inclusion of the nonadopting parent (Goldberg et al., 2007).

In addition to structural and institutional barriers, prospective LGBT parents face discrimination both on cultural and personal levels. Because dominant culture often deems men as not being nurturing, gay men in particular face questions as to how they can parent without a woman in the family (Downs & James, 2006; Lev, 2004; Mallon, 2004). Gay men face sexist assumptions, therefore, that only women can be good parents, and heterosexist assumptions about how families should consist of a married heterosexual couple. Lesbians also face heterosexist understandings about families (Mallon, 2004). Similarly, biases against bisexuals and transgender people as parents due to their assumed "abnormal" or "pathological" sexual and gender practices can lead to biases in the adoption and foster care process (Appell, 2012; Downs & James, 2006; Lev, 2004). To worsen matters, many LGBT people receive limited social support from friends and families thus limiting the emotional support needed to endure sometimes difficult adoption and foster processes (Brown et al., 2009; Downs & James, 2006; Goldberg et al., 2007). Therefore, while the adoption and foster care process leads many LGBT people to become parents, the process is often rife with structural and cultural barriers causing the adoption process to be particularly difficult for LGBT people.

Despite barriers, LGBT people are becoming parents in record numbers; and the data suggest that such trends are good for children and society in general. Most LGBT parents make intentional parenting decisions such that they desire and carefully plan for nearly all of the children they birth.

LGBT parents are also more likely to adopt and foster children in need of stable homes, and they are often better equipped to deal with racial and cultural differences than their heterosexual counterparts. Without LGBT parents adopting and fostering children, the nation would face a loss of up to $27 million in funds trying to care for children through public means. And as discussed in both Chapter 2 and above, LGBT parents raise children who are as healthy, if not more, than heterosexual parents. Therefore, while conservatives argue that LGBT parents are a blight on society, the data clearly suggest that their fears are grossly unfounded and in fact harmful to society.

LGBT Parenting Experiences and Issues

Once parents come out as LGBT, or once LGBT people become parents, their parental experiences are both similar to and different from the experiences of heterosexual parents. Just like heterosexual parents, LGBT parents have to feed, bath, nurture, and take care of their children. They have to negotiate big vision issues like where to live, what schools to enroll their children in, and how to balance work responsibilities with family life. They have to manage emotions and stress and find time for themselves. Just like heterosexual parents, LGBT parents have to deal with the minutia of parenting and household chores that accompany parenthood, such as cooking dinner, making lunches, doing the laundry, taking children to afterschool activities, and shopping. They have to negotiate illness and extended families and deal with separation and divorce. In fact, put any parents in a room with other parents—regardless of sexual or gender identity—and they will no doubt have a lot in common to talk about regarding parenting and their children.

So what makes being a LGBT parent different from a heterosexual parent? For that matter, what makes being a lesbian parent different from being a gay or bisexual or transgender parent? To answer the above questions, we should remember that the structural barriers that heterosexism and homophobia present, the cultural beliefs concerning who makes a good parent, and how LGBT people choose to parent given their own structural and cultural experiences all interact to shape their lives as parents. The following discussion addresses the major issues that LGBT parents deal with and how those issues are both similar to heterosexual families and also specific to their being LGBT. These issues include diverse family forms, parenting strategies, redefining family roles, teaching children to address prejudices against their families and themselves, and dealing with separation and divorce.

Diverse Family Forms

As LGBT people transition from heterosexual to LGBT parents and as LGBT people create intentional families within their LGBT identities, they often create a variety of new family forms, including stepfamilies, heterogay families, families with multiple and polyamorous parents, and families with social but not legal or biological connections. I define and discuss these family forms below.

LGBT stepfamilies are composed of two major forms: previously heterosexual partners in which at least one parent has entered a LGBT relationship and remained connected to their children from a previous marriage or relationship; and LGBT partners who had children together, then separated or divorced, and then entered into a new LGBT relationship. Regardless of the origin, the relationships that develop from LGBT stepfamilies are often socially and legally undefined, which makes them vulnerable to social and legal prejudice (Tasker, 2013). The absence of legal recognition has created some differences between LGBT stepfamilies and heterosexual stepfamilies. In particular, LGBT stepparents often have few legal rights and little way to gain legal connections to their stepchildren. The exception is when a second-parent adoption was or can be performed (Tasker, 2013), but as discussed earlier, such adoptions are often difficult depending on the state in which the LGBT family lives. The lack of marriage equality and the lack of second-parent or joint adoption creates a very tenuous situation for the "other" or stepparent because that parent has no legal connection to the other adults or children in the family (Goldberg, 2012; Moore, 2011; Muzio, 1999; Sullivan, 2001). The status of being a social parent without the status of being a legal or biological parent or partner affects interpersonal relationships such as the household division of labor (as discussed below). Having the status of "other parent" can also make that parent feel awkward and isolated in relationship to his or her partner, as well as to institutions and situations outside of the family.

For example, in her study of lesbian mothers, Sullivan (2001) found that in social situations, "other mothers" needed to negotiate how they would identify themselves to outsiders in order to explain their relationships to their children. Sometimes they would disclose their nonlegal and nonbiological status, and other times they would not. Similarly, several gay men in Goldberg's (2012) study stated that they often felt invisible, isolated during the adoption process, and worried about not having a legal connection to their child, although other men in that study were less bothered by their "other" parent status.

Regardless of the emotional toll that being an "other" parent might take, the legal risk is real. In the case of separation, if the biological or legal parent wants full custody of the child, the other parent often has little legal recourse, particularly in states in which LGBT families remain stigmatized by the courts. Similarly, in cases where the biological or legal parent dies, other family members with biological or legal ties to the child (e.g., grandparents, aunts, uncles, cousins, etc.) often fight for legal guardianship even when the other parent has raised and cared for his or her children for years (Hunter, Joslin, & McGowan, 2004; Minter & Wald, 2012b; Richman, 2009). As discussed in Chapter 2, the lack of marital rights often prevent parental rights, therefore creating emotional distress, social isolation, and legal threats to parental rights among LGBT parents.

The challenges that a lack of legal connections pose notwithstanding, the relationships between stepparents and stepchildren sometimes differ from relationships in heterosexual stepfamilies in a positive way because of the same-gendered nature of lesbian and gay stepfamilies. Studies have found that in both lesbian and gay male stepfamilies, although the transition into stepparenting is often challenging, the stepparents have integrated more patiently, with more flexibility, and in a less controlling way than in heterosexual stepparent families. This is partly because the stepparents tend to take on less of a gendered parent role (e.g., nurturing mother or controlling father) and more of the role of a friend or playmate. In addition, qualitative studies suggest that LGBT stepparents are aware of the negative pressures coming from outside their families and therefore attempt to create a more secure environment within their families (Current-Juretschko & Bigner, 2005; Tasker, 2013; Wright, 1998, 2001).

Despite the differences between LGBT and heterosexual stepfamilies, many of the issues that these two groups of families face are similar to one another (Current-Juretschko & Bigner, 2005; Moore, 2011; Tasker, 2013; Wright, 1998, 2001). For example, "children in both types of stepfamilies have more of an emotional tie to their parent than their stepparent; they also have a closer tie to their nonresident parent than their stepparent" (Tasker, 2013, p. 10). Challenges concerning how to integrate and blend multiple families together, as well as how to divide household labor and what type of parenting role to assume are also inherent to most stepfamilies (Current-Juretschko & Bigner, 2005; Moore, 2011; Tasker, 2013; Wright, 1998, 2001). In fact, recognizing the similarities, and in an attempt to normalize their families, lesbian and gay stepparents often report that their families really are not much different from heterosexual stepfamilies (Current-Juretschko & Bigner, 2005; Wright, 1998). Although I understand the reasons why LGBT people want to normalize their families, doing so hides two important facts: (a) The lack of legal support makes the very formation and sustainability of LGBT families harder for LGBT people, and

(b) LGBT families actually present a positive model from which heterosexual couples can gain important information about how to improve upon their own stepfamily relationships.

In addition to stepfamilies and families with a combination of legal or biological and other parents, LGBT families are creating families with a variety of other parental configurations. For example, there are LGBT families with multiple parents, LGBT polyamorous families, and heterogay families. LGBT families with multiple mothers and/or multiple fathers arise when couples choose to parent with other couples. For example, a lesbian couple may use the sperm of a gay male couple; then, the four biological parents become parents together. Polyamorous families (aka polyfamilies) are families in which the people involved create non-monogamous and open relationships such that the people involved are aware of the other people involved (Pallotta-Chiarolli, Haydon, & Hunter, 2013; Sheff, 2011). According to sociologist Elisabeth Sheff, "many polyamorous families live together and share domestic, financial, and child-care responsibilities, though some maintain separate residences" (Sheff, 2004, p. 1). Heterogay families are families that are intentionally formed by both heterosexual and gay parents together, for example, a heterosexual mother and a gay father (Segal-Engelchin, Erera, & Cwickel, 2005). All of these families face similar challenges to LGBT and heterosexual stepfamilies, as discussed above. As such families become more widespread and more research is conducted, our information on the details of how such families form, the experiences they have, and what we can learn from them, will become more evident.

Division of Labor and Work-Family Balance

Because of the many different types of LGBT families and because LGBT families are often created and exist in degendered, or at least differently gendered relationships than heterosexual couples, LGBT families often redefine how to raise their children, how to divide household and child-care division of labor and parental roles, and how to balance work and family responsibilities. Lesbian mothers often raise children without fathers, thus simultaneously maintaining socially accepted nurturing roles and taking on the breadwinning role as well. Similarly, by taking on nurturing roles, gay fathers challenge cultural and traditional views of fathers as primarily being breadwinners. Families with bisexual and transgender parents also challenge conventional definitions of family, and bend the rules of how to structure families along lines of gender and sexuality (Downing, 2013; Goldberg, 2010; Moore, 2011; Schacher et al., 2005; Stacey, 2006). In creating their families, therefore, LGBT parents tend to degender parenting by focusing on each parent's strengths and interests, rather than on preconceived dominant cultural notions about what mom or dad "should" be doing to fulfill their parenting and partner roles. As Schacher and her colleagues (2005) wrote about the gay fathers in their study, the fathers

> felt free to write their own rules, define their own parenting roles, and create new norms. They created a hybrid, degendered parent role that encouraged both partners to be adept at most childcare duties rather than creating a "mommy role" in which one partner over-functioned in caretaking, and a "daddy role" in which the other partner over-functioned in the public world of work. (p. 45)

This rethinking and degendering of family roles is common within LGBT families and can be seen clearly throughout the research on the household division of labor and work-family balance within LGBT families, as discussed next.

There is a burgeoning body of studies focusing on the household division of labor and work-family balance among White, middle-class lesbians and gay men. There is only one such study on African American lesbians (see Moore, 2011), only one study that focuses specifically on the division of labor in transgender families (see Pfeffer, 2010), and no studies to my knowledge that examine the division of labor in bisexual families. This discussion focuses largely, therefore, on how a small group of lesbians and gay men organizes their families, with the two exceptions mentioned above.

How GLT families (the *B* is purposefully omitted here due to lack of information) organize their household and family responsibilities depends on the gender of the couple (e.g., women, men, or transgender), on the legal and biological status of the parent, and on personal preferences and desires. Many gay men and lesbians believe in an egalitarian division of labor and strive toward this goal. In fact, many report that they have an egalitarian household structure, even if more objective standards of researchers question this claim (Carrington, 1999; Weeks, Heaphy, & Donovan, 2001). As sociologist Jeffrey Weeks and his colleagues (2001) wrote,

> The dominant belief in the non-heterosexual world is that same sex-partnerships offer unique possibilities for the construction of egalitarian relationships. A democratized, flexible, model of couple relationships has become the ideal. The reality, inevitably, is more complex: non-heterosexuals strive to achieve equality in terms of intimacy, sexual relations and the division of labour in the household against all the inequalities that continue to structure our societies. (p. 109)

Even if GLT couples do not always achieve equality, however, they at minimum spend time reflecting on and communicating with each other their desires for equality and often work toward that goal (Hines, 2006; Hybarger, 2000; Johnson & O'Connor, 2002; Weeks et al., 2001).

Within their attempts at consensus and equality, studies suggest that some GLT families do achieve an egalitarian division of labor, while others do not. In lesbian families where parents do not have egalitarian divisions of labor, studies show that the biological, legal parent, or the parent who had a greater desire to have children, tends to shoulder more of the child-care responsibilities, while the other parent focuses more on other household chores or on paid labor (Carrington, 1999; Downing & Goldberg, 2011; Gartrell, Rodas, Deck, Peyser, & Banks, 2006; Goldberg, 2010; Johnson & O'Connor, 2002; Moore, 2011; Panozzo, 2010; Sullivan, 1996). Carrington (1999) found that in order to "normalize" their families, sometimes lesbians and gay men protect their partners from appearing too much like a breadwinner (for women) and nurturing (for men) by overemphasizing the traditionally gendered work that they do.

Despite some unequal divisions of labor within lesbian and gay male families, researchers still find that lesbians' families (both women-born lesbians and transgender lesbians) are more egalitarian than gay male families; and both have a more egalitarian division of labor than do heterosexual families in general (Goldberg, 2010; Hines, 2006; Hybarger, 2000; Johnson & O'Connor, 2002; Kurdek, 2007). Family form (e.g., stepfamilies, adoptive families, or biological families) not withstanding, lesbians and gay men agree that they do not want to organize their families around specializations (e.g., a breadwinner and homemaker). Instead, they try to organize their work according to the skills and desires of each parent (Moore, 2011; Patterson, Sutfin, & Fulcher, 2004).

Regardless of how lesbian and gay couples *want* to balance work and family, much of their reality relies on their relationship to the paid labor market. Both gay fathers and lesbian mothers grapple with the balance between work and family. Gays and lesbians who want one parent to stay at home and one to remain in the work force rely on several major factors when deciding who should stay at home and who should go to work (Goldberg, 2012). The person who earns a higher salary or has more earning potential tends to remain full-time in the paid labor force. In addition, partners with greater job flexibility tend to remain at work because they have a greater ability to share child care and participate in their children's lives despite their need to work. People with greater job dissatisfaction tend to carry more child-care responsibilities. In fact, some parents are eager to leave their paid jobs for parenthood (Mallon, 2004; Mezey, 2008a). In addition, some LGBT parents feel that they are better suited for parenthood than their partners, leading them to stay at home (Goldberg, 2012).

Studies on White gay men suggest that these men were unsure they wanted to give up their breadwinner roles. For example, in their qualitative study of 21 mostly White (mixed with several Asian American), middle-class gay fathers, Schacher and her colleagues (2005) found that even though the fathers wanted "to be very involved in caregiving, many expressed feeling conflicted about giving up their primary role as breadwinner. They spoke of the strong ethic ingrained in them to be providers" (p. 44). The fact that many gay fathers did not want to be full-time caregivers led to friction with their partners about who should stay home. In the end, the partner with less earning potential did more child care. Interestingly, even though the stay-at-home partner cared greatly about his paid work prior to becoming a parent, paid labor became less important to him after the child arrived.

Researchers have also found that some middle-class, White gay and lesbian families who earn enough money can have one parent stay at home, or they can hire help to minimize their household and child-care responsibilities and to create more leisure time or time to be in the paid labor force (Goldberg, 2010; Sullivan, 1996). However, some White lesbian mothers and gay fathers who want to remain at home are unable to because they need to earn a salary to maintain financial stability (Mallon, 2004; Reimann, 2001).

As stated earlier, very little research exists on the division of labor in Black, Latino, and Asian American lesbian and gay families. One exception (Moore, 2011) suggests that because Black women's relationship to work in the United States is historically different from White women's relationship to work, in African American lesbian families, both women are likely to be employed, particularly as economic independence is very important to many Black women. In fact, Moore's study suggests that similar to African American heterosexual women, African American lesbians see paid labor as part of what it means to be a good mother. Regardless of race, however, data show that lesbian mothers are more likely than heterosexual mothers to be in the workforce whether they want to be in the paid labor force or not (Moore, 2011; Reimann, 2001).

While heterosexual parents must also decide who will work and who, if anyone, will stay at home, the difference between heterosexual and LGBT parents is that in heterosexual couples, fathers tend to earn more than mothers, because men in general tend to earn more than women. Overall, heterosexual mothers are the ones who stay home. In addition, heterosexual women and men often think that women should be mothers, and so they may perceive the women in their families as being better equipped as parents. This is not the case for LGBT parents. As Schacher et al. (2005) wrote, gay fathers in their study "*degendered parenting* where parental roles and duties are not ascribed by gender." Gay parenting, by necessity, makes the gender role distinctions between "mommy" and "daddy" obsolete" (p. 44). This sentiment is true among most gay and lesbian parents.

The result of gay men and lesbians organizing their division of labor and balancing their work and families is that they have to determine how to share their money. In order to maintain autonomy, the women in Moore's study maintained separate financial accounts instead of pooling their money. Unlike African American lesbians in Moore's study, Solomon, Rothblum, and Balsam (2004) studied the sharing of money among mostly White lesbians and gay men who had civil unions in Vermont. They found that White lesbians share their money in more egalitarian ways than White gay men, and both lesbians and gay men share their money in more egalitarian ways than married heterosexual couples.

The two studies on transgender families provide evidence of differences between those families and lesbian and gay families. In one study, sociologist Carla Pfeffer (2010) drew on qualitative narratives from 50 women whose partners were transgendered and transsexual men. Some of these relationships began with both partners identifying as lesbians; that is, the women had women partners. However, at some point, one woman transitioned to a transman. In the study, Pfeffer (2010) examined both division of household labor and emotion work (i.e., work that manages the emotions of other family members). She found that most of the women she interviewed identified as feminists and were aware of the unequal division of labor that exists in the majority of heterosexual relationships. Despite that understanding, most of them experienced an unequal division of labor in their own families. This division was based on gender, in which they (the women) did more housework than their transmen partners. Pfeffer found, in other words, that women and transmen had a similar unequal division of labor as heterosexual couples. In addition, women in these families do most of the emotion work, particularly in helping their partners' transition, which often involved working through their partners' depression, suicidal thoughts, administration of testosterone shots, and support through surgery. Thus, due to the amount of domestic and emotion work, women in these relationships sometimes gave up their own work and educational aspirations.

In contrast, Sally Hines (2006) studied 30 transgender women and men in Great Britain. She found that transgender women (men who transition to women) living in lesbian relationships created more egalitarian divisions of labor. The two existing studies suggest that the social gender with which a person identifies plays a large part in how couples divide their labor, giving credence to the notion that gender divisions of labor are socially constructed, not biologically mandated. However, although both the research by Pfeffer (2010) and Hines (2006) provide insight into how transgender families divide household labor, because of the diversities within transgender families, we need further research before we can draw any reliable conclusions.

Parenting Strategies

In addition to creating ways of dividing household labor and balancing work and family, LGBT parents create parenting strategies to help their children develop in healthy and productive ways. Many of the parenting issues that LGBT parents need to address are similar to those of heterosexual parents. However, two major issues—transracial families and external homophobia and heterosexism—are regular experiences of LGBT families because of transracial adoptions and discrimination against LGBT families. As discussed earlier, because many LGBT parents are White, and because many of the children they adopt are not, many LGBT families are transracial in nature. Regardless of sexual or gender identity, parents who adopt children with different racial-ethnic backgrounds from their own need to be prepared to help their children maintain their racial-ethnic identity and help them address, deflect, and combat racial discrimination (Ausbrooks & Russell, 2011). Ausbrooks and Russell (2011) posited that LGBT parents are specifically equipped to help their adopted children with these needs because LGBT parents have experienced and understand oppression. As discussed in Chapter 2, studies suggest that experience with one form of oppression creates "a greater awareness of other forms of oppression" (Boyer, 2007, p. 234). In addition, in their parenting strategies, LGBT parents often create open lines of communication to help discuss issues of gender and sexuality. These lines of communication may create opportunities to discuss other issues or problems such as racism and questions about identity that their children of color may be experiencing (Gianino, Goldberg, & Lewis, 2009). Ausbrooks and Russell (2011) also argued that LGBT families are resilient and rely on support communities that can help their children cope. While their support groups often consist of other LGBT parents, LGBT parents have the skills to seek out or create racial-ethnic support networks for their children as well.

Despite findings that LGBT parents may have some skills that can make them adept at helping their children of color adapt to a racist world, there is also evidence that many White LGBT people are racist themselves; in fact, racism in LGBT communities is well documented (Boykin, 1997). Furthermore, some White LGBT parents have commented that they do not think that race really matters or that they do not "see in Black and White"

(Moore & Brainer, 2013; Schacher et al., 2005, p. 45). Sociologists argue that "color blind" approaches that ignore racial discrimination actually exacerbate racial inequality, rather than make such discrimination disappear (Bonilla-Silva, 2009). Therefore, while LGBT parents may have the potential skills to address racial discrimination and racial identity formation, they must first acknowledge and address their own racist thoughts and practices, just as White heterosexual parents who adopt children of color must do (Moore & Brainer, 2013).

In addition to addressing transracial factors in families, as discussed throughout this chapter and in the previous two chapters, homophobic attitudes and heterosexist practices and policies that exist outside of LGBT families shape and filter into these families in a variety of ways. One way is that LGBT families, including the children in those families, face discrimination from people in larger communities. Therefore, similar to other ostracized groups in the United States (e.g., racial-ethnic minority families, immigrant families, and Muslim families), LGBT parents need to develop strategies for both protecting their children from discrimination and equipping their children with the emotional tools needed to deflect and combat discrimination.

In her work on lesbian mothers, Wright (2001) wrote that "children in lesbian families encounter an ongoing tension between their experience within their families, which feels 'normal' and safe and nurturing, and their experience outside their families, in which they often feel invisible or vilified" (p. 288). Although she was writing specifically about lesbian mothers, LGBT parents in general have to negotiate homophobia that exists outside their families. If parents do not openly confront homophobia in others, then they risk reinforcing for their children the notion that their family is shameful or something is wrong. And yet, in their daily lives and in the public arena (e.g., in schools, work, shopping malls, parks, etc.), parents have to pick and choose which homophobic remarks or heterosexual assumptions they want to confront (Goldberg, 2010).

Studies show that the homophobic and heterosexist attitudes, words, and actions of people around LGBT families have a negative impact on children growing up in those families (Bos & Gartrell, 2010). To minimize exposure to discriminatory comments and actions, parents with sufficient financial means may seek out progressive communities, schools, child-care programs, and extracurricular activities that are more accepting of their families (Byard, Kosciw, & Barkiewicz, 2013). Regardless of where they live, however, most parents are concerned about the homophobic comments, bullying, and other hurtful actions that people will inflict upon their children (Bos & Gartrell, 2010).

In order to prepare their children for homophobic encounters, help their children deal with being bullied because of their family structure, and teach their children to be accepting of others, LGBT parents employ a variety of strategies that differ depending on the age and situation of the child. For example, some parents create open communication with their children about diverse sexual and gender identities (Breshears, 2011). They talk about the different types of families that exist in the world and emphasize the importance of appreciating diversity. They may do role-playing to responses to possible homophobic comments that others might make (Goldberg, 2010). One successful strategy parents use to help their children cope with negative outside influences is to inundate their children with positive images of LGBT people. These images are available through the media, by identifying famous LGBT people, and by parents seeking out other LGBT people and heterosexual allies who can reinforce those positive images (Goldberg, 2010).

In addition to the above strategies, working-class parents and parents of color may need to teach their children to negotiate racial and class discrimination. For example, in her study of seven White, working-class lesbian parents in northeastern England, Nixon (2011) found that the mothers taught their children how to live on a tight budget, and stressed doing well in school, and being independent and autonomous. Similarly, Moore (2011) found that Black lesbian mothers teach their children by example to stand up and be proud of their families. To combat homophobia within Black communities, by being out and active as lesbian mothers, their families teach and increase "awareness among Black people of what Black homosexuality can mean" (p. 198). Moore found that "Black lesbians, interacting in Black communities invites a struggle to avoid portraying to others—and perceiving within themselves—that their sexuality is something for which they should be ashamed or sorry" (p. 199). Lesbian mothers in Moore's study interacted within their communities by simultaneously being respectful of others' cultural and religious beliefs without hiding their sexual identities or family structures to those others.

Parents may also need to work with teachers and school officials to combat homophobia in the schools (Byard et al., 2013). This often requires the parents to reveal their sexual identities or come out to those people, which may not be comfortable for the parents. Coming out exposes the parents to potential homophobic treatment, but it also helps them stand up for their children (Goldberg, 2010; Nixon, 2011). Furthermore, Nixon's study suggests that some working-class lesbian parents might have had particularly negative experiences in schools when they were growing up. Therefore, walking into a school and speaking up on behalf of their children can be intimidating. However, because these parents were often bullied and felt left out of school when growing up, they pushed past that intimidation to help their children cope with the difficulties in school (Nixon, 2011). In addition, some parents try to work with schools to incorporate into the school curriculum positive messages about and images of LGBT families. Although some of the efforts to shape curriculums have been successful, not all schools are receptive to such change (Byard et al., 2013; Goldberg, 2010; Wright, 2001).

Despite challenges to their families, or perhaps because of them, most LGBT parents feel that their children benefit from growing up in LGBT families. Studies show that parents think that their children learn to be more tolerant and accepting of others and to appreciate diversity in ways that children of heterosexual parents may not. Children of LGBT parents may also be more willing to discuss difficult topics with their parents because parents have already opened communication around issues of sexual and/or gender identities. And some studies suggest that because their families are based on a nongendered egalitarian division of labor, children benefit from seeing how functional and loving different families can be (Goldberg, 2010; Johnson & O'Connor, 2002; Lynch & Murray, 2000).

Separation and Divorce

Even with the best intentions and efforts to create supportive and egalitarian families, some LGBT families do not stay together. Unlike the abundance of research on divorce among heterosexual couples, there is little research on relationship dissolution among LGBT couples. The limited research is most likely because LGBT relationships are not often legally or socially recognized; therefore, some heterosexual people do not take the dissolution seriously. In addition, researchers have a hard time pinpointing the start or end dates of the relationship because there are few, if any, official markers (e.g., marriage and divorce).

Unlike recorded divorces among heterosexual couples, there are few records of how many LGBT parents separate unless they were legally married or had a civil union or domestic partnership. Without legal guidance or recognition, trying to end a relationship, particularly one that involves children, is often difficult. Therefore, "lesbian and gay parents are forced to creatively and independently manage the details of their separation and to agree upon the mutual roles and obligations of each partner to each other and to their children" (Goldberg, 2010, p. 114; see also Mallon, 2004). Legal and biological connections can create an unequal power dynamic between parents where the biological or legal parent has the upper hand regarding custody. Therefore, as discussed earlier, separation can be particularly scary for the nonbiological or nonlegal parent who is more likely to lose child custody. The power dynamic exists among separating lesbians even though research suggests that lesbians tend to minimize differences between biological or legal and social mothers while their relationships are intact (Goldberg, 2010). Therefore, creating legal connections between adults and their children prior to a separation is critical. For example, one study found that lesbian mothers who shared legal joint custody prior to separating were much more likely to share custody of the children once they separated. Furthermore, upon separation, "The percentage of adolescents who reported closeness to both mothers was significantly higher in families with coparent adoption" (Gartrell, Bos, Peyser, Deck, & Rodas, 2011, p. 572).

Family relationships among LGBT couples dissolve for a variety of reasons, many of which are similar to those of heterosexual couples. For example, similar to heterosexual couples, LGBT couples separate because they grow apart, have infrequent sexual intimacy, are incompatible, are unfaithful, and have different parenting styles (Gartrell et al., 2011; Mallon, 2004). In addition, as with heterosexual couples, having a child may delay some lesbian couple's decision to separate (Gartrell et al., 2011). However, for some gay fathers, children hastened the demise of their relationship because once they brought children into the family, preexisting relationship problems resurfaced.

Research also suggests that external stressors specific to being LGBT—in particular, coming out and transitioning, and a lack of support—play a factor in why LGBT couples separate.

For example, as discussed above, for people who have children within heterosexual relationships and then later come out as LGBT, the transition from one identity to another can disrupt relationships enough to cause a separation. One study suggests that relationships dissolve during the transition period in about 45% of transgender relationships (Levi, 2012). When these couples separate, transgender partners often assume (correctly or not) that the break up was due to their transition. And transitioning and coming out places LGBT parents at great risk of losing not only their spouses but also their children because of bias in the courts (Crozier, 2012; Levi, 2012).

In addition, a lack of support might lead to a higher number of separations among LGBT couples than among heterosexual couples. For example, in a long-term study of lesbian mothers, 80% of 40 couples studied had separated before they could have had civil unions in Vermont in 2000. The study also found that lesbian mothers separated at slightly higher rates than heterosexual couples (Gartrell et al., 2011). Gartrell and her colleagues (2011) speculated that the higher number may be due in part to the external stressors that LGBT families experience, as well as the lack of economic, legal, and social support for LGBT families in general. Thus, while the evidence suggests that LGBT parents create more egalitarian, open, and nurturing homes for their children than do heterosexual couples, the research also suggests that the lack of support for LGBT families due to heterosexist practices and policies and to homophobic attitudes may compel such families to separate.

What We Know About LGBT Grandparents

Although the focus of this chapter is on LGBT parents, approximately 50% of parents nationwide become grandparents. Conservative estimates suggest that there are between one and two million LGBT grandparents in the United States (Orel & Fruhauf, 2006). Given the growing number of LGBT parents, we can certainly expect this number to grow as well. Very few studies have examined the experiences of LGBT grandparents, and those that do focus primarily on lesbian and bisexual women (Orel, 2005; Orel & Fruhauf, 2006; Whalen, Bigner, & Barber, 2000) and on gay men (Fruhauf, Orel, & Jenkins, 2009).

The studies to date suggest three major findings. First, how lesbian and bisexual women define and experience being a grandmother is similar in many ways to heterosexual grandmothers (Orel, 2005; Whalen et al., 2000). For example, a study of lesbian and bisexual grandmothers saw themselves as an important source of help and support for their adult children and grandchildren (Orel, 2005). Second, the relationship that LGBT grandparents have with their adult children greatly shapes their relationships with their grandchildren (Fruhauf et al., 2009; Orel, 2005; Orel & Fruhauf, 2006). Regardless of sexual or gender identity, adult children decide where and when their own children will see their grandparents. Because heterosexism and homophobia sometimes negatively affect the relationship between LGBT parents and their children, adult children do not always allow their LGBT parents to visit with their children. However, many adult children facilitate the grandparent-grandchild relationship by helping their parents answer grandchildren's question about sexuality in positive and supportive ways (Fruhauf et al., 2009; Orel & Fruhauf, 2006). Third, GLB grandparents often encourage their grandchildren to respect gender flexibility, moving their grandchildren away from strict gender roles. And once they disclose their sexual identities to their grandchildren, GLB grandparents can provide "their grandchildren opportunities to explore issues related to homophobia and heterosexism" (Orel & Fruhauf, 2006, p. 66).

Research to date has not adequately explored LGBT grandparents. As the number of LGBT parents become grandparents, the opportunity to learn more about the lives of this growing elderly population will expand.

What We Learn From LGBT Parents

As this chapter suggests, the number of issues facing LGBT families in creating, maintaining, and dissolving their families are vast and complicated. Furthermore, while LGBT parents experience similar parenting challenges and joys, many of those challenges vary by gender and sexual identities, as well as by race and class. Clearly, the majority of research conducted on LGBT parents has focused on not only lesbian and gay parents but also specifically on middle-class, White lesbian and gay parents who have intentionally created their families after they came out. In contrast, most of the research on transgender families focuses on relationships that began prior to transitioning, rather than examining transgender relationships that people create once they have already transitioned. And virtually no research exists on bisexual parents. Much research helps us understand the interpersonal relationships within LGBT families, as well as how external pressures shape LGBT families. However, much more research is needed in order to better understand the diversities in lesbian and gay families along lines of class, race, nationality, and age, and to understand the parental relationships within bisexual and transgender families.

Despite the need for further research, what the existing research tells us is that we have much to learn from LGBT parents and grandparents. Because many LGBT parents make intentional parenting decisions, few are birthing children that they did not plan on having or did not want. In addition, LGBT parents often adopt and foster children and are well equipped to deal with racial and cultural differences between themselves and their children; and by adopting and fostering children, LGBT parents save the nation millions of dollars. Thus, when LGBT parents make intentional parenting decisions, they do so because they want and are prepared to be parents. As the research tells us, not all LGBT adults become parents by birthing or adopting their own children. When LGBT adults become stepparents, they are more patient, flexible, and less controlling than are heterosexual stepparents, thus creating healthier environments within their families. And when they become grandparents, they work to help their grandchildren make sense of issues of gender and sexuality that often plague children's minds.

We also learn that LGBT parents hold as an ideal, work toward, and often create a more equal division of labor in their families than their heterosexual counterparts. Rather than having the division of labor dictated by historical patriarchal inequalities, many LGBT couples divide their household labor on what each person is better suited and prefers to do. These same parents also often teach their children to be more accepting of people from diverse backgrounds. And while LGBT couples separate at similar rates as heterosexual couples, part of the reason they do so is due to the lack of support from a heterosexist world, not on their lack of desire to stay in committed relationships. So what we learn from LGBT parents is how to create families that can be equal, accepting, and nurturing.

GLOBAL BOX

by Morganne Firmstone

As stated at the beginning of this chapter, the data are clear—LGBT couples are having children and creating families. Adoption, co-parenting arrangements (such as stepparenting), donor insemination, and surrogacy are among the most popular ways for LGBT couples to have children. However, based on geographic location, access to these parent pathways is not the same for each couple. For instance, Australia allows same-sex couples to file a joint adoption petition in only three states: New South Wales, Australian Capital Territory (ACT), and Western Australia (Adoption.org, n.d.). Other Australian states allow single-parent adoption, while several opt for stepparent adoption. According to Solodnikov and Chkanikova (2010), adoption of children by same-sex couples has been authorized by law in places such as Andorra, Belgium, the Netherlands, Sweden, and South Africa, as well as several provinces and states of Canada and the United States.

There is no question that couples are finding ways to have children, but are states and public and private institutions recognizing them as legal or legitimate parents? Law and policy regarding the creation of families are shaped by many factors—cultural practices, historical views, politics, religious beliefs, and even cultural philosophies about what it means to be a "good parent." Who should be able to have children? Who can provide for a child? What kind of environment is suitable to raise a child? The answer to these questions, however, does not contain a one-size-fits-all solution, which is why we see such variance in the international guidelines regarding parenting.

Millbank (2003) made note that Australian law does not necessarily protect the rights of nonbiological mothers. For example,

> If a co-mother dies, her child is not eligible to automatically inherit her estate, superannuation [Australian pension], or worker's compensation. If a biological mother dies, the co-mother has no automatic right to maintain residence of the child and continue to parent him/her. (p. 572)

Such policies have very real, tangible effects on LGBT couples and their ability to become and remain parents in a way that ensures security and stability for their children and themselves.

(Continued)

(Continued)

Interestingly, vulnerability under the law is a major factor in lesbian couples' decisions about how they will have children. Research conducted by Donovan and Wilson (2008) offers evidence of such decisions through in-depth interviews with lesbian couples from the United Kingdom. Similar to the sentiments of lesbians in the United States, the researchers found that respondents who opted for donor insemination oftentimes emphasized the threat to their family that a *known* donor could pose. The nonbiological parent's status is often in jeopardy given the lack of protection for lesbian co-mothers under the law, much like the case of Australia. Donovan and Wilson (2008) found that when deciding about becoming parents, the couples in the study tended to reject known donors so as to "give clarity and protection to their family vision" and to allow them to "realize that theirs is a vision of joint parenting and family without the contingencies of donor involvement" (p. 656).

Restricted access to parenthood could also mean health risks for some groups of LGBT people. Glover, McKree, and Dyall (2009) used in-depth interviews and focus groups to analyze a LGBT subpopulation, also known as the Takatapui, of the indigenous Maori people of New Zealand. The research analyzed the Takatapui and their views on the importance of fertility, responses to infertility, and assisted human reproduction technologies. This study found that the Takatapui faced added challenges when considering assisted human reproduction technologies: "A [Takatapui] preference for do-it-yourself arrangements and methods could be denying Takatapui the same level of medical and legal safety available to users of fertility services" (p. 309). These "do-it-yourself arrangements" include "finding their own donors and negotiating how conception will be achieved" (p. 306). In most cases, this means that Takatapui couples do not consult any type of fertility experts or services. Without adequate donor screenings that identify genetic abnormalities, sexually transmitted diseases, and HIV, potential Takatapui parents are at risk for serious health consequences (Daniels & Burn, 1997, as cited in Glover et al., 2009, p. 307). The authors found that homophobia might play the most critical role in LGBT Maori opting for the do-it-yourself arrangements or even deciding not to have children at all. The study revealed that fertility service practitioners "may object and refuse to provide assisted human reproduction technologies to lesbians, gay men, and transgender individuals" (p. 305). Despite the passing of the New Zealand Human Rights Commission Act of 1977, anecdotal evidence suggests that health-care providers in New Zealand are still refusing service to lesbians because of their sexuality.

Some LGBT couples turn to their own communities for advice and support when deciding about children. For instance, Solodnikov and Chkanikova (2010) used qualitative and quantitative analyses of Internet blogs and communities devoted to the upbringing of children by same-sex Russian couples and concluded that there is very real, concrete presence of LGBT couples who are motivated to have children. However, the couples in this online community tended to shy away from having to deal with "costly, legally formalized methods of artificial insemination" (p. 58). Instead, they resorted to turning to LGBT communities for "strategies of cooperation" in which "lesbians get pregnant with gays and agree in advance what role the father is going to play in the future upbringing of the child" (p. 58).

Complex kin arrangements are not unheard of when LGBT couples are deciding about how they will have children. Bos (2010) conducted a survey of planned gay fathers (gay men who become fathers after coming out) and their relationship with their children, their experiences of parental stress, and their children's well-being. A survey of 37 Dutch gay fathers revealed that "all of the participants were involved in kinship arrangements with lesbian couples, were the biological fathers of their children (they had donated sperm to lesbian couples), and were sharing the child-rearing responsibilities with the children's mothers" (p. 366). Bos concluded that we can attribute parenting arrangements such as this to the fact that in the Netherlands, gay men who want to become parents face limited options because Dutch law often prohibits surrogacy and adoption by same-sex couples. Furthermore, joint same-sex international adoption in the Netherlands is possible only for heterosexual married couples or single individuals. Dutch law also prohibits paid surrogacy, which also adds to the appeal of entering into kinship arrangements (Bos, 2010).

Interestingly enough, despite advances made in marriage equality throughout the globe, as discussed in Chapter 2's Global Box, policy has not strongly supported the issue of parenting. Many LGBT couples face discrimination, diminished access, and even exclusion from the world of becoming parents.

ADDITIONAL RESOURCES

Compiled by Morganne Firmstone

Websites

- ACLU American Civil Liberties Union—LGBT Parenting
  - http://www.aclu.org/lgbt-rights/lgbt-parenting
- COLAGE
  - http://colage.org
- Family Equality Council
  - http://www.familyequality.org
- Family Pride Coalition
  - http://www.familypride.org

- LGBTQ Parenting Network
  - http://www.lgbtqparentingconnection.ca/home.cfm
- Our Family Coalition
  - http://www.ourfamily.org

Book

- *Families Like Mine: Children of Gay Parents Tell It Like It Is (by Abigail Garner)*
  - Drawing on a decade of community organizing and interviews with more than 50 grown sons and daughters of LGBT parents, Garner addresses such topics as coming out to children, facing homophobia at school, co-parenting with ex-partners, the impact of AIDS, and the children's own sexuality.

Films

- *All Aboard! Rosie's Family Cruise (2006 Documentary)*
  - Follows Rosie O'Donnell and her family along with several other families on the first-ever cruise specified for gay parents and their families, which was arranged and planned by Rosie O'Donnell and her life partner Kelli O'Donnell.
- *Fatherhood Dreams (directed & produced by Julia Ivanova; 2007 Documentary)*
  - A documentary that gives people a glimpse into the day-to-day lives of gay dads Scott, Steve, Randy, and Drew, who are fathers through adoption, co-parenting, and surrogacy.
- *No Dumb Questions (2001 Documentary)*
  - A documentary about three sisters, aged 6, 9, and 11, struggling to understand why and how their Uncle Bill is becoming a woman.

4

LGBT Youth

I haven't come out to my daddy yet, and I don't think I want to do that, because I love my life and I want to live it. That would put me six feet under.

—18-year-old African-American homeless
gay male from Detroit, Michigan (Ray, 2006)

My auntie caught me and my ex-girlfriend . . . we were just in bed together, and she told the whole church. She told the whole church!

—19-year-old homeless lesbian
from Ann Arbor, Michigan (Ray, 2006)

The main difference between now and before is that I don't have to suffer through sexuality issues by myself. The more people I come out to, the more people I have to cheer me up when I have a "bad sexuality day." . . . Coming out is an ongoing trial, and as more people find out, I'm thankful to my sorority for continuing to accept me; the process has been almost seamless. I'm thankful that the atmosphere of my chapter is one in which I feel safe to be myself and in which I know instinctively that the love of my sisters is unconditional.

—"Mary Baker," a female student
talking about coming out as bisexual
to her college sorority (Baker, 2001)

A s the above quotes suggest, the experiences of LGBT youth vary by how much support they receive from their families and peers, as well as from teachers, religious leaders, and other significant people in their lives. While scholars have been studying LGBT adults since the 1940s and 1950s, the study of LGBT youth did not start in earnest until the late 1990s. Over the past decade or so, research on LGBT youth has grown significantly. This burgeoning body of research originally focused on gay and bisexual boys in the United States, but it has since expanded to studies on girls, as well as youth from diverse racial-ethnic backgrounds around the world (Saewyc, 2011). Over the years, the quality and types of research—both qualitative and quantitative—has greatly improved, most recently incorporating theoretical lenses through which researchers can better analyze and explain their research findings (Friedman et al., 2011; Saewyc, 2011).

Within the past two decades, the research on adolescents has grappled with how to define and measure sexual orientation, or the "erotic inclination toward people of one or more genders, most often described as sexual or erotic attractions" (Saewyc, 2011, p. 257). In measuring and defining sexual orientation, some research focuses specifically on what arouses youth, others on their behaviors, and others on self-labels. Recommendations from experts in the field encourage the use of multiple measurements; however, most studies still solely rely on the use of attraction, behavior, or identity—despite the fact that attraction, behavior, and identity do not always agree with one another (Saewyc, 2011). For example, youth might hold sexual desires that they act on; they might behave in ways that go against their sexual desires; and they might identify in ways that do not reflect their desires or behaviors.

While such definitional and measurement issues are concerns for those studying both adults and youth, studying youth becomes more complicated because youth involves a fast-changing time period through puberty and adolescence that research on adults avoids. As professor of nursing Elizabeth Saewyc (2011) commented, adolescence occurs anywhere between ages 7 and 13, involves the changing of bodies and sexual organs, and the development of sexual feelings, but not necessarily with the experiences of romantic relationships. Therefore, studying LGBT youth is particularly challenging because trying to measure "any developmental aspect across the intense physical, cognitive, and behavioral transformations of adolescence is fraught with such difficulties and limitations" (Saewyc, 2011, p. 258).

Despite difficulties in measurement, the past 10 to 15 years have yielded important studies on LGBT youth. Such studies have been particularly helpful in estimating the number of youth who identify as LGBT, specifically through school surveys. One study estimates that approximately 2% to 4% of youth in the United States and Canada identify as GBL (transgender children were not included in this study) (Homma, Chen, Poon, & Saewyc, 2012). Studies also suggest that boys tend to identify more as bisexual than do girls, and African American and Hispanic youth tend to identify more as bisexual than do White youth (Rodriguez Rust, 2000b). Regarding transgender children, no study to date has produced very reliable numbers, although estimates suggest that approximately 1 in 500 children identify as transgender (Skougard, 2011).

Regardless of how many LGBT or questioning children and youth there are, studies are clear that without strong family support, and support from other social institutions, such as schools, health care, and legal services, LGBT youth suffer greatly as they come to terms with their sexual and gender identities. Because LGBT children often have different identities than their parents and siblings, their parents may not be emotionally equipped to teach them about how to positively negotiate conflicting feelings. Thus, heterosexual parents may not always protect their LGBT children from outside discrimination and psychological or physical harm, and they may actually be the cause of such discrimination and harm. Therefore, in addition to living through the trying times that plague many adolescents regardless of gender and sexual identity, LGBT youth often live double lives and juggle multiple identities and challenges (Connolly, 2006; Ragg, Patrick, & Ziefert, 2006).

Given the trajectory of the gay liberation movement, the visibility of LGBT people in general, and particularly the visibility of LGBT families over the past 50 years, the fact that LGBT youth are now more visible is not surprising. Indeed, LGBT youth often create their own spaces and define their own identities on their own terms. A full spread article in *The New York Times* labeled the growing visibility of "out" youth as "Generation LGBTQIA" (lesbian, gay, bisexual, transgender, queer/questioning, intersex, ally/asexual; Schulman, 2013). Despite—or perhaps because of—the growing number of visible and out LGBT youth, dominant culture in the United States is both acclimating to and fearing this new youth culture. The result is that similar to LGBT adults, LGBT youth may simultaneously occupy both safe and harmful spaces in which to develop their identities.

Research points to several key areas that shape the experiences of LGBT youth. In particular, studies focus on how youth develop and respond to their own sexual and gender identities, how parents react to their LGBT children, how people in related social institutions (e.g., schools, medicine, legal, and social agencies) respond to LGBT children and youth, and how

LGBT youth respond to attitudes of those around them. This chapter will focus on these areas, as well as discuss how the fear and loathing of LGBT youth creates much harm, and what we can learn from our LGBT youth.

Youth Coming to Terms With LGBT Identities

Because of heterosexism and homophobia conveyed daily through parents, schools, the media, and religious organizations, among others, most youth are well aware that many people disapprove of and feel threatened by people of diverse sexual and gender identities (Ragg et al., 2006). In order to negotiate their gender and sexual identities, LGBT youth make daily decisions about those with whom they want to share their feelings. As a result of homophobia and heterosexism, as well as hegemonic masculinity and emphasized femininity, many LGBT youth "experience confusion, feel misunderstood, internalize hostility, and worry about their future" (Ragg et al., 2006, p. 244; see also Jennings, 2003; Mallon & DeCrescenzo, 2006; Russell, 2011; Saewyc, 2011).

In describing the processes that LGBT youth go through to develop and grapple with their gender and sexual identities, scholars and practitioners have developed several models of the stages associated with coming out (see, for example, Jennings, 2003). Although those models can be useful, I prefer to describe some of the major issues that LGBT youth go through as they develop their identities. Worth noting is that coming out processes differ by identity. For example, one main difference between LGB and transgender youth is that although many LGB children and youth do not conform to dominant gender identities, they still see themselves as the gender that medical professionals and their parents assigned to them at birth. However, some transgender children see themselves as being born in the wrong bodies (Mallon & DeCrescenzo, 2006; Skougard, 2011). Therefore, as transgender children begin to go through puberty, they face serious challenges that are difficult to mask or hide without the help of parents and medical professionals. In the discussion below, I highlight major issues that transgender youth, as well as LGB youth face in exploring and developing their sexual and gender identities.

In coming out, LGBT youth often realize that they are different from their peers. Perhaps because of the visibility of LGBT people in general, LGBT youth report coming out approximately 4 to 5 years earlier today than they did in the 1960s (Cloud, 2005). Some scholars argue that children do not recognize sexuality until later in life (Mallon & DeCrescenzo, 2006; Skougard, 2011). However, noticing gender differences can begin as young as 3 or 4 years old, although most are between 8 and 10 years old before gender issues become prominent (Skougard, 2011). Gender differences might include girls and boys having an interest in activities stereotypically reserved for the opposite sex (e.g., girls liking sports rather than dolls; boys liking dolls rather than sports).

In addition to the realization that they are different from their peers, LGBT youth often question their own identities, wondering if they are in fact LGBT. During their periods of questioning, youth might separate themselves from their families and heterosexual friends, or they might "obsessively date the opposite sex—to prove they're straight" (Jennings, 2003, p. 123). What complicates such periods of questioning for transgender children is that they come from diverse sexual identities (Mallon & DeCrescenzo, 2006). They may not be lesbian, gay, or bisexual. The confusion for them about whether or not they are LGB or transgender makes this time particularly difficult for transgender youth.

Another part of the coming out process occurs when youth start accepting their own identities and begin revealing those identities to select family members and close friends. For LGB adolescents, the coming out process is often stressful. The amount of internalized homophobia and external support a youth has will often shape the coming out process (Haas et al., 2011; Rosario, Schrimshaw, & Hunter, 2006). The process can also be particularly difficult for transgendered youth because they often have a specific need "to match one's exterior with one's interior, to achieve harmony of spirit and shape, of body and soul" (Mallon & DeCrescenzo, 2006, pp. 224–225). To create such harmony of body and soul, as transgender youth begin to approach puberty, they may start using hormone blockers or hormone enhancers to prevent certain bodily changes (e.g., developing breasts) and encourage others (e.g., growing facial hair) (Mallon & DeCrescenzo, 2006; Minter & Wald, 2012a; Skougard, 2011).

Provided youth are able to come out with support from those around them, many LGBT youth not only accept but also actually start feeling good about their gender and sexual identities. Many LGBT youth participate in gay-straight alliances in their schools, get involved with LGBT pride organizations, such as GLSEN, or participate in other LGBT advocacy and support programs. As I discuss below, however, not all LGBT youth reach a point in their coming out processes where they feel good about themselves. In addition, for transgender youth, a sense of pride often only comes with a sense of "realness" in which their outward gender identity matches their internal sense of self. As discussed below, such a sense of "realness" often requires medical intervention with parental consent and support.

For many youth, being LGBT becomes a significant part of their master identity. However, at some point, many LGBT youth not only integrate their gender and sexual identities into their personalities but also "move beyond thinking of themselves as an LGBT person to a person who is LGBT as well as funny, smart, talented, etc." (Jennings, 2003, p. 124). In other words, being LGBT becomes part of who they are, but it does not define them or dominate their overall identities.

As mentioned above, the process of recognizing and coming to terms with one's gender and sexual identity often lead youth to eventually move into a positive emotional space. However, studies show that the coming out process can be difficult for many LGBT youth. According to a meta-analysis of school-based studies between 1980 and 2009, LGBT youth "were on average 3.8, 1.2, 1.7, and 2.4 times more likely to experience sexual abuse, parental physical abuse, or assault at school or to miss school through fear, respectively" than non-LGBT students (Friedman et al., 2011, p. 1481). The analysis also found that boys experienced more sexual abuse than girls, girls were assaulted more at school than boys, and bisexual youth experienced more parental physical abuse and missed more school through fear than did lesbian and gay youth (Friedman et al., 2011). These findings are consistent throughout the research. In fact, LGBT youth show higher rates of "emotional distress, depression, self-harm, suicidal ideation, and suicide attempts than do their heterosexual peers," and bisexual boys appear to be at higher risk for suicide than gay boys (Saewyc, 2011, p. 263). In writing this chapter, I cannot overemphasize the seriousness of such distress. One study of 246 LGBT youths between the ages of 16 and 20 years showed that gender and sexual victimization place youth at 2.5 times the risk of inflicting self-harm (Liu & Mustanski, 2012).

In addition, LGBT youth are almost 3 times more likely to report substance abuse, including an earlier use of alcohol, than their heterosexual peers (Coker, Austin, & Schuster, 2010; Marshal et al., 2008; Saewyc, 2011), with bisexual girls showing particularly high rates of substance abuse (D'Amico & Julien, 2012). These high rates place LGBT youth at higher risks of binge drinking in later years (Saewyc, 2011). And while LGBT youth are less likely to have sex while drinking or drunk (Saewyc, 2011), higher rates of physical abuse, sexual abuse, and stress lead LGBT youth to engage in risky sexual behavior overall. This risky behavior places them at higher risk of contracting HIV and other sexually transmitted diseases (Friedman et al., 2011; Grossman & D'Augelli, 2006; Grossman, Anthony, Nickolas, & D' Augelli, 2006; Mallon & DeCrescenzo, 2006; Rosario et al., 2006). These findings are consistent among a variety of populations. For example, a study conducted on Asian Canadian LGB youth found that LGB adolescents were more likely than heterosexual adolescents "to use alcohol, marijuana, or other illicit drugs. Particularly, sexual minority girls were at increased risk for substance use" (Homma et al., 2012, p. 32).

A major cause of the increased emotional distress and risky sexual and drug-related behavior occurs because as LGBT youth try to come to terms with their gender and sexual identities, they "have fewer supportive resources to draw upon, especially bisexual adolescents; they have lower family connectedness or support as well as lower connectedness to school, lower connectedness to other adults, and lower peer support" (Saewyc, 2011, p. 266). A study conducted on North American youth found that bisexual youth may have fewer protective resources through their families and peers, which possibly leads them to engage in risky sexual and drug/alcohol-related behavior (Saewyc et al., 2009). One response of unsupported or abused LGBT youth is to run away from home. According to the U.S. Department of Health and Human Services, an estimated number of 575,000 to 1.6 million youth are homeless or runaway each year (Robertson & Toro, 1998). The National Gay and Lesbian Task Force estimates the number of homeless youth who identify as LGBT range between 20% and 40% of all homeless youth, thus, placing LGBT youth at higher rates of homelessness than the general youth population (Ray, 2006). Those who leave home face serious discrimination in terms of finding work. The result is that many engage in sex work to survive. And homeless transgender youth may start injecting hormones on the street and without medical supervision, which can be lethal (Mallon & DeCrescenzo, 2006).

What the research tells us, therefore, is that supportive social institutions and the relationship that children have with their parents and their parents' responses to their children's gender and sexual identities are critical in helping children develop healthy senses of self. The next section discusses parental responses to their LGBT children and the importance of parental support in the emotional and physical outcomes of LGBT youth.

Parental Responses to, Reactions by, and Consequences for LGBT Children

Parents respond differently to their children coming out depending on their own feelings about gender and sexuality. Parents who are heterosexist, follow strict gender rules, or follow religious doctrines may have difficulties with their children coming out as LGBT (Chung, Oswald, & Wiley, 2006; Jennings, 2003). Some parents are devastated; others are relieved to have their suspicions confirmed or the reasons for their children's anxiety made known (Jennings, 2003). Many parents go through a grieving process because they mourn the "loss" of their heterosexual or particularly gendered child, "as well as their own loss–of the hopes and dreams they had for a traditional life for their child" (Jennings, 2003, p. 125). Parents often blame themselves for something they did wrong as parents that caused their child to be LGBT; and often parents take months, if not years, to arrive at an emotional point where they accept their child and care less about what other people think. The more LGBT youth move away from dominant gender displays, the more their families and others tend to reject them (Grossman & D'Augelli, 2006).

Similar to the processes that LGBT youth go through in coming out, so parents of LGBT children also go through processes of understanding. Because some parents internalize and are influenced by homophobic and heterosexist images and messages about LGBT people spread throughout our social institutions (e.g., family, work, politics, medicine, law, religion, media, sport), they may have negative responses to their children's coming out as LGBT. Therefore, the processes parents go through may involve denying that their child is LGBT, or feeling angry, fearful, embarrassed, or disappointed. Some religious parents may bargain with God, asking some higher power to change their children back. Some parents become depressed, particularly around concerns that they (the parents) will never have grandchildren. However, there are many parents who readily accept their children's identities and show pride in their children's decisions to come out. Some parents also engage in activist and advocacy activities and organizations to fight for their children's rights. These parents often see their children as normal kids who happen to identify as LGBT (Jennings, 2003; Saewyc, 2011).

From a sociological perspective, there is nothing inherently wrong with being LGBT. However, because our society attributes a negative meaning to LGBT identities and privileges heterosexuality and specific gendered behaviors, those who are LGBT pay a high price. As discussed in Chapter 1, many people assume that being LGBT is bad for society. However, as a sociologist, I take the position that what is bad for individuals and society is how people perceive LGBT people, and particularly LGBT youth, a point I will discuss at the end of this chapter.

Research on parents' reactions to their LGBT children clearly indicates that negative reactions lead to negative outcomes for the children, communities, and parent-child relationships. Similarly, positive parental responses lead to better support systems and fewer problems for LGBT youth (Coker et al., 2010; D'Amico & Julien, 2012; D'Augelli, Grossman, Starks, & Sinclair, 2010; Friedman et al., 2011; Grossman et al., 2006; Jennings, 2003; Mallon & DeCrescenzo, 2006; Ragg et al., 2006; Rosario, Schrimshaw, & Hunter, 2011; Ryan, Huebner, Diaz, & Sanchez, 2009; Saewyc et al., 2009). As the quotes by gay and lesbian youth at the beginning of the chapter suggest, families play a pivotal role in the physical, emotional, and mental well-being of their LGBT children (Ryan et al., 2009). Although times are changing and becoming easier for LGBT children, the evidence is clear that LGBT children still struggle through adolescence, even though they often come through adolescence as healthy as their heterosexual peers (Saewyc, 2011).

In the not-so-distant past, some parents sent their children who showed diverging gender identities to psychiatric facilities (see, for example, Scholinski & Adams, 1998). Parents' responses now more commonly are to reach out to support groups, medical professionals, and legal services for advice on how to help their children successfully negotiate their identities, and in the case of transgender youth, transition and live as transgender people (Minter & Wald, 2012a). The best predictor of how parents will respond to their children's identity development is the quality of the parent-child relationship prior to disclosure of that identity (i.e., prior to coming out) (D'Amico & Julien, 2012). When children fear parental rejection, they tend to fear coming out to their parents (D'Augelli et al., 2010). This fear may be the reason why parents are not often the first people LGBT children come out to when they first start disclosing their identities (D'Augelli et al., 2010). In addition, the earlier children recognize their own identities, the earlier they tend to come out to their parents. Youth who disclose their identities to their parents report higher levels of acceptance from their mothers and fathers (D'Amico & Julien, 2012).

In general, parents tend to accept diverging identities from their daughters more than their sons (D'Amico & Julien, 2012). However, some cultures dictate that girls follow strict gender rules as well, which means being heterosexual. For example, research suggests that Korean American girls would shame their families if they came out as lesbians. Shaming their parents means the possibility that their parents would be censored or exiled from their Korean American communities (Chung et al., 2006). In general, however, dominant definitions of masculinity penalize boys who stray from acceptable gender roles (Pascoe, 2012). Because boys tend to recognize their gender and sexual differences before girls (D'Augelli, 2002), and because boys in general are more ostracized for gender-bending than girls, boys may suffer longer than girls if they chose not to come out or if they have unsupportive parents.

The timing of when and how children come out to their parents affects how parents react. Because of a great fear of rejection, children often keep their LGBT feelings to themselves until the point where living a lie becomes unbearable for them. The result is that some children may come out to their parents without the parents realizing their children had any feelings about being LGBT. The surprise to parents can trigger feelings of "shock, denial, anger, grief, misplaced guilt, and shame" as well as real concerns about the safety, health, employment, and intimate relationships of their children, as well as surgery concerns if their children are transgendered (Mallon & DeCrescenzo, 2006, p. 224). Parents therefore must go through a quick adjustment period that requires not only understanding what is happening to their children but also how to handle their own emotions and their children's needs.

Studies suggest that parents' reactions to their children coming out is affected both by how suddenly children share their news and the age at and openness with which they do so. For example, in a 2-year study of 196 LGB youths, D'Augelli et al. (2010) examined the responses of parents who were either aware of their children's sexual identity prior to the start of the study, who learned about their children's identities during the time of the study, and who never came to learn about their children's identities. The youth came from a variety of social classes and racial-ethnic backgrounds, with less than 25% being White. D'Augelli and his colleagues found that children who disclosed their identities to their parents at younger ages tended to have "more gender atypical behavior in childhood and less internalized homophobia than youths whose parents were not aware" (p. 180). Interestingly, these children also reported greater verbal persecution by their parents, even though the children reported greater family support and fewer worries about future abuse and rejection. D'Augelli et al. (2010) suggested that parents may be frustrated by their children's "abnormalities" when parents do not understand them. However, once parents are aware of their children's feelings, they become more sympathetic and supportive.

Some LGB children who came out to their parents found their fathers less accepting than their mothers. Overall, youth who came out to their parents found that they experienced a significant decrease in victimization by their parents after they came out. The decrease in victimization was due to parents' increased compassion regarding their children's differences once their children shared the reason for those differences. On the other hand, closeted youth (i.e., youth who did not come out) "reported the least sexual orientation victimization" (D'Augelli et al., 2010, p. 194) because they kept their diverging sexual identities a secret from their parents. Closeted youth also experienced better relationships with their fathers overall, and in some instances better relationships with their mothers, than those who came out. Despite their better relationships, however, closeted youth had the highest fear of parental rejection if they were to come out.

Although closeted youth reported less victimization by their parents than out youth, they also showed higher levels of internalized homophobia and were less involved in LGB social activities outside the home, thus, providing them with fewer positive LGB role models. Studies show that the more integrated into a variety of activities LGB youth are, the higher their self-esteem, the lower their levels of depression, and the fewer conduct issues they have (Haas et al., 2011; Saewyc et al., 2009). As D'Augelli et al. (2010) concluded, "If parents do not reject the youth or are unduly punitive, they are likely to begin a process of integrating the youth's sexual orientation into the family" (p. 195).

While the study by D'Augelli et al. (2010) looked only at LGB youth, studies specifically on transgender youth find that once transgender youth come out to their parents, they are quick to want to transition. Therefore, coming out as transgender often leads parents to work with medical professionals to determine how best to help or prevent their children from transitioning (Mallon & DeCrescenzo, 2006). At a similar time, transgender youth will ask their parents and others to call them by a different name and use pronouns consistent with their desired gender, highlighting how the transitioning process is both medical and social in nature.

For parents who are unaccepting of their transgender children, the children suffer greatly. For example, in a study of 31 male-to-female transgender youth, over two thirds said "they were verbally harassed by their parents, and approximately one-half reported being harassed by their brothers or sisters. Consequently, for many of the MtF [male-to-female] transgender youth in this study, their families of origin were not always safe havens" (Grossman et al., 2006, p. 85). In another study of 24 participants in which 95% were transgender youths of color, one participant stated, "When my mother, who is a PhD, found out what I was (i.e., transgender), she used to hurt me with things. She hit me on the head with an iron once, and I had five staples. Finally, she disowned me" (Grossman & D'Augelli, 2006, p. 118). Because of racism and transphobia within LGB communities, the youth of color in this study who were kicked out of their homes had few places to go. In addition, due to their limited financial means and legitimate ways of earning money, many transgender youth entered into illicit activities, such as sex work, thus increasing their chances of contracting STDs (Grossman & D'Augelli, 2006).

The findings discussed above concerning transgender children are consistent with studies on LGB youth as well. For example, a survey of 224 White and Latino LGB young adults, aged 21 to 25, found that those who experienced family rejection during adolescence

were 8.4 times more likely to report having attempted suicide, 5.9 times more likely to report high levels of depression, 3.4 times more likely to use illegal drugs, and 3.4 times more likely to report having engaged in unprotected sexual intercourse compared with peers from families that reported no or low levels of family rejection. (Ryan et al., 2009, p. 346)

The study also showed that Latino LGB boys experienced the highest rate of negative reactions from their families based on their sexual identities during adolescence. These findings as well as findings from Grossman and D'Augelli (2006) suggest that LGBT youth of color are at higher risk for family rejection than are their White counterparts, have fewer options if kicked out of their homes, and have higher risks of depression, suicidal thoughts and attempts, illicit substance use, and risky sexual behavior.

What the research shows, therefore, is that when parents support their children, their children learn to positively integrate their gender and sexual identities into their general sense of self with fewer emotional and physical problems than those children whose parents do not support them. That is, when parents prevent their children from expressing their gender or sexual identities, the children become depressed, anxious, and angry, often leading to self-harm and self-mutilation, low self-esteem, risky sexual behavior, drug abuse, and thoughts or attempts of suicide (Liu & Mustanski, 2012; Mallon & DeCrescenzo, 2006). Parents and service professionals in turn often take these at-risk behaviors "as further evidence that something is wrong with the child, rather than the normal response to attempting to accommodate oneself to a hostile environment" (Mallon & DeCrescenzo, 2006, p. 217).

Responses of Other Social Institutions to LGBT Youth

An extreme result of unsupportive parents is that the parents reject their LGBT children. Because these youth have few personal networks or support systems, they often rely on social services and private organizations to help them survive. As discussed above, rejected LGBT youth are at higher risk of becoming involved in illegal activities to survive; at which point they may find themselves in youth detention facilities. In contrast, LGBT youth—and particularly transgender youth—who come from supportive families may access other social institutions, including mental health professionals and physicians, to help them transition more smoothly. In addition, because there are very few support systems in schools and few child welfare agencies for LGBT children, parents who try to advocate on their children's behalf are often met with resistance and hostility from school officials and other care providers (Mallon & DeCrescenzo, 2006).

This section briefly discusses the responses of other social institutions, such as schools, medicine, social welfare agencies, juvenile justice agencies, and legal agencies, in addressing LGBT youth. A lengthy discussion of LGBT youth outside the family is beyond the scope of this book. However, understanding how related social institutions compound family support (or lack thereof) is important, particularly when trying to understand how LGBT youth cope when their families reject them or choose to engage outside institutions to help them through the process of developing positive gender and sexual identities.

Educational and Medical Services

I have grouped the responses of educational and medical services together for two reasons. First, these institutions can potentially support LGBT youth in significant and positive ways; or they can seriously abuse and harm them in negative ways. Second, parents may look to these institutions to help advocate for their LGBT children, or parents may find themselves struggling against these institutions because both share a great deal of gender and sexual phobias and biases.

Educational Responses. When parents begin to realize that their children are LGBT, they may want to work with school administrators and teachers to help their children negotiate the one place outside of home that children spend a significant amount of time. In addition, youth who are experiencing problems at home may also look to school officials and teachers for guidance. Unfortunately, schools are often some of the most unsafe places for LGBT youth (Grant, Mottet, & Tanis, 2011; Jennings, 2003). For example, of the 6,450 diverse transgender and gender-nonconforming participants in the National Transgender Discrimination Survey, 51% reported that students, administrators, and teachers harassed and bullied them at school. Broken down by type of offense, while in grades K–12 the participants "reported alarming rates of harassment (78%), physical assault (35%) and sexual violence (12%); harassment was so severe that it led almost one-sixth (15%) to leave a school in K–12 settings or in higher education" (Grant et al., 2011, p. 3).

Similarly, in their 2011 National School Climate Survey, GLSEN found that 71.3% of LGBT youth frequently heard homophobic remarks and 56.9% reported hearing negative remarks about gender expression from teachers or other school staff. In addition, 63.5% felt unsafe because of their sexual orientation, and 43.9% because of their gender expression. Because of homophobia, nearly 82% were verbally harassed, 38.3% were physically abused, and 18.3% were physically assaulted (e.g., punched, kicked, injured with a weapon) in the past year because of their sexual identity. Because of transphobia, 63.9% of transgender youth were verbally harassed, 27.1% were physically harassed, and 12.4% were physically assaulted because of their gender identity. Approximately 55% of LGBT students also experienced electronic harassment or cyber-bullying via text messages and postings on Facebook. To make matters worse, GLSEN reported that the school staff rarely, if ever, intervened on behalf of the LGBT students. Over 60% of "the students who were harassed or assaulted in school did not report the incident to school staff, most often believing little to no action would be taken or the situation could become worse if reported" (Kosciw, Greytak, Bartkiewicz, Boesen, & Palmer, 2011, p. xv). Students' lack of trust was with good cause as "36.7% of the students who did report an incident said that school staff did nothing in response" (Kosciw et al., 2011, p. xv).

The result of harassment and abuse at school is that approximately 30% of LGBT students avoid and miss school at least 1 day per month; and the more severe the abuse, the more days they miss, thus leading to lower grade point averages, lower educational aspirations, lower self-esteem, and increased psychological problems (Kosciw et al., 2011). The lack of support in and from schools often intensifies problems that LGBT youth and their parents may be experiencing at home.

In several instances, abuse and bullying in schools becomes so severe, and school administrators are so unresponsive, that parents rely on legal help to resolve their children's problems. Under the Fourteenth Amendment of the U.S. Constitution, all students have the right to equal protection. This means that schools cannot discriminate against youth because they are suspected or known to be LGBT (Estrada & Marksamer, 2006). In perhaps the most high profile case (as portrayed in the 2010 documentary titled *Bullied*), Jamie Nabozny, a student in a rural town in Wisconsin who was bullied by his peers, sued his school district. School officials knew of the bullying; however, when confronted, school administrators told Jamie he should expect such abuse given that he is gay. After Jamie ran away from home and attempted suicide, Jamie sued the school district in 1996, calling on lawyers from Lambda Legal Defense and Education Fund, two national LGBT legal groups. The court found the school district guilty, stating that

> The Equal Protection Clause . . . require[s] the state to treat each person with equal regard, as having equal worth, regardless of his or her status. . . . We are unable to garner any rational basis for permitting one student to assault another based on the victim's sexual orientation. (Estrada & Marksamer, 2006, p. 187)

The trial concluded with the court awarding Jamie Nabozny $1 million in damages. While this victory sent a warning message to school administrators and a positive message to LGBT students around the country, the lack of support from schools for both parents and LGBT children remains a serious problem in the United States.

Medical Responses. In addition to schools, LGBT youth and their parents at times need to become involved with medical professionals. Because transgender youth often require medical intervention to help them through puberty, this section addresses their specific needs rather than focusing on the needs of all LGBT youth.

As stated in this chapter's Global Box, most medical professionals in the United States and Europe follow the recommendations by the Standards of Care of the World Professional Association for Transgender Health (WPATH). According to WPATH (2012), less than 25% of children who show gender variance as children are actually diagnosed as "gender dysphoric" as adults. The number of girls who remain transgender into adulthood is greater than the number of boys, and the remaining group of people often identify as gay or lesbian (WPATH, 2012).

WPATH suggests a three-stage process when treating adolescents. The first stage includes fully reversible interventions, such as hormone-blockers, "to suppress estrogen or testosterone production and consequently delay the physical changes of puberty" (p. 18). Some children may approach this stage as young as 9 years old, but recommendations are to start interventions closer to 12 years of age. The second stage involves partially reversible interventions, such as hormone therapy, that can masculinize or feminize the body. Reconstructive surgery may need to accompany some of these hormones, while others may produce irreversible changes, such as voice changes caused by testosterone. While WPATH does not suggest a particular age range for this stage, WPATH recommends that the adolescent, family, and treatment team make the decision together. The third stage involves irreversible interventions that involve surgical procedures. WPATH recommends that the person seeking such treatment be a legal adult who can make an informed decision. Research suggests, however, that the younger a person starts transitioning, the easier time they will have both emotionally and physically. As lawyer Erika Skougard (2011) wrote, "If a child receives puberty delaying hormones (or hormone-blockers) at an early stage of puberty, followed by cross-gender hormones later in adolescence, full gender transition in adulthood is significantly less traumatic (both physically and emotionally) and generally more successful" (pp. 1171–1172).

Despite the 120-page manuscript that WPATH produces to help medical professionals work more effectively with transgender people of all ages, medical schools provide physicians with extremely limited, if any, training on how to address transgender children or adults (Skougard, 2011). Furthermore, the training that medical professionals receive is largely based on the American Psychiatric Association's *Diagnostic and Statistical Manual of Mental Disorders (DSM)*. When the American Psychiatric Association removed homosexuality from the revised *DSM-III* in 1986, they added Gender Identity Disorder (GID), which persisted through the *DSM-IV*. In the latest version of the DSM (the *DSM-5*) released in May 2013, the association changed the name from GID to "gender dysphoria." According to the American Psychiatric Association, they changed the name "to better characterize the experiences of affected children, adolescents, and adults" (American Psychiatric Association, 2013). This change is more than semantics, as the American Psychiatric Association (2013) explained in their fact sheet on gender dysphoria:

> DSM not only determines how mental disorders are defined and diagnosed, it also impacts how people see themselves and how we see each other. While diagnostic terms facilitate clinical care and access to insurance coverage that supports mental health, these terms can also have a stigmatizing effect. . . . DSM-5 aims to avoid stigma and ensure clinical care for individuals who see and feel themselves to be a different gender than their assigned gender. It replaces the diagnostic name "gender identity disorder" with "gender dysphoria," as well as makes other important clarifications in the criteria. It is important to note that gender nonconformity is not in itself a mental disorder. The critical element of gender dysphoria is the presence of clinically significant distress associated with the condition.

The last two sentences of this quote are critical because they show the American Psychiatric Association's move away from understanding gender variance as a mental illness to understanding that people who are transgender face serious emotional challenges caused by external and internalized transphobia. The statement also recognizes that in order to receive health insurance coverage for hormones and other treatment to help people successfully transition, there needs to be a medical diagnosis, which the DSM continues to provide.

Equally notable is that the American Psychiatric Association did not make the change from GID to gender dysphoria until 2013. Prior to 2013, mental health professionals and physicians had used the DSM to shape their understanding of transgender as a mental illness. Therefore, the many transgender people (youth and adults alike) who have interacted with the medical profession, as well as with social workers and other mental health counselors, have done so with physicians and mental health workers assuming that they are mentally ill and thus often trying to "cure" them of what they believed to be a disease. As Mallon and DeCrescenzo wrote in 2006, "Children are particularly vulnerable to medical and mental health injustices in the name of treating GID. As minors, children have no legal standing to make an informed choice to refuse 'treatment' " (p. 220). The result has been that with limited exceptions, few mental and physical health professionals truly understand the experiences of transgender children, or how best to help those children transition. Indeed, to date the "treatment" that many transgender people in general have undergone involved attempts to "cure" their "disease" or "correct" their behavior (Mallon & DeCrescenzo, 2006).

As with schools, at times lawyers and courts become involved in medical issues, particularly regarding some transgender children. According to American civil rights attorney Shannon Price Minter and family law practitioner Deborah H. Wald (2012a), "Parents have a constitutionally protected fundamental right to the custody, care, and raising of their children" (p. 133). The state can only intervene in cases of abuse and neglect, although the state intervenes disproportionately in the lives of poor people and people of color because those people tend to interact more frequently with public agencies and therefore are under greater scrutiny (Minter & Wald, 2012a). Therefore, children of color, or those from economically disadvantaged families, may face greater state intervention than those from wealthier White families.

Regarding transgender children, given parents' constitutional right to care for their children without state intervention, if parents agree to hormone-blockers for their children under medical guidance, the state should not intervene. However, in a few cases, the state has removed children from their parents' care when parents permitted children to live as the child's preferred gender. Studies show that removing a child from a supportive family or home situation is distressing and harmful for the child and the family. In such instances, the child is often returned to the home after the social worker or court is educated about the situation. However, the "fear that the state may intervene and remove a transgender child is a source of great anxiety and stress for many parents with transgender children" (Minter & Wald, 2012a, p. 134).

Some parents involve legal counsel and the courts when they do not agree with each other on how to address their transgender child. This often happens during custody cases where one parent wants to allow the child to transition and the other parent does not. Often the noncustodial parent takes the custodial parent to court. Courts are not supposed to intervene in a parent's medical decision unless that decision harms the child. Some courts assume that simply supporting a child's decision to transition with medical help is harmful to the child. In those instances, the court will support the petition by the noncustodial spouse to have the child moved to the noncustodial parent (Minter & Wald, 2012a).

Foster Care and Juvenile Detention Centers

Legal officials not only become involved when parents ask them to help mitigate issues regarding schools and medical treatment but also when parents, caregiving facilities, or detention agencies are abusing an LGBT child or if caregivers cannot agree on how best to address gender and sexual identity issues that a LGBT youth may be facing. The lack of knowledge about LGBT youth among medical and mental health professionals is mirrored, if not exacerbated, by professionals in social service and foster care settings. This is particularly true for those who encounter transgender children. According to Mallon and DeCrescenzo (2006), in their combined

> 60 years of experience in child welfare, they rarely have come across a mental health professional or social worker who is knowledgeable and proficient about working with a transgender child in an affirming manner. Most do not understand the condition, and few have ever had training to prepare them for competent practice with transgender children and youth. (p. 229)

Other research echoes this concern for LGBT youth in general (Jennings, 2003). Given the lack of training and knowledge, when LGBT youth are kicked out of, run away from, or are removed from their homes by the state, they face difficult times in foster care and state care systems (Estrada & Marksamer, 2006; Jacobs & Freundlich, 2006; Ragg et al., 2006).

Despite research that shows the need for LGBT youth in foster care to have access to physical and mental health services, as well as educational services, LGBT youth face particular difficulties in foster care systems because of several key factors and challenges (Jacobs & Freundlich, 2006). Having a greater likelihood of experiencing physical and sexual abuse prior to arriving at the social service agency or juvenile facility, they may enter with multiple issues to address. Transgender youth are particularly at high risk of experiencing additional harassment and abuse when living in foster care group homes that compound their problems and assault their self-esteem (Jacobs & Freundlich, 2006). Furthermore, because the rate of care worker turnover is high, and foster children often face multiple placements, finding stable and supportive mentors is difficult for LGBT youth. Even when LGBT youth find some supportive professionals in the foster care system, as Mallon and DeCrescenzo (2006) stated, those people are often ill-equipped to help LGBT youth.

In addition, many of the policies and procedures that agencies have in place present obstacles for LGBT youth to effectively communicate their emotions and experiences (Jacobs & Freundlich, 2006; Ragg et al., 2006). This is particularly true for religious and other agencies that are intolerant of, biased against, or try to convert LGBT youth (Ragg et al., 2006). Studies also show that some foster care and residential systems "screen out gay and lesbian foster parents inhibiting the development of supportive relationships and potential mentors" (Brooks & Goldberg, 2001 and Hicks, 2000 as cited in Ragg et al., 2006, p. 246). As a result of the multiple problems that LGBT youth face largely due to the ignorance and fear of those around them, services have not focused on placing LGBT youth in safe and permanent homes. The consequence is that "these youth continue to leave foster care—often running away or being emancipated—without caring, committed adults in their lives" (Jacobs & Freundlich, 2006, p. 300).

To rectify the problem of agencies being ill prepared to address the needs of specific populations, some states have implemented laws to protect LGBT youth. For example, California

enacted the 2004 Foster Care Nondiscrimination Act (AB 458) to prohibit harassment and discrimination against youth and adults in the California foster care system based on whether they are lesbian, gay, bisexual, or transgender, or whether they are believed to be. (Jacobs & Freundlich, 2006, p. 306)

The law also protects youth in foster care who have faced harassment or discrimination "based on race, ethnic group identification, ancestry, national origin, color, religion, sex, mental or physical disability, or HIV status" (Jacobs & Freundlich, 2006, p. 306).

Regardless of the state in which a LGBT youth resides, as stated above, under the 14th Amendment of the U.S. Constitution, everyone in state custody has the right to safety in foster care and juvenile justice systems. Such constitutional protection is "called the 'substantive due process liberty interest in safety,' or the 'right to safety' for short" (Estrada & Marksamer, 2006, p. 174; see also Skougard, 2011). Regarding foster care, this right includes the right to protection against threats of physical, emotional, and sexual violence by social agency workers and foster care families; the right to supervision of one's situation; and the right to services that prevent harm (Estrada & Marksamer, 2006). Regarding juvenile detention and correctional facilities, like all minors, LGBT youth have

the right to reasonably safe conditions of confinement, freedom from unreasonable bodily restraint, freedom from conditions that amount to punishment, access to treatment of mental and physical illnesses and injuries, and minimally adequate rehabilitation. These rights extend to children whether they are confined in juvenile detention centers, adult jails, training schools, or other secure institutions for delinquent children. (Estrada & Marksamer, 2006, p. 180)

Despite such constitutional protections, LGBT youth regularly face violations. For example, foster care and juvenile detention workers routinely fail to protect LGBT youth from harassment by caregivers, peers, and other workers. Some juvenile detention and correctional facilities force LGBT youth to participate in conversion therapies (i.e., therapies that attempt to convert LGBT people to heterosexual), therapies that research shows is detrimental to LGBT people. In fact, many such therapies are being banned on the state level, as is the case in New Jersey and California (Eckholm, 2012). Some facilities also assume that LGBT youth are sex offenders and thus isolate them from others in the facility (Estrada & Marksamer, 2006).

Despite laws meant to protect LGBT youth, many youth do not know their rights, and they are thus quiet about the abuse they experience while in foster care or detention centers. Given some parents' concerns raising their LGBT children, and given the multiple problems children face both within and outside of families, academics and clinicians who study and work with LGBT youth offer recommendations which I discuss in Chapter 6 for how to best support this group of children (see for example, Jennings 2003; Mallon & DeCrescenzo, 2006; Skougard, 2011; WPATH, 2012).

What We Learn From LGBT Youth

The research presented throughout this chapter provides strong evidence that although some parents are comfortable raising LGBT youth, many parents struggle with the thought or actuality of raising LGBT children, often because they themselves are deeply committed to maintaining dominant gender and sexual orders. Most parents also fear that their children will struggle with both internal and external homo- or trans- or biphobia, sexism, and heterosexism. What the research also clearly presents is a picture of what happens to LGBT youth when they lack social, psychological, and physical support from their families, peers, teachers, physicians, mental health professionals, and social workers. LGBT youth face not only increased incidences of verbal, physical, sexual, and emotional abuse, but also they are more likely to become depressed, drop out of school, lose academic ambition, run away, abuse drugs and alcohol, and engage in risky sexual behavior. Furthermore, studies show that conversion therapy often causes more damage than good, and generally does not work (Skougard, 2011). In other words, all evidence points to the fact that external factors, not the youth themselves, cause the increased problems LGBT youth experience.

In discussing the family values debate in Chapter 1, I raised the question of cause and effect. Here I raise the question again: Do LGBT children cause social problems, or do gender and sexual inequalities in the form of hegemonic masculinity and emphasized femininity, as well as homophobia and heterosexism, cause problems for LGBT youth who in turn engage in problematic behavior? Conservatives in the family values debate argue that families divergent from the "traditional family" model cause social problems. By blaming LGBT youth for social problems and for continuing to ostracize youth for being LGBT, what we find is that social problems among youth rise unnecessarily, causing strain not only for individual children and their families but also for society as a whole. As clinical social worker Caitlyn Ryan and her colleagues (2009) wrote,

> Because families play such a critical role in child and adolescent development, it is not surprising that adverse, punitive, and traumatic reactions from parents and caregivers in response to their children's LGB identity would have such a negative influence on their risk behaviors and health status as young adults. (p. 350)

Similarly, it is not surprising that supportive families have such a positive influence on the lives of LGBT youth.

The lesson learned from the research on LGBT youth, therefore, is if individuals, social institutions, and society as a whole embraced our children's multiple gender and sexual identities, then we would see rates decrease among child abuse and neglect, homeless youth, drug and alcohol abuse, STDs and HIV rates, suicide attempts, and depression. The strain on our families, schools, foster care systems, shelters, social services, and detention facilities would also decrease. The question we must ask, therefore, is what we want for our children, families, and society. Is the trade-off—that is, having happier, healthier children and families (albeit LGBT ones)—really worse than having the plethora of social problems associated with discrimination against LGBT children and youth?

LGBT children learn quickly about the disdain people in their families and larger society hold for them. Even if many of us cannot fully understand why some people and the social institutions they occupy direct such hatred toward our children, we know that when parents are unwilling to care for their children because those children's gender and sexual identities stray from the parents' own, that their children face serious emotional and physical challenges.

The good news is that a growing number of parents are embracing and supporting their children's differences. For example, in working with transgender youth and their families, lawyers Shannon Price Minter and Deborah H. Wald (2012a) have found that

> for the first time in contemporary Western culture, there is a generation of transgender children and youth who have a chance to grow up with parental and familial nurturance and support, and to live their entire lives authentically—without suffering the debilitating pain and trauma of suppressing their gender identity for years. This is a watershed moment, and one that will make a huge difference in the quality of life for many transgender people. (p. 132)

In addition to receiving new support, equally good news is that children are resilient. As Saewyc (2011) wrote, despite all of the hardships LGBT youth encounter, ultimately most of those who survive are able to overcome "the stigma and discrimination they encounter" (p. 256).

We can certainly learn more about resiliency and survival by looking closely at the success stories presented by LGBT youth. We can learn about how to be supportive parents, teachers, coaches, administrators, social workers, medical professionals, policy makers, lawyers, judges, religious and spiritual leaders, and community members by understanding how our actions can help or hinder our youth. We can work to understand how to create safe spaces for our youth, spaces that LGBT youth are already creating through face-to-face and online social networks (Russell, 2011).

Equally importantly, we can learn from our LGBT youth how to create positive labels for diverse groups of people or resist labels altogether. Throughout this chapter, a question arose that I often ask in my sociology and gender studies classes: Why do gender and sexual categories matter so much that children and adults alike think that they have to define or redefine their identities at all? Why can't we all just be people without a gendered or sexualized identity? Our biology will be what it is, but if the biology has no social meaning other than to create pleasurable relationships and procreate when we choose, then why do gender and sexuality matter at all?

Research suggests that resisting labels is a strength we can learn from LGBT youth in general, and bisexual and transgender youth more specifically, who so often cross multiple sexual and gender boundaries (Russell, 2011). In *The New York Times* article on "Generation LGBTQIA" (Schulman, 2013) mentioned earlier, a student named Santiago listed a host of labels associated with diverse gender and sexual identities: lesbian, gay, bisexual, transsexual, queer, homosexual, asexual, pansexual, omnisexual, trisexual, agender, bigender, third gender, transgender, transvestite, intersexual, two-spirit, hijra, polyamourous, undecided, questioning, other, human. Santiago's point is well taken: We are so diverse and occupy and cross so many categories that perhaps the easiest and healthiest way (both for individuals and society) of referring to people is just that: human. If a new generation of youth can recognize, accept, and deconstruct diverse categories until we all boil down to equal humans, then we have much to learn from these youth.

GLOBAL BOX

by Morganne Firmstone

How do youth who want to transition from male-to-female, or female-to-male do so around the world? Transgender youth who wish to transition from one gender to another, often because of their age, face added difficulties regarding treatment options, such as hormone therapy or surgery. Issues of diagnosis, access, and consent are three of the major factors that transgender youth, their families, and medical professionals need to consider when thinking about transitioning. The diagnostic process alone can be a challenging one. For instance, the term *Gender Identity Disorder* (GID) is the diagnostic category historically used by the American Psychiatric Association to describe children who often feel as though they were born with an assigned sex that does not align with their socially prescribed gender (Gibson & Catlin, 2010a). However, as discussed in this chapter, the most recent installation of the *Diagnostic and Statistical Manual of Mental Disorders* (*DSM-5*) removes GID and replaces it with "Gender Dysphoria." The reclassification of GID to Gender Dysphoria is a more contiguous definition considering the latest research on transgender individuals. In fact, Shields (2007) noted that "researchers have found no correlation between non-normative gender identification and mental illness" (as cited in Gibson & Catlin, 2010a, p. 53). This new definition allows those who wish to seek gender reassignment therapies to do so without the stigma of having a "disorder."

The American Psychiatric Association's classification change affects youth who wish to transition in a profound way. Historically, according to Gibson and Catlin (2010a), there have been two approaches when dealing with children who wish to transition—acceptance (which entails using mental and physical health interventions to aid in transition) or treatment (which considers gender incongruence a disease that physicians and mental health professionals can treat). In addition, the diagnosis of GID relies heavily on a "subjective report of

(Continued)

(Continued)

a person verified by a mental health professional using diagnostic criteria as spelled out in the widely used psychiatrist classification system" (Cohen-Kettenis, Delemarre-van de Waal, & Gooren, 2008, p. 1892). Under the new Gender Dysphoria classification, transgender youth may be more able to seek services that aid in their choice to transition rather than forcing them to seek treatment with a "reprogramming" method.

As discussed in this chapter, many health professionals around the world choose to follow the Standards of Care of the World Professional Association for Transgender Health (WPATH), and for adolescents, guidelines also exist in the British Royal College of Psychiatrists (Cohen-Kettenis et al., 2008). Under these guidelines, the diagnosis takes place in several stages. According to Cohen-Kettenis et al. (2008), there is a "diagnostic phase in which the actual diagnosis of GID is made, and an estimation is made of potential risk factors for post-treatment regret" (p. 1893). Following the diagnosis, there is a "real life test" in which "both clinician and patient check whether the applicant is able to live satisfactorily in the desired gender role" (p. 1893). The applicant is eligible for sex reassignment surgery only if the real life experience test is successful.

The issue then becomes consent, which is perhaps one of the most heavily debated areas when considering gender reassignment surgery. Some medical professionals believe that the diagnostic process described above does not provide enough of a basis to proceed with hormone therapy or surgery. Many believe that waiting until patients reach young adulthood or the age of legal consent is the best course of action.

What, then, establishes consent regarding medical procedures for minors? In a series of court cases, the general standard that establishes where parental rights terminate and adolescent power of decision begins when pertaining to medical treatment is something called "Gillick competent" (Jones, 2005). Originating in England, this term refers to when "the child is aware of the nature and the consequences of a course of action" (Jones, 2005, p. 121). In 1985, in the historic *Gillick v. West Norfolk and Wisbech Area Health Authority*, the English House of Lords ruled that a 15 year old can seek contraceptive advice and receive contraception without parental consent (Jones, 2005). The "Gillick competence" test is not based on age but rather the decision-making capability of the adolescent.

The High Court of Australia also upheld Gillick competent in the 1992 case of *Secretary of the Department of Health and Community Services v. JWB and SMB*, or more commonly known as *Marion's Case*. In this instance, the parents of a 13-year-old girl, "Marion," sought sterilization of their daughter who suffered from severe mental handicap (Jones, 2005). The High Court found that because Marion was in fact *not* Gillick competent, she would not have the capacity to consent to the medical procedure suggested by her parents; therefore, there was a significant risk that the wrong decision would be made (Parlett & Weston-Scheuber, 2004). In *Marion's Case*, the Australian High Court downplayed the role of parental guardianship and instead emphasized that it was actually the courts, acting in the best interest of the child, who had the authority to grant consent to such radical medical procedures.

According to Dutch law, "adolescents from 16 years on are legally competent to make a treatment choice, even without parental consent, because it is assumed that they are able to fully understand the pros and cons of a treatment" (Cohen-Kettenis et al., 2008, p. 1895). Cohen-Kettenis et al. (2008) noted that by this point in time, the adolescent who seeks gender reassignment hormone treatment or surgery has already been briefed on the potential benefits and risks of such procedures as they have already undergone the diagnostic process. Dutch children between the ages of 12 and 16 can also make treatment decisions, but only with parental consent.

Once consent is determined, transgender youth can take several different paths. Many youth first consider puberty suppression through hormone therapy as the first option. According to lead gender transition researchers emerging from the Netherlands, adolescents at the Amsterdam gender identity clinic are "eligible for puberty suppression when they are diagnosed with Gender Identity Dysphoria, have shown persistent gender dysphoria since childhood, live in a supportive environment, and have no serious comorbid psychiatric disorders that may interfere with diagnostic assessment" (De Vries, Steensma, Doreleijers, & Cohen-Kettenis, 2011, p. 2). Gonadotropin-releasing hormone analogues (GnRHa) are used in the process of puberty suppression to "prevent the emotional problems many young transsexuals experience when puberty has started" (De Vries et al., 2011, p. 2). Through hormone treatment, transgender adolescents can bypass physical changes to their bodies during puberty and thus prevent having to undergo surgery in the future (Gibson & Catlin, 2010a). As Gibson and Catlin (2010a) described, "Female-to-male transitions might avoid the need for mastectomy, and male-to-females might avoid the need for reduction thyroid chondroplasty and voice modification therapy" (p. 56).

In pursuing gender reassignment, cross-sex hormone (CSH) treatment, a partially reversible procedure, would be the next course of action for transitioning youth. CSH is the second stage of physical intervention, which includes prescribing the client the opposite gender's hormones (testosterone or estrogen) in order to develop masculine or feminine characteristics (Gibson & Catlin, 2010a). CSH is an option for Dutch adolescents when they reach the age of 16 and meet the puberty suppression criteria discussed previously; gender reassignment surgery, however, is not an option until adulthood at the legal age of 18 (De Vries et al., 2011).

(Continued)

(Continued)

The final option for transgender people who wish to transition is sex reassignment surgery. Considered a permanent treatment option, this type of medical procedure involves "surgical procedures to change an individual's genitals and/or secondary sexual characteristics" (Gibson, 2010, p. 112). WPATH sets specific universal medical standards and guidelines that prospective patients must meet in order to undergo such procedures (Gibson, 2010). Those transitioning from female-to-male may choose a mastectomy. This procedure involves removal of "breast tissue, excess skin, and the inframammary fold" (Gibson, 2010, p. 113). According to Gibson (2010), female-to-male transitioning patients may also choose a hysterectomy (removal of the uterus and cervix), a salpingo-oophrectomy (removal of the fallopian tubes and ovaries), a vaginectomy (removal of all or some of the vaginal mucosa), urethral lengthening (vaginal tissue is used to create urethral length), scrotoplasty (surgical creation of a scrotum) and insertion of testicular prostheses, a metoidioplasty (the creation of a neophallus using hormonally enlarged clitoral tissue), or a phalloplasty (creation of a neophallus using free tissue grafts). Furthermore, rhinoplasty, calf or pectoral implantation, and liposuction are all methods utilized to achieve complete gender transition (Gibson, 2010). Male-to-female patients may opt for breast enlargement, penectomy (the removal of the penis without vaginoplasty), orchidectomy (removal of the testes), vaginoplasty (the creation of a vagina), labiaplasty (creation of the labia using male genital skin segments), or clitoroplasty (creation of the neoclitoris) (Gibson & Catlin, 2010b). Additional surgeries for transitioning males include reshaping of the eyelids and of the nose, cheek augmentation, chin and jaw reduction, and lip augmentation as well (Gibson & Catlin, 2010b).

De Vries et al. (2011) noted that across the globe, medical professionals do not agree on these courses of treatment. Some are concerned that the use of puberty-suppressing hormones may pose risks for adolescents—both physical and mental. Gibson (2010) identified general risks for those undergoing sex reassignment surgeries as "infection, deep vein thrombosis, pulmonary embolism, and death," depending on how invasive the procedure (p. 115). Furthermore, many doctors believe that "one's gender identity is still subject to change during adolescence and that adolescents are therefore unable to make decisions regarding gender reassignment" (De Vries et al., 2011, p. 2).

Medical cohesion across the globe involving youth who wish to transition will no doubt evolve in coming years, as people's understanding of this growing phenomenon is experiencing a major paradigm shift from a more disease-based field to an identity-based area of interest (Bockting, 2009). Bockting (2009) described the identity-based model as one "that assumes gender variance is merely an example of human diversity" and that the health problems transgender youth experience may be a result of "social stigma attached to gender variance" (p. 103). Prominent Norwegian physician and transperson, Benestad (2009), echoed that claim and noted that instead of viewing transgender youth as "disturbed," they should be considered "children who disturb those around them" (p. 215). The social disruption that develops is reflected back to the child as "sanctions of denial and rejection" (Benestad 2009, p. 215). Benestad (2009) argued the negative social interaction fueled by cisgender (i.e., non-transgender people) and aimed at transgender people causes "pain and trauma" among transgender youth (p. 215). The solution, Benestad argued, is directing educational and therapeutic work toward individuals who are disturbed by the children; in essence, it means developing a network of "transpositivity" that can help lessen a child's proclivity to trauma (p. 215).

ADDITIONAL RESOURCES

Compiled by Morganne Firmstone

Websites

- The Gay Alliance Youth Program
  - http://www.gayalliance.org/programs/youth.html
- Gender Education & Advocacy
  - http://www.gender.org
- GLBT National Help Center
  - http://www.glnh.org/index2.html
- It Gets Better Project
  - http://www.itgetsbetter.org
- Transgender Europe—TGEU
  - http://www.tgeu.org
- The Trevor Project: Providing crisis intervention and suicide prevention services to LGBTQ youth
  - http://www.thetrevorproject.org
- World Professional Association for Transgender Health
  - http://www.wpath.org

Book

- *Trans Forming Families: Real Stories About Transgendered Loved Ones (Jessica Xavier, Mary Boenke and Arlene Istar Lev, Oak Knoll Press, 2003)*

Films

- *Becoming Me (In the Life Media) (2012)*
  - http://www.youtube.com/watch?v=IxzKlPVceWg
  - A documentary that follows eight families with transgender and gender non-conforming children ranging in ages from 5 to 25. With the healthy development of their children at stake, parents must confront binary perceptions of gender, widespread transphobia, and controversial parenting decisions.

- *Bullied: A Student, a School and a Case That Made History (2010, Teaching Tolerance)*
  - A 40-minute documentary film that chronicles Jamie Nabozny's ordeal at the hands of antigay bullies in school and offers an inspiring message of hope to those fighting harassment today.

- *I'm Not Les: A Transgender Story (2012, KCTS 9 Documentary)*
  - *I'm Not Les* is the deeply personal account of one woman's journey to create an identity and find her place in the world. Follow Sherri, from childhood to womanhood, as she struggles to fit in, to find love, and to accept herself.

- *The Infamous T (2012)*
  - Homeless, bullied, and failing out of high school, 18-year-old Jonathon moves in with gay foster parents, transfers to an alternative school, and forms a J-sette dance crew. *The Infamous T* chronicles Jonathon's struggle for a stable life as he discovers that home is more than four walls, everyone needs a family, and friendship can transforms us.

- *Red Without Blue (2007 Documentary)*
  - The intimate bond between two identical twin brothers is challenged when one decides to transition from male-to-female; this is the story of their evolving relationship and the resurrection of their family from a darker past.

- *TransGeneration (Jeremy Simmons and Thairin Smother) (2005)*
  - An eight-episode documentary series depicting the lives of four transgender college students during the 2004–2005 school year as they attempt to balance college, their social lives, and their struggle to merge their internal and external selves while gender transitioning.

5

Intimate Partner Violence

I was grabbed from behind by my partner's girlfriend, and I heard the click of a gun, and I'll never forget the words. She said, "They'll never find your body." And I knew that could be true. I knew I had to get out immediately . . . I moved seven times in two-and-a-half years. I ended up with a debt in excess of $25,000.

—Jan, survivor of intimate
partner abuse (Quinn, 2010, p. 7)

After a lengthy courtship, during which I was treated like gold, my partner and I moved in together. Almost immediately he began to turn on me, demanding separate rooms, bringing strange men home for sexual encounters, subjecting me to verbal abuse privately and in public. At one incident, he started an argument, slapped me, pushed me into oncoming traffic at an intersection in front of a very populated café.

—Dave, survivor of intimate
partner abuse (Quinn, 2010, p. 8)

As a trans-man who is a survivor, I wasn't allowed into certain survivor spaces because I was now male, even though at the time I experienced domestic violence I was living as a lesbian in a relationship with another lesbian.

—Gunner Scott, Massachusetts Transgender
Political Coalition and survivor of
intimate partner abuse (Quinn, 2010, p. 8)

D uring the 1970s and 1980s, feminist activists and social scientists began raising awareness and questions about violence within families. Early researchers and activists were concerned about women whose husbands were physically abusing them. Beginning with the recognition of "family violence" and "wife battering," activists and researchers alike have moved to a broader understanding of "domestic violence" and now "intimate partner violence" (IPV). In defining IPV, I draw on the broad and inclusive definition provided by women's studies and social work professor Betty Jo Barrett and applied social psychologist Melissa St. Pierre (2013). They defined IPV as "any form of psychological/verbal (e.g., name calling, threats, manipulation), financial (e.g., controlling access to monetary resources), physical (e.g., the use of physical force), or sexual (e.g., verbal and/or physical coercion to engage in unwanted sexual activity) violence directed at another individual" (p. 2).

Much of the research on IPV to date has focused at least in part on the gendered nature of such violence, including a discussion of whether women or men are more likely to be battered, and what causes men to both physically and emotionally abuse and control women with whom they are intimately involved (Johnson, 1995; Kurz, 1989; Straus, 1973). Some of the research suggests that women and men may experience physical violence at similar rates, but that women experience more severe violence at the hands of men, than do men at the hands of women (Tjaden & Thoennes, 2000). In addition, women—and particularly elderly women—experience more emotional and psychological abuse than do men (Mezey, Post, & Maxwell, 2002). Other research estimates that 85% of all victims of IPV are women. In addition, "30 percent of female homicide victims are murdered by their intimate partners compared with 5 percent of male homicide victims, and . . . 22 percent of victims of nonfatal intimate partner violence are female but only 3 percent are male" (National Institute of Justice, 2010, para. 10).

In the 1990s, sociologist Michael P. Johnson tried to make sense of why some research found the major perpetrators of violence against women to be men and why other studies found that men and women are victims of physical violence at nearly equal rates. Johnson suggested that there are two types of IPV: situational violence and patriarchal terrorism. Situational violence involves "occasional outbursts of violence from either husbands or wives," while patriarchal terrorism involves the physical and emotional terrorizing of women through systematic male violence (Johnson, 1995, p. 283). Drawing on the idea of patriarchal terrorism, the sociological analysis around why men are more likely to abuse their female partners than women are to abuse their male partners lies squarely, therefore, in the understanding that violence against women occurs because we live in a patriarchal society that gives men greater control over women. This control exists within most social institutions, including the family.

Understanding of how patriarchal terrorism works is best illustrated through the Power and Control Wheel (see Figure 5.1), developed as part of the Domestic Abuse Intervention Project (DAIP) in 1984 by staff and women

Figure 5.1 Power and Control Wheel for Heterosexual Relationships

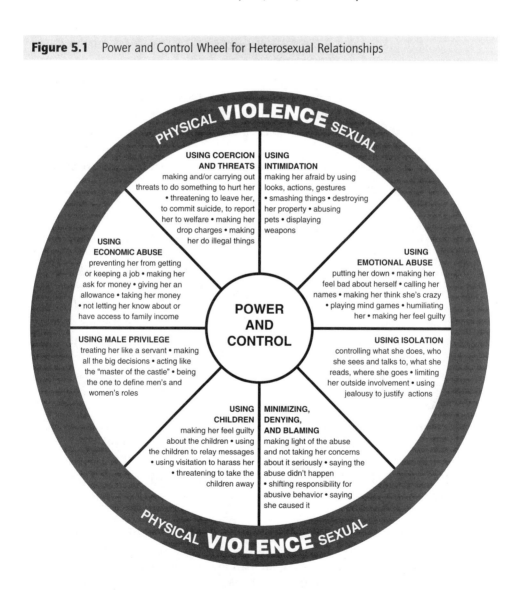

Source: The Duluth Model (http://www.theduluthmodel.org/training/wheels.html)

seeking refuge at a shelter in Duluth, Minnesota. The wheel is widely used by activists, educators, and researchers. As the Power and Control Wheel illustrates, men maintain power and control over women through physical and sexual violence, or the threat of such violence, and through emotional, psychological, and/or economic abuse. Feminists argue that men are able to maintain power and control because of how men maintain positions of power throughout society, not just within their families. Therefore, the macro-level force of gender inequality throughout society allows men to maintain power and control on a micro-level of intimate relationships (Eitzen, Baca Zinn, & Smith, 2011).

If IPV is the result of patriarchal terror in which men abuse female partners, then how can IPV possibly exist within LGBT relationships? To what extent does such violence and abuse exist within LGBT relationships? What does that violence and abuse look like? What do LGBT people do when they experience IPV? What can we as a society do to help those LGBT people in abusive relationships? This chapter attempts to answer these questions.

Prevalence of IPV Within LGBT Relationships

As indicated by the quotes by survivors at the beginning of the chapter, IPV within LGBT communities is a serious issue. According to the Lesbian, Gay, Bisexual, Transgender, Queer, and HIV-Affected (LGBTQH) Intimate Partner Violence report of the National Coalition of Anti-Violence Programs (2012), in 2011 there were 19 IPV-related homicides, "the highest number of LGBTQH IPV homicides ever recorded. This represents an increase of more than three times 2010's six LGBTQH IPV homicides" (p. 7). Of these homicide victims, 42.1% were people of color and 36.8% were White. In addition, 57.9% were gay men and 21.1% were lesbians.

Although homicide lies at the extreme spectrum of IPV, recent studies suggest that lesbians and gay men report being the victim of IPV more than heterosexual women and men (Messinger, 2011; Ristock, 2011). For example, in their analysis of the National Violence Against Women (NVAW) survey, Ard and Makadon (2011)

> found that 21.5% of men and 35.4% of women reporting a history of cohabitation with a same-sex partner had experienced physical abuse in their lifetimes; the corresponding rates for men and women with a history of only opposite-sex cohabitation were 7.1% and 20.4%, respectively. (p. 630)

However, what Ard and Makadon acknowledge, but what many reporting similar statistics overlook, is that the data do not specify whether or not those who experienced violence did so within a same-sex or heterosexual relationship (Barrett & St. Pierre, 2013; Ristock, 2011). Therefore, we cannot say with confidence that lesbians and gay men experience more or less IPV than heterosexual women and men.

Studies on IPV within LGBT relationships are problematic in other ways as well. For example, Barrett and St. Pierre (2013) listed a variety of methodological concerns in the collection of data regarding IPV among LGBT people. These problems include using data that are typically from nonrepresentative convenience samples, the lack of consistency in defining IPV, problems concerning the validity and reliability of the measures used, not accounting for the participation of both partners in a single study, and not assessing the gender of the perpetrators (p. 5). In addition, LGBT people are not a homogeneous population, and many studies do not look at differences of IPV among lesbians, gay men, bisexual people, and transgender people. Therefore, our knowledge about the prevalence, severity, and nature of IPV among LGBT people remains limited.

What we do know about LGBT IPV is that variations exist depending on the group of LGBT people under question. For example, according to one of the most comprehensive studies conducted on IPV that includes same-sex couples, Tjaden and Thoennes (2000) found that lesbians experience violence in their relationships less than gay men and less than women living in heterosexual relationships. In fact, Tjaden and Thoennes (2000) found that slightly

> more than 11 percent of the women who had lived with a woman as part of a couple reported being raped, physically assaulted, and/or stalked by a female cohabitant, but 30.4 percent of the women who had married or lived with a man as part of a couple reported such violence by a husband or male cohabitant. (p. iv)

Regarding gay men, Tjaden and Thoennes (2000) found that around

> 15 percent of the men who had lived with a man as a couple reported being raped, physically assaulted, and/or stalked by a male cohabitant, while 7.7 percent of the men who had married or lived with a woman as a couple reported such violence by a wife or female cohabitant. (pp. iv–v)

Other studies have found both similar and varying rates among gay men and lesbians, ranging from 8% to 60% among lesbians and from 11% to 44% among gay men (Turell, 2000).

The data on the prevalence of IPV among bisexual and transgender people are even scarcer than that on lesbian and gay people. With the exception of one study that employed snowball sampling to interview 81 LGBT people (Turell, 2000), the extant research suggests that bisexual people experience IPV at higher rates than do gay men and lesbians. For example, when looking specifically at IPV in dating relationships, Freedner, Freed, Yang, and Austin (2002) reported, in their study of 521 adolescents at an LGB youth rally, that bisexual males between the ages of 13 and 22 were more likely to experience IPV (57.1%) than gay (44.6%) and heterosexual males (28.6%) in the same age group. Similarly, when studying the victimization of a largely White sample consisting of 557 lesbian or gay, 163 bisexual, and 525 heterosexual adults over the life course, Balsam, Rothblum, and Beauchaine (2005) found that when compared to lesbians and gay men, bisexual women and men were more likely to experience sexual coercion and rape. And in a study drawing on data from the 2004 General Social Survey of Canada (GSS), Barrett and St. Pierre (2013) found that 46.8% of bisexual people experienced emotional or financial IPV, compared to 26.6% of gay men or lesbians in the study. In addition, nearly one third (28.6%) of the bisexual people reported experiencing physical or sexual IPV, compared to 15.5% of gay men and lesbians (Barrett & St. Pierre, 2013). One possible reason for the heightened levels and severity of IPV among bisexuals is that such violence may be more likely to occur when the female partner experiences the IPV at the hands of her male partner (Messinger, 2011). What the data suggest, therefore, is that those who have male partners—regardless of sexual or gender identity—may experience more IPV than those who have female partners. In other words, unequal gender relations intersecting with oppressed sexual identities might be an important cause of IPV (Barrett & St. Pierre, 2013).

In addition to lesbians, gay men, and bisexual people, the limited research on transgender people suggests they too experience serious levels of IPV. According to lawyer Kae Greenberg (2012), the Gender, Violence, and Resource Access Survey estimates that 50% of transgender respondents reported that their partner had assaulted or raped them. In addition, "the comprehensive National Transgender Discrimination Survey (NTDS), which compiled the responses of over 6,000 transgender and gender nonconforming people, found that nineteen percent of respondents had been subjected to domestic violence specifically *because* they were trans or gender nonconforming" (Greenberg, 2012, pp. 200–201). While more research on IPV within LGBT relationships needs to be conducted, the numbers strongly suggest that IPV is a serious issue within those relationships (Pattavina, Hirschel, Buzawa, Faggiani, & Bentley, 2007).

Not only do levels and types of IPV vary by gender and sexuality but also by race, class, immigrant status, HIV-status, and mental abilities, although the data focusing on diverse groups of people are limited. One study suggests that IPV rates are as high as 25% to 40% among African American lesbians, particularly due to poverty, past traumatic experiences, mental health issues, and "multiple and intersecting forms of oppression," such as racism, classism, sexism, and heterosexism (Hill, Woodson, Ferguson, & Parks, 2012, p. 401). Similarly, a study that included a probability sample of 912 Latino gay and bisexual men from three U.S. cities found that when looking at psychological, physical, and sexual abuse together, 52% reported some type of abuse, and the abuse was also associated with being HIV-positive (Feldman, Diaz, Ream, & El-Bassel, 2007). In addition, Barrett and St. Pierre (2013) found that LGB people with lower educational levels and greater physical and mental limitations were more likely to experience IPV than those with higher education levels and fewer limitations. Although some studies suggest that facing multiple forms of oppression can make some groups of people more resilient (Hill et al., 2012), the fact remains that such forms of oppression place specific groups of LGBT people at particular risk of facing IPV. And while further research is needed, existing data strongly suggest that rates of IPV vary depending on the group of people under study. As discussed later in the Issues of IPV Specific to LGBT People section, the experiences of LGBT people vary by gender, race, and class as well.

Causes of IPV Within LGBT Relationships

Despite the dearth of research, our understanding of LGBT IPV has certainly increased over the past several decades. In the early 1990s, when two books—one on "battered gay men and domestic violence" (see Island & Letellier, 1991) and one on "partner abuse in lesbian relationships" (see Renzetti, 1992)—were published, researchers and the general public knew very little about IPV within LGBT relationships. Considering that social scientists started recognizing "family violence" and violence against women as a serious problem in the early 1970s, perhaps the 20-year lag time is not surprising, particularly as LGBT relationships were hardly publically recognized prior to the 1980s. For gay men, the public's unwillingness to take gay male relationships seriously was perhaps part of the reason why IPV remained deeply closeted (Island & Letellier, 1991). Regarding lesbians, the misguided belief that "gay, and especially lesbian, relationships are not characterized by the power struggles that plague heterosexual relationships" prevented many family violence researchers from even looking into the question of violence within lesbian relationships (Renzetti, 1992, p. 1). In addition, because of fierce homophobia within the United States at that time, many lesbians and gay men did not want to draw negative attention to their relationships (Renzetti, 1992).

In many ways, the nature of IPV in LGBT relationships is similar to that of IPV in heterosexual relationships. As in abusive heterosexual relationships, physical and sexual violence, economic and psychological abuse, and threats of violence and abuse exist within violent LGBT relationships (Greenberg, 2012; Island & Letellier, 1991; Renzetti, 1992; Tjaden & Thoennes, 2000; Wittenberg, Joshi, Thomas, & McCloskey, 2007). However, even while some of the types of abuse and experiences of such abuse are similar, there are important distinctions between IPV within heterosexual relationships and IVP within LGBT relationships.

Just as the most insidious and long-standing IPV within heterosexual relationships is due to patriarchal terrorism, the most insidious and long-standing IPV within LGBT relationships is due to homophobia (both internalized and external) and heterosexism (Barrett & St. Pierre, 2013). Homophobia and heterosexism shape the nature and experiences of IPV for LGBT people from the very micro-experiences of interpersonal relationships and what happens between two people, to the very macro-experiences of how interconnected social institutions, such as law enforcement and social services, respond to LGBT IPV.

Figure 5.2 illustrates the redrawing of the Power and Control Wheel to help explain how homophobia and heterosexism cause and shape IPV among LGBT people. The existence of homophobia and heterosexism affects IPV in a variety of ways, including types of abuse specific to LGBT people and access to legal and social services. For example, in 1994, the U.S. federal government passed the Violence Against Women Act (VAWA) with the goal of both holding offenders accountable for their crimes and providing services for the victims of IPV (The White House, n.d.). The VAWA, which the U.S. Congress reauthorized in 2000 and 2013, requires governments and local agencies to examine rates of IPV among marginalized groups, such as same-sex couples, racial and cultural minority groups, and immigrants (Pattavina et al., 2007). However, such data are still lacking. In addition to the lack of data collected on marginalized populations, and despite the good programs the VAWA has helped secure for heterosexual couples, those governing the VAWA have failed to fully recognize or incorporate protections for LGBT people (Pattavina et al., 2007). Although laws are changing, most states do not specifically grant same-sex couples the option of pursuing an order of protection against an abusive partner (ABA Commission on Domestic Violence, n.d.; Pattavina et al., 2007). In fact, in its

Figure 5.2 Power and Control Wheel for LGBT Relationships

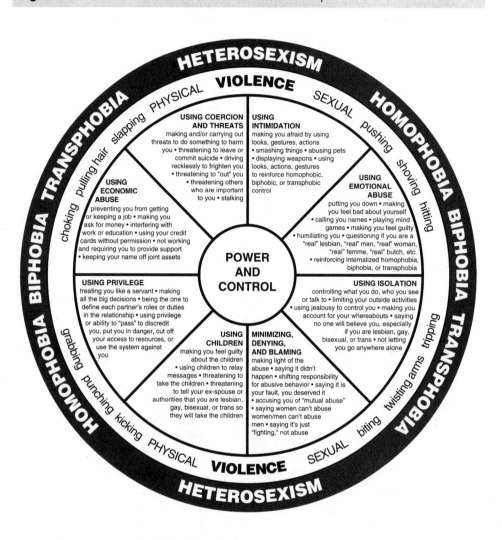

Source: Developed by Roe & Jogodinsky; adapted from The Duluth Model (http://www.theduluthmodel.org/training/wheels.html).

reauthorization of the VAWA in 2013, the U.S. House of Representatives specifically left out LGBT people from the act. Because the Senate countered the House's omission, Congress ultimately reissued the VAWA, thus, providing LGBT people with the same protections and rights as heterosexual people.

Despite the recent inclusion of LGBT people in the VAWA, a lack of understanding and training about LGBT IPV, as well as homophobic beliefs and heterosexist practices, have led law enforcement agents and agencies to commit egregious acts of their own. Similar to the earlier responses of the police to calls of heterosexual IPV, police officers' lack of understanding of LGBT IPV lead to police often minimizing the seriousness of abuse, failing to arrest the perpetrator, and disregarding standard procedures that require the officer to identify who is the primary aggressor (Comstock, 1991; Pattavina et al., 2007; Peterman & Dixon, 2003). Similarly, in states with mandatory arrest policies, police officers often arrest both partners. This double arrest means that in some cases of LGBT IPV, "both parties were arrested and subsequently held in the same jail cell where the 'real' victim was reassaulted" (Letellier 1994, as cited in Pattavina et al., 2007, p. 380). Transgender people report similar problems of double arrests as well (Greenberg, 2012).

The police are not alone in their lack of training for addressing LGBT IPV. Even among agencies whose mission is to help survivors of IPV, a lack of training around the specific issues that LGBT people face leaves IPV workers with good intentions, but few tools to actually help (Duke & Davidson, 2009). Furthermore, even if IPV workers themselves may not be homophobic, their fear of losing funding by providing services to LGBT people may force or encourage them to participate in homophobic and heterosexist practices (Duke & Davidson, 2009).

In addition, the structure of shelters and help agencies in the United States makes seeking refuge from an abusive partner difficult for many LGBT people. Most shelters are set up specifically for biologically born women to seek help (Douglas & Hines, 2011; Greenberg, 2012). Thus, gay men, bisexual men, bisexual women who are abused by their female partner, lesbians, and transgender people have difficulty seeking or finding adequate refuge and help when trying to leave an abusive partner. And when such LGBT people find a shelter where they can stay, they are often reluctant to reveal their identities or the nature of their intimate relationships for fear of the response they will receive by those in positions to help (Greenberg, 2012; Hardesty, Oswald, Khaw, & Fonseca, 2011).

Issues of IPV Specific to LGBT People

In addition to laws, policies, practices, and attitudes that can prevent LGBT people from receiving the help they may need when involved in IPV, the heterosexism and homophobia, as well as the patriarchal constructions of masculinity that are built around homophobic sentiments (Kimmel, 1994), contribute to the causes, experiences, and patterns of abuse in LGBT relationships. This section discusses the specific issues that make LGBT people vulnerable to being victims and perpetrators and how these issues differ by sexual and gender identities.

Because of the intersections of structures of gender, sexuality, race, and social class, when LGBT people experience physical violence in their relationships, their experiences vary from other groups of people. For example, because hegemonic definitions of masculinity in the United States include men as being strong and aggressive, men and women alike expect that men should be able to protect themselves. The result is that not only do outsiders have trouble seeing men as victims of IPV, but also men have trouble seeing themselves as victims of IPV. Therefore, gay men may not identify themselves as victims until they are seriously injured (Poon, 2011). In addition, people both within and external to gay intimate relationships may see the couple as mutually combative, thus, creating difficulties in knowing who the perpetrator is and who the victim is (Duke & Davidson, 2009). Indeed, one form of abuse within LGBT relationships is the abusers' efforts to convince their partner that the partner is a mutual batterer, rather than someone who is retaliating in self-defense (Pattavina et al., 2007). As a result of our cultural understandings of gender and masculinity, not only do abused gay men wait until they are seriously injured to see themselves as needing help, but police tend also not to make an arrest until there are serious injuries (Pattavina et al., 2007). The trivializing of men's violence also results in very few services for battered gay men; and those services that do exist are "underfunded, understaffed, and often run on a volunteer or ad hoc basis" (Durish, 2011, p. 239; see also Duke & Davidson, 2009).

In addition, based on socially constructed gender and sexual norms, lesbians' experiences of violence differ from that of gay men and heterosexual women. Lesbians may be reluctant to report the abuse because if they do, they may feel like—or fear other lesbians as perceiving them to be— "'traitors' to their gender and sexuality" (Hattery & Smith, 2012, p. 297) or "betraying the feminist sisterhood" (Durish, 2011, p. 239). Social worker Patricia Durish (2011) speculates that this feeling of betrayal may be particularly strong for White, middle-class lesbians who have historically been closely connected to a feminism that idealizes a unified lesbian sisterhood.

Furthermore, lesbians who abuse their partners challenge the cultural ideal that women are nonviolent. Therefore, unlike situations involving gay men, when physical violence occurs within lesbian relationships, both those within and external to lesbian communities may be surprised (Duke & Davidson, 2009). The result of the general understanding that women are nonviolent is that police are likely to make an arrest for lower acts of violence when two women are involved because any female act of violence is surprising (Pattavina et al., 2007). The combination of not wanting to betray other women and fearing what will happen when they call the police often leads lesbians to underreport to authorities the abuse they are experiencing.

A new area of research on IPV examines lesbian mothers in abusive relationships with other women. The limited research suggests that being able to rely on LGBT support networks is critical to whether or not an abused lesbian mother will seek help or not (Hardesty et al., 2011). For example, Hardesty et al. (2011) interviewed 24 lesbians and bisexual women (12 African American, 9 White, and 3 Latina) who had children and who had been in abusive relationships with another woman. The study suggests that when women have a strong and proud sense of identity, have economic resources and strong social networks, believe that IPV can happen to anyone, and have legal rights over their children and home (e.g., homeowner, name is on the lease), they are likely to talk openly with their children and friends and family, and to seek professional help from the police, health-care workers, and IPV workers. However, when lesbians believe that either being a lesbian or bisexual is shameful, that being abused is shameful, and when they have fewer legal rights over their children and homes, then they are less likely to talk with friends and family about the abuse and less likely to seek formal help (Hardesty et al., 2011).

Hardesty et al.'s (2011) study not only suggests that being a parent in an abusive relationship complicates matters (as is true with heterosexual parents) but also that homophobia and heterosexism, internalized ideals of gender roles, and internalized homophobia can shape patterns of abuse and how LGBT people respond to that abuse. In fact, studies on other groups of people provide evidence that homo/bi/trans-phobia shape IPV in most LGBT relationships. For example, LGBT people who have faced the disdain of their family, friends, and community members, as well as absorbed messages from educational systems, religious organizations, political leaders, and the media, tend to internalize the message that they are immoral people, undeserving of human dignity (Barrett & St. Pierre, 2013; Carvalho, Lewis, Derlega, Winstead, & Viggiano, 2011; Greenberg, 2012; Mendoza, 2011). For many LGBT people, such negative messages and images are reinforced when their partners perpetrate violence against them.

Social science researchers call the internalization of discrimination "minority stress" (Carvalho et al., 2011; Hequembourg & Brallier, 2009; Mendoza, 2011; Meyer, 1995). Minority stress occurs when a person in an oppressed group experiences "psychological and social stresses that arise from one's minority status (i.e., stigmatization), and the discrimination associated with" that discrimination (Mendoza, 2011, p. 170). Minority stress may lead some LGBT people to hide their gender and sexual identities from others. Hiding identities makes LGBT people vulnerable such that their partners, in order to maintain power and control over them, may threaten to "out" them, or reveal their identities to others. This fear of being "outed" by their partners forces some LGBT people to remain in abusive relationships (Mendoza, 2011; Ristock, 2005).

The issue of outing someone as a means of IPV holds particular issues for bisexual people. As Duke and Davidson (2009) wrote, abusive partners may threaten to out their bisexual partners

> as lesbian or gay to their families, even though that may not be how they readily identify. In addition, abusers may threaten to out survivors as bisexual to the gay or lesbian community, further increasing the isolation experienced by bisexuals within the LGB community and heterosexual society. (p. 803)

In addition, bisexual survivors are nearly twice as likely as LGT people to experience verbal abuse (National Coalition of Anti-Violence Programs, 2012). Thus, the effects of different types of abuse vary depending on the status of that group not only within larger heterosexual circles but also within specific LGBT communities.

In addition, being HIV-positive might heighten minority stress for LGBT people, thus putting LGBT people who are HIV-positive at greater risk of being abused. Research suggests that the same factors that make gay and bisexual men more likely to become HIV-positive (e.g., chaotic and violent childhoods, marginalization, substance abuse, mental illness, reliance on sex-work due to a lack of other job opportunities) also place these men at heightened risk of being abused (Feldman et al., 2007; Pantalone, Lehavot, Simoni, & Walters, 2011). Among Latino men, although psychological, physical, and sexual abuse are all associated with increased intercourse with an unprotected and non-monogamous partner, sexual abuse is the most important indicator of such behavior (Feldman et al., 2007). Furthermore, some HIV-positive partners—regardless of race—may threaten to infect their partner as part of the abuse they inflict (Pattavina et al., 2007).

Researchers have found that minority stress can lead LGBT people to be both more vulnerable to abuse and more likely to abuse their partners (Balsam & Szymanski, 2005; Carvalho et al., 2011). For example, in a study of mostly White, educated, and middle-class lesbian and gay men (138 who were abused and 51 who were abusers), psychologist Amana Carvalho (2011) and her colleagues found that minority stress was a key factor in whether or not someone was abused and/or was the abuser. Similarly, psychologist Jesmen Mendoza (2011) studied the effects of minority stress on 150 men (also mostly White, highly educated, and older) in same-sex relationships living in the United States and Canada. Mendoza "conceptualized minority stress as having three factors: internalized homophobia, perceived stigma, and discrimination" (p. 178). He found that these three factors together are strong predictors of whether or not a gay man will perpetrate violence against his same-sex partner. Mendoza (2011) explained his findings by stating that some gay men who perpetrate IPV "may rationalize their use of force as a way of dealing with their own internal struggles, or as a way to regain a sense of power when they have faced discrimination" (p. 179). Although Mendoza makes clear that minority stress does not justify IPV among gay men, his research illuminates some of the issues specific to LGBT IPV. Mendoza's research also suggests how mental health workers and policy makers might treat those who abuse and as a result create policies to help prevent discrimination in the first place.

The limited research suggests that transgender people face additional challenges to those that LGB people face. As psychologist Nicola Brown (2011) stated, "The marginalized status of trans people is a central construct in the relationship abuse against them, as well as in the relationship abuse they perpetrate" (p. 162). Regarding the abused person in a transgender relationship, research suggests that transgender people are nearly three times as likely as LGB people to experience sexual abuse (National Coalition of Anti-Violence Programs, 2012). In addition, because some transgender people may fear that they have limited options for finding another partner, they may risk staying in abusive relationships. Transgender people may also fear that their partners will out them as transgender, thus forcing them to remain in the abusive relationship. Additional factors exacerbate abusive situations for transgender people, preventing them from leaving abusive situations. For example, lack of job security, fear of the police, mistreatment by medical professionals, and legal identification (e.g., driver's licenses) with a different gender identification than as presented in person, all act as barriers preventing transgender people from calling the police or considering leaving an abusive situation (Greenberg, 2012). In other words, the abuse that many transgender people experience outside of their families often prevents them from leaving the abuse they experience within their families.

Even if transgender people decide to leave an abusive relationship, they need some place to go. If transgender people are alienated from family and friends, then they may not have many safe options, particularly as community shelters can be very dangerous places for transgender people (Brown, 2011). As Greenberg (2012) wrote, many transgender people cannot seek shelter with their birth family because of estrangement or lack of support. When their abusers are prominent in the local LGBT community, trans women victims may not wish to turn to LGBT-specific services. However, they may also be unwelcome in mainstream shelters, where transphobia or outright bans on trans women may present insurmountable barriers to access. (p. 235)

In addition, according to the National Transgender Discrimination Survey (NTDS), transgender people are almost four times as likely to have an income under $10,000 as the general population (Greenberg, 2012). The survey also found that transgender people in general have two times, and transgender people of color have closer to four times the unemployment rate as the general population. Not only may the lack of economic resources "lead trans people to be more susceptible to the economic control that abusers often utilize" (Greenberg, 2012, p. 202), but may also prevent them from leaving an abusive relationship because they have limited money with which to travel or find another—and safer—place to live.

Regarding the abuser, some cisgender (i.e., non-transgender) people who are with transgender people state they themselves become abusive because they feel left out of the transgender community or feel the vulnerability of being with a transgender person. Futhermore, some transmen say they abuse because of hormones; and some transmen try to establish hegemonic masculinity. In addition, some transgender abusers know that their partners are reluctant to call the police because they fear what the police will do to their abusive transgender partners (Brown, 2011).

By examining not only differences in how LGBT people experience IPV from heterosexual people but also how LGBT people experience IPV differently from one another, we can understand how structures of gender, sexuality, race, and social class intersect to create a variety of causes, types, and responses to IPV. By studying LGBT IPV in depth, therefore, we can learn how best to respond to IPV in inclusive and comprehensive ways.

What We Learn From LGBT IPV

In returning to my three main questions stated in Chapter 1, we can understand that our knowledge about and increased research and services concerning LGBT IPV comes out of the historical context of taking LGBT relationships more seriously in general. The irony of my second question—why are new family forms so threatening to certain groups of people in society—is that concerning IPV, the opposite is true: Because most people in society do not take LGBT IPV seriously, IPV within LGBT relationships is virtually invisible and, therefore, not threatening to a larger heterosexual consciousness.

The lack of perceived threat has led to a lack of much needed support for LGBT people who are in abusive relationships. In addition, as the discussion throughout this chapter suggests, pressure from the heterosexual world that already deems LGBT people to be abnormal and problematic, and pressure from within LGBT communities themselves to hide IPV because of the blight such violence places on their communities, means that LGBT people are caught between external and internal systems of homophobia and heterosexism. As the research also suggests, these systems intersect with, and become compounded by, other systems of oppression, such as sexism, racism, and classism. The result is the culmination of police, legal, and support systems that continuously fail to meet the needs of abused LGBT people who desperately need external help. Unless LGBT people have the emotional, economic, and human resources, as well as the personal gumption, they are unlikely to acknowledge, report, or seek help for the IPV that they are experiencing.

So what can we learn from studying LGBT IPV? Perhaps we can best understand the most important lesson through the following quote from Barrett and St. Pierre (2013):

> Feminist theories posit that IPV is a manifestation of power and control, in which patriarchal social structures at the macro level support the use of male-perpetrated violence against women at the micro level. While feminist approaches to IPV initially focused solely on IPV as a gendered construct within male-female dyads, and thus were largely dismissed as being able to account for IPV in sexual minority communities, these theories have evolved to reflect a more sophisticated understanding of IPV in diverse populations. Such evolutions in thought include an analysis of the way in which patriarchal social structures support and are intertwined with heteronormativity, and, as such differentially position sexual minority identities within patriarchal culture (Johnson 1997). Such inequalities create distinct vulnerabilities for LGB[T] individuals in relation to IPV that are unique from those experienced by heterosexual-identified persons. (p. 18)

When feminists and other scholars began studying IPV, because they focused on the gendered nature of heterosexual IPV, they focused on patriarchy as the cause of male-dominated violence. Patriarchy and hegemonic masculinity are certainly part of the cause of IPV. But research on LGBT IPV provides evidence to support the notion that IPV is the result of power and control in general, not just one particular form of power and control (i.e., patriarchal). For example, one study that questioned feminist models focusing on heterocentric and patriarchal explanations of IPV moved the center from gender to emotion work (i.e., the work required to manage love and other emotions in intimate relationships) (Donovan & Hester, 2011). That is, rather than looking at the gendered nature of IPV, the researchers examined the type of reproductive labor the partners did within their relationship. In their qualitative study of 67 lesbians, gay men, bisexual, and heterosexual participants, Donovan and Hester (2011) concluded that those who do most of the emotion work in a relationship—regardless of gender or sexual identity—are most vulnerable to abuse. Their study suggests that IPV is the result of power inequalities that develop from a variety of social structural systems, including heterosexism, racism, classism, nationalism, and sexism. We need more research to examine how a variety of power inequalities leads to violence within intimate relationships of all kinds. The acknowledgment of and research regarding LGBT IPV has helped lead scholars to consider and practitioners to examine a variety of explanations for IPV. Although there is nothing positive about the existence of IPV, examining LGBT IPV is beginning to increase our understanding of IPV in general—as LGBT IPV forces us to look beyond gender and focus more broadly on power inequalities overall. The advantage of taking a broader view is that practitioners and policy makers can work to end a variety of IPV, not just violence against women. I offer some suggestions for ending LGBT IPV in Chapter 6.

GLOBAL BOX

by Morganne Firmstone

Violence—emotional, physical, sexual, and verbal—is no stranger to many LGBT people. In 2007, "1,265 LGB-biased hate crimes were reported to the FBI, which is a 6-percent increase from 2006" in the United States (Marzullo & Lbman, 2009, p. 2). Even as disturbing as these rates of violence are, one must consider that these are only the *reported* hate crimes committed against LGBT people. In fact, many cases go unreported because victims are not publically "out" or they may face a lack of support and resources in pursuing their cases.

The rate of violence against LGBT people may also be much higher for people living in geographic regions other than the United States that have differing cultural ideals regarding sexual identities. For instance, in southern India, men who have sex with men and transgendered individuals (MSM-T) face an elevated

(Continued)

(Continued)

risk of experiencing violence due to "strongly entrenched societal and structural sanctions against same-sex relationships" (Shaw et al., 2012, p. 1). Additionally, the prevalence of sexual violence among this population in India may go under-reported due to "stigma attached to reporting of sexual violence by men, as well as the marginalization of MSM-T communities in India" (Shaw et al., 2012, p. 1). Thus, acts of violence committed against people in the LGBT community most likely occur at much higher rates than data may reveal.

Similar to men in India, women of diverse sexualities around the world also report violent acts and threats committed against them. In a 2011 survey conducted by the Society Against Sexual Orientation Discrimination, an advocacy group in Guyana, "Twenty-three women from six of the ten administrative regions in Guyana reported experiencing verbal harassment" (GuyBow, IGL-HRC, & SASOD, 2012, p. 4). The survey also revealed that lesbian and bisexual women in Guyana reported harassment on a regular basis because of their gender nonconforming physical appearance, mannerisms, and way of dress:

> One woman reported being threatened by a strange man with a scissors to cut her dreadlocks because she was "a disgrace to Rasta" and had a "dirty lifestyle." Another woman said, "I get harassed all the time. Because I don't dress or act like a woman." Yet another said, "sometimes people will make comments about the fact that I'm always wearing pants." (As cited in GuyBow, IGLHRC, & SASOD, 2012, p. 4)

Disturbingly enough, according to the Human Rights Watch, hate violence is inflicted upon LGBT not only by heterosexual people in general but also at the hands of law enforcement officials in some regions around the globe (Kidd & Witten, 2008). For example, in Nepal, the Nepalese police have specifically targeted transgender people, referred to as *metis*:

> On March 14, 2006, 26 metis were arrested, detained, and denied legal counsel. In the end, they were charged with "public nuisance." The report [by the Human Rights Watch] also details a 2004 incident in which police "rounded up" 39 metis and arrested them. Several of these individuals told reporters stories of the abuse they endured during their two-week detention. (Kidd & Witten, 2008, p. 45)

Not only are people outside LGBT communities committing acts of violence, but as discussed in this chapter, violence is also prevalent *within* LGBT relationships in the form of intimate partner violence (IPV), not just within the United States but also throughout the world. Finneran, Chard, Sineath, Sullivan, and Stephenson (2012) studied several risk factors for IPV among over 2,000 men who have sex with men (MSM) and are from six different countries: Brazil, Canada, the United States, the United Kingdom, Australia, and South Africa. The research revealed that 5.75% of respondents from the United States reported experiencing physical IPV compared to 7% of men in Brazil, 7.02% in Canada, 8.54% in the United Kingdom, 9.01% of men in Australia, and 11.75% in South Africa. Experiences of sexual IPV were less frequent but still existent across the six countries, ranging from 2.54% in Australia to 4.52% in the United States.

Similar to findings discussed throughout this chapter, Finneran et al. (2012) found that of all the risk factors tested (e.g., age, education, race), experiences of heterosexism proved to significantly increase the odds of reporting IPV. Although the ways in which heteronormativity was expressed varied among the six countries Finneran et al. studied, particular experiences based on heterosexism consistently emerged as a risk factor. The authors suggest that there may be "associations between violence and homophobia that are necessarily unique to MSM" (p. 269). Finneran et al. (2012) cited larger social practices like "social stigmatization and marginalization" and "a lack of formal recognition of gay partnerships" as reasons why MSM may be at an increased risk of IPV (p. 269). In addition, "lack of safeguards against IPV normally afforded married or otherwise legally recognized couples" leave MSM little opportunity in seeking relief (Finneran et al., 2012, p. 269).

Clearly, IPV is not exclusive to the heterosexual community. According to Ard and Makadon (2011), there are several similarities among LGBT couples and heterosexual couples in abusive relationships. "Power dynamics, the cyclical nature of abuse, and the escalation of abuse over time" are all just as likely to occur in both heterosexual and LGBT relationships (p. 630). However, the authors make note that there are in fact unique experiences in LGBT IPV cases. For instance, the concept of "outing" may be used as a weapon of abuse. "LGBT individuals often hide outward expression of their sexual orientation or gender identity for fear of stigma and discrimination; abusive partners may exploit this fear through the threat of forced outing" (p. 630). This vulnerability may cause a victim of IPV to stay in a relationship for fear of others learning about their sexual identity. Heterosexism and homophobia may also hinder a victim's ability to reach out to friends and family for help. Much like Finneran et al. (2012), Ard and Makadon (2011) pointed out that IPV within LGBT communities occurs with a background of "stigma and discrimination" (p. 630). Thus, many LGBT people have experienced some sort of discrimination or psychological and/or physical trauma in their lifetime solely based on their sexual identity. The authors concluded that "prior experiences of violence and discrimination, coupled with the failure of the community to adequately respond, may make LGBT victims less likely to seek help when they experience IPV" (p. 630).

(Continued)

(Continued)

Culture can also play a serious role in shaping the actions of partners in relationships. Téllez Santaya and Walters (2011) conducted a study among Cuban male couples living in the city of Santiago. The researchers identified several factors leading to IPV in same-sex male relationships such as culture, power dynamics, and economic hardship. Some of the men in the study regarded violence as a cultural act or "the natural consequence of being raised as male in a Latin society" (p. 166). Many of the men recalled that the punishments and socialization practices they experienced while growing up were centered around the idea that men are the head of the family and thus must emit a masculine identity in order to "achieve both self-respect and respect of others" (p. 166). Because heterosexism is an extension of masculinity (Kimmel, 1994), the participants spoke of the shame they felt when their families rejected their gay identities. Consequently, many carried this shame and guilt with them into their romantic lives and approached these intimate relationships "as a quest—or a battlefield—for power and esteem" (Téllez Santaya & Walters, 2011, p. 167). The resulting power struggle, and subsequent acts of violence, were often motivated by "a man's self-possession of a masculine ideal—to embody a privilege of masculinity" (p. 169). Téllez Santaya and Walters (2011) also made note that among the Cuban male couples sampled, some quarrels and disagreements that incited emotional acts of violence were due to financial concerns and a "palpable fear of poverty" (p. 170).

Social institutions, culture, attitudes, beliefs, religion, and personal experience can all contribute to incidents of violence. Across the globe, LGBT people experience violence not only through hate crimes but also within their own relationships. Negative attitudes, discriminatory policies, the absence of resources, little trust in law enforcement, limited means of legal protection, and general lack of acceptance of LGBT people and relationships put these individuals at a heightened risk of experiencing violence. Until law-making bodies around the globe directly address the legitimacy of LGBT intimate partner relationships, as well as the rights of LGBT people in general, we will have a population of people who are at great risk of experiencing discrimination, harassment, and physical attack around the world.

ADDITIONAL RESOURCES

Compiled by Morganne Firmstone

Websites

- Anti-Defamation League
  - http://www.adl.org

- The Anti-Violence Project
  - http://www.avp.org

- Global Respect In Education—GRIN
  - http://www.grincampaign.com/Home.html

- National Sexual Violence Resource Center
  - http://www.nsvrc.org

- OutServe-SLDN
  - http://www.outserve-sldn.org

- Southern Poverty Law Center
  - http://www.splcenter.org

Films

- *Accessory to Murder: Our Culture's Complicity in the Death of Ryan Skipper (director & coproducer Vicki Nantz and coproducer Mary Meeks, 2008 Documentary)*
  - Explores the rampant homophobia which is present in our culture's institutions, from religion, education, and law enforcement to politics.

- *Beyond Gay: The Politics of Pride (directed by Bob Christie, 2009 Documentary)*
  - Examines relevance of Gay Pride celebrations internationally, against the backdrop of opposition to such events in a number of countries. The documentary tries to portray Gay Pride as more than just a parade, but rather an important step on the road to equality and fight against homophobia and discrimination.

6

Learning From LGBT Families

I just can't imagine how if some of these people who oppose gay marriage saw your family, that they could ever think that how you and your partner, together for almost 20 years, raising two wonderful children, could be doing this country any harm.

—Judy Mezey, Assistant Director of Community
Based Programs for Student Assistance Services
Corporation and the author's sister, in a phone
conversation after listening to a radio program
regarding the United States Supreme Court
decision on DOMA, July 2, 2013

I think lesbians are one of the strongest people I know. And you've got all these kids who are being raised in that environment and they're strong kids. They just are. They're being encouraged to do a lot of things and think.

—Lilly, a middle-class, White lesbian interviewed in
2000 for the author's doctoral research on lesbians'
decisions to become mothers or remain childfree

As I was writing the final chapter of this book, one of my sisters called me on the phone. The comment she made, transcribed above, brought me back to the original question posed in Chapter 1: Why are new family forms so threatening to certain groups of people in society? A comment made by one of the women I interviewed for my doctoral research, also quoted above, also returned me to an initial question of how new family forms are beneficial to the society in which they exist. Of course someone could ask how new family forms are harmful to society. That is a legitimate question as well. As a trained social scientist, I base my understanding of the social world on research and evidence. In writing this book, I presented as much evidence as possible to ensure that the information I provided was thorough and honest. I drew on studies conducted by sociologists, psychologists, social workers, lawyers, political analysts, physicians, nurses, journalists, and scholars from a variety of other fields. I asked hard questions about LGBT families, discussed methodological limitations in a variety of studies, and tried to present as unbiased a story about LGBT families as the research would allow. What I found is that, with the exception of one very methodologically flawed study (Regnerus, 2012) which I discussed in Chapter 3, the research coming from the social, behavioral, and natural sciences is extremely clear and consistent: LGBT families are at least as healthy as heterosexual families.

My statement above does not mean that readers cannot find literature about how harmful LGBT families are to society. Of course such reading material exists. But the information presented in those books and manuals is not based on scientific evidence. Rather, information discussing how harmful LGBT families are for society is based on belief systems that perpetuate hatred toward, or at least a strong disdain for, a particular group of people. The main problems facing LGBT families today—that is, the main reasons LGBT elderly people fall into poverty and face elder abuse in care facilities; the main problem that children of LGBT parents state they face; the biggest reason that LGBT youth drink more, drug more, are depressed more, commit suicide more, engage in more risky sexual behavior, and run away more than heterosexual children; and one of the most serious catalysts for LGBT IPV—all rest on the shoulders of belief systems that are fueled by heterosexism and homo/bi/trans-phobia and that are built into our laws, policies, practices, and attitudes.

Therefore, if someone were to ask how LGBT families are harmful to society, after reading and analyzing the research for this book, I can only answer emphatically, "They are not harmful at all." Do LGBT families change existing gender and sexual orders? Of course they do. But the volumes of books and articles and research conducted on the dangers of that order—written over centuries and beyond the scope of this book—suggest that gender and sexuality have been continuously changing throughout time, and the ways in which they are changing are creating greater equality for more people. How is greater equality bad for society?

In fact, what does it mean to say that a social phenomenon is beneficial or harmful to society? Certainly, we know that there are social problems, but how we determine what is a social problem and what is not relies on a subjective understanding of "good" and "bad." As sociologists D. Stanley Eitzen, Maxine Baca Zinn, and Kelly Eitzen Smith (2011) wrote in their book, *Social Problems*,

> There is an **objective reality to social problems:** There *are* conditions in society (such as poverty and institutional racism) that induce material or psychic suffering for certain segments of the population; there *are* sociocultural phenomenon that prevent a significant number of societal participants from developing and using their full potential; there *are* discrepancies between what the United States is supposed to stand for (equality of opportunity, justice, democracy) and the actual conditions in which people live. (p. 7)

Based on these criteria and the evidence I present throughout this book, I argue that heterosexism, homo/bi/trans-phobia, hegemonic masculinity, and emphasized femininity are social problems; LGBT families are not.

As the first five chapters of this book have explained, LGBT families have developed out of the coalescing and intersections of specific social, political, economic, and cultural factors and are therefore a product of their time. While LGBT families are more prevalent and visible in society now than ever before, they are also living under political and cultural scrutiny, and facing serious challenges in forming and maintaining themselves. Yet LGBT families are not only surviving, but they are flourishing. So how are LGBT families beneficial to society? This chapter aims to answer that question by providing a summary of what we learn from studying LGBT families and how LGBT families help society in general. The chapter concludes by making recommendations about how families of origin, communities, private and public agencies, and public policies can support LGBT families to ensure that they are as healthy as possible.

Lessons Learned From Studying LGBT Families

This section highlights five main lessons that we learn from *studying* LGBT families. The first lesson is that families in general, including LGBT families, are socially constructed. As explained in Chapter 1, being socially constructed means that how we define family, who we think should be included or not included in our families, the functions of families, and the structure of families, change over time and by geographic location. There is nothing fixed, innate, or natural about families. In other words, what families look like and how we think about them depends on the social and historical context and moment in which we are thinking about them. Understanding families as socially constructed moves us away from the myth that families are based on a biological mandate and helps us understand how people decide what families in their particular societies should consist of. As society, culture, and economics shift, our understanding of, and indeed the shape of, our families shift as well. Therefore, LGBT families are a result of societal shifts and, in turn, have the opportunity to shape society in a variety of ways.

The second lesson we learn is that social categories and definitions are messy. As discussed in Chapter 1 and exemplified throughout the book, the categories we use to define different groups of people are somewhat mythical; or at least their boundaries can be very blurry. What being lesbian, gay, bisexual, or transgender means varies not only based on personal definitions but also on the social and cultural context in which those people live. One might ask why categories are important at all. Sociologist Michael Kimmel (2012) argued that inequality creates difference. In other words, we create categories so that we know to whom to give certain societal benefits (e.g., good education, good jobs, tax breaks, safe communities, leisure time, safety, social legitimacy, etc.) and from whom to deny those benefits. Applied to LGBT people, we like to know who is lesbian, gay, bisexual, transgender, or heterosexual because we want to know who we should value and who we should not. We want to know who should receive certain benefits (e.g., marriage, housing, jobs, safety, respect, etc.) and who should not. Without gender and sexual categories, we would have difficulty knowing who to value more and who to value less; indeed, we would need to value everyone equally. The research I have presented in this book certainly points to the fact that we do not value LGBT people as much as we value heterosexual people in the United States, or around the world. Therefore, the lesson learned is that by studying LGBT families, we realize that the categories we use are problematic, and consequently, we should question why we value some categories of people more than others. Hopefully, that questioning will lead us to a more equal society.

The third lesson we learn from studying LGBT families is that LGBT people are diverse. Throughout this book, I have represented a variety of LGBT people and families. I do not claim to have represented all LGBT families, but most of the time when I did not present information on a specific group of LGBT people or type of family, the omission was due to a lack of available research. What we learn is that we cannot assume that all LGBT families share the same experiences. Differences by race, class, immigration status, age, and a multitude of other factors shape the experiences of all families, including LGBT families. For those interested in researching LGBT families, there remains much work left to do.

The fourth lesson we learn from studying LGBT families is that discrimination makes life harder for all members of the family. Heterosexism, homophobia, sexism, racism, classism, nationalism, and ageism all mean that children, adults, and elderly members of families have to negotiate reduced or lacking resources in ways that privileged heterosexual people and families do not. For example, as discussed in Chapter 2, LGBT families are fighting for marriage equality not only because they want to be part of a legitimate social institution but also because marriage offers 1,138 federal benefits to those who can legally access a marriage license. Because of the June 26, 2013, U.S. Supreme Court Decision in the *United States v. Windsor*, same-sex couples living in one of the 18 states or the District of Columbia that honor marriage equality can access those benefits. However, the millions of same-sex couples living outside those legal jurisdictions cannot. Thus, institutionalized and government-sanctioned discrimination is not only denying rights to millions of American families that heterosexual families have access to, but it is also forcing those families to make difficult choices about how to best support their families because they need to spend their limited resources on legitimizing their families in ways that married heterosexual families do not need to.

The fifth lesson we learn from studying LGBT families is that intimate partner violence (IPV) is not just about gender inequality that exists throughout society but is also about other forms of inequality, such as sexual, racial, and social class inequality. What studying LGBT IPV has forced family and feminist scholars to consider is that IPV is the result of power and control in general, not just one particular form of power and control (i.e., patriarchal). The advantage of taking a broader view is that practitioners and policy makers can work to end a variety of IPV, not just violence against women.

We have much to learn by studying any group of families that sits outside the margins of the dominant family form. Research on African American and Latino families, impoverished families, immigrant families, global families, and other types of families have taught us much about unequal power structures as well as the diverse experiences people have both in the United States and around the world. What we learn about and from LGBT families adds to our knowledge of how discrimination and resilience can lead to new family forms that come out of the social context and more often than not benefit the new social context into which they emerge.

How LGBT Families Benefit Society

Given that LGBT families have risen out of a history of discrimination and resilience, and given that these families have clearly and permanently emerged into and are shaping the current family landscape, this section examines how LGBT families benefit society by strengthening the quality of relationships within families both for adults and children.

LGBT people strengthen the quality of relationships of adults in families (whether married or not) in two major ways. First, LGBT people present a potential model for egalitarian relationships that heterosexual couples can emulate. Research on heterosexual couples shows that many heterosexual women and men strive to live in "peer marriages," or marriages in which husbands and wives share equally in household and child-care responsibilities (Schwartz, 1994). Over the past several decades, heterosexual marriages have indeed been trending toward more equally shared paid and unpaid labor. However, in 2013, married mothers still spent 32 hours per week on household chores and child care, as opposed to 17 hours for married fathers. And married mothers spent only 21 hours per week in the paid labor force, as opposed to the 37 hours that married husbands spent earning a living each week (Parker & Wang, 2013). Thus, although many heterosexual couples, and particularly women, would like to move away from the father/breadwinner-mother/homemaker model, they are still struggling to do so. As discussed in Chapter 3, although research shows that LGBT couples have not perfected equality within their adult partnerships, some LGBT couples offer a potential model for how to develop nongendered ways of sharing household responsibilities. Lesbian couples in particular base such ways of sharing on desire and skills rather than economic earnings and preexisting (and unequal) formulas of how to divide paid and unpaid work among family members.

The second way in which LGBT people strengthen the quality of adult relationships within families is by presenting hope for an increase in stable relationships and a reduction of divorce and separation. The research in this area is new and therefore speculative. However, as discussed in Chapter 2, in Massachusetts—the state with the longest experience with marriage equality thus far—as the numbers of lesbians and gay men getting married has increased, the rate of divorce has held steady. This trend is similar to many of the other states that allow lesbians and gay men to legally marry (Kirk & Rosin, 2012; Kurtzleben, 2011). In other words, the fear that LGBT people will destroy the institution of marriage is unfounded and untrue. In addition, the fight for marriage equality has brought much attention to the personal and social benefits of marriage. Therefore, for those who believe that marriage is an institution worth saving, evidence suggests that particularly those LGBT people within the marriage equality movement are helping with that mission.

In addition to benefiting the quality of adult relationships, LGBT families—most specifically LGBT parents and grandparents—are good for children. As the number of LGBT adults become parents, the number of intentional parents also increases. Therefore, LGBT parents present a way of reducing the number of accidental pregnancies, unplanned pregnancies, and unwanted births. The result of increased intentional parenting could possibly mean a decreased need for abortions and foster or adoption services. In addition to the potential benefits of intentional pregnancies, LGBT parents are good for children in terms of adoption. LGBT parents are more likely to adopt children, particularly children of color and children with special needs, thus helping to relieve the burden placed on social services to find good, stable homes for a large number of currently disadvantaged children born from unplanned pregnancies.

Once in LGBT families, children of LGBT parents are at least as emotionally and mentally healthy as children of heterosexual couples, even when faced with discrimination against their families. Children of LGBT parents are also less likely to experience sexual molestation from either their fathers or mothers than they would if they had heterosexual parents. Moreover, children in step or blended LGBT families are more likely to find their stepparents to be more patient and flexible and less controlling than children who have heterosexual stepparents. Those same children of LGBT parents and stepparents are more likely to grow up in households that teach about accepting people who are different from themselves. And if children are fortunate to have LGBT grandparents, the children will most likely find that their grandparents can help them make sense of issues concerning gender and sexuality that often occupy the minds of children.

In addition to being good for the adults and children in families, LGBT families are good for children and society in general. Through their gender and sexual expressions, many LGBT parents, grandparents, and youth help challenge hegemonic masculinity and emphasized femininity that cause much emotional and physical violence in the world. As Kimmel (2012) explained, the most violent societies are ones in which the ideals and practices of hegemonic masculinity are similar to those in the United States. LGBT men in particular offer a variety of masculinities that may be less violent than the dominant masculinity offered by the current heterosexual model. Therefore, for the LGBT children in the world who are wading through a fearful and difficult adolescence, LGBT families and parents offer much hope that life indeed does get better. And LGBT parents often serve as positive role models and offer an important support network for LGBT youth and their parents who are trying to make sense of budding gender and sexual identities that do not fit into hegemonic ideals.

In short, how do LGBT families benefit society? They do so by presenting a new model of equality into an ever-changing and revered institution historically based on inequality; they offer children safe, stable, secure, and healthy homes in which to thrive; and they offer LGBT children—and indeed all children—a vision of and pathway to a less violent and more inclusive world.

Suggestions for Strengthening LGBT Families

Because we can learn from studying LGBT families and because LGBT families benefit society, we have much to gain from supporting LGBT families and helping them grow. This section highlights a few key policy areas that could help alleviate some of the problems facing LGBT families and thus strengthen LGBT families. As mentioned throughout the book, most problems that LGBT people face both in the United States and around the world are due to heterosexism, homo/bi/trans-phobia, and dominant gender norms that define masculinity and femininity in ways that leave little if any room for variation. Recently, the United Nations recognized this point by naming May 13 the International Day Against Homophobia. The purpose of creating such a day was to issue a yearly "call on Governments worldwide to protect the rights of lesbian, gay, bisexual and transgender (LGBT) individuals, and strike laws that discriminate against them" (United Nations, 2013). Following the lead of the United Nations, this concluding section to my book is a call to community members and policy makers particularly in the United States, but certainly not excluding those worldwide, to help support LGBT families.

To legitimate and fully support LGBT families, we need full marriage equality throughout the United States and beyond. Marriage equality cannot rely on "geographic happenstance" (Kendell, 1998) such that where an LGBT couple lives determines what benefits they might receive. Marriage equality must exist at both state and federal levels for everyone, regardless of the state in which one lives. The benefits of marriage equality need to be enforced throughout all social institutions, such that schools, workplaces, elder care facilities, courts, police, and other officials and agencies honor the rights of LGBT family members. And recognizing that not all families contain couples and not all adults want to marry, policy makers need to either expand marriage or create new systems (perhaps by expanding or bolstering civil unions) to include the diversity of families that exist, regardless of gender and sexual identities, of family structure, or of marital status.

In addition, policies and practices should facilitate processes to help LGBT people foster, adopt, and birth children. This means that states such as Utah and Mississippi that specifically ban LGBT people from adopting, and other states such as Florida that make adoption particularly difficult, need to revisit and reverse their laws. Furthermore, adoption agencies need to provide training so that their workers can more effectively work with prospective LGBT parents. Similarly, fertility specialists and sperm banks should be encouraged to work with potential LGBT parents who want to have biologically connected children. And if insurance policies cover infertile heterosexual people, then they should also cover LGBT people who are technically fertile but need access to sperm and/or egg through infertility treatments and sperm banks.

Regarding LGBT children, all states should institute, implement, and enforce pro-LGBT curriculum in their public schools, as well as strong anti-bullying programs, such as the state of New Jersey's Anti-Bullying Bill of Rights Act. This bill states,

> Each school district shall adopt a policy prohibiting harassment, intimidation or bullying on school property, at a school-sponsored function or on a school bus. The school district shall adopt the policy through a process that includes representation of parents or guardians, school employees, volunteers, students, administrators, and community representatives. (Anti-bullying Bill of Rights Act, March 2012 Amendment, p. 1)

The bill specifically defines harassment, intimidation, or bullying to include

> any gesture, any written, verbal or physical act, or any electronic communication, whether it be a single incident or a series of incidents, that is reasonably perceived as being motivated either by any actual or perceived characteristic, such as race, color, religion, ancestry, national origin, gender, *sexual orientation, gender identity and expression* [emphasis added], or a mental, physical or sensory disability, or by any other distinguishing characteristic, that takes place on school property, at any school sponsored function, on a school bus, or off school grounds. (Anti-bullying Bill of Rights Act, 2012, P.L. 2010, p. 2, no. 7)

In order to comply with the Anti-bullying Act, public schools around New Jersey have held trainings and have specific school personnel assigned to anti-bullying programs. Other states should follow suit.

In addition to educating school administrators, teachers, students, and community members, each state needs to educate youth services about how best to support LGBT youth when in crisis situations or foster care, or when entering juvenile detention facilities. The issue of detention facilities is particularly crucial for transgender children who need to work with a trained professional who can determine whether the state should place the child in a facility that suits their gender identity or their biological sex. Social workers in all settings should receive specific training as well, to help them work more effectively with LGBT youth.

Other than youth facilities, adult care facilities should also implement such training so that elderly LGBT adults do not need to return to the closet or be separated from their life partners when entering the last stages of their lives. Helping LGBT elders live and die with dignity is critical to their mental well-being and requires specific training and policies to both sensitize staff and enforce rules that support elderly LGBT people.

In addition to supporting elderly LGBT people, we must also work to help the significant number of LGBT people who experience IPV in their lives. I list here some recommendations on how to help victims and survivors of LGBT IPV. I have borrowed many of these recommendations (as indicated) from the National Coalition of Anti-Violence Programs (NCAVP, 2012) and Duke and Davidson (2009):

- Congress must continue to support VAWA and make the act as inclusive as possible so as not to exclude any group of people based on their race, class, gender, sexual, immigrant, or other status/identity;
- Federal, state, and local governments must increase funding on all levels to support "LGBTQH-specific anti-violence programs, particularly for survivor-led initiatives" (NCAVP, 2012);
- Public and private agencies should provide adequate training to their staff in order to more effectively help and support victim service providers and IPV survivors;
- Local police should provide training to their officers on how best to respond to LGBT IPV calls;
- All groups—public and private—should work to raise public awareness within LGBT and heterosexual communities about the prevalence of LGBT IPV;
- In order to gain a more accurate understanding of the prevalence and nature of IPV, researchers and government agencies should collect reliable information and data on LGBT IPV through a variety of methodological means;
- Extended families, friends, and community members (both LGBT and heterosexual) must work at recognizing, identifying, and holding responsible people who are violent or abusive in their relationship with a LGBT friend, family member, or acquaintance.

By thinking about IPV as only a woman's issue created by patriarchal terror and by shying away from recognizing IPV within LGBT communities, the problem of LGBT IPV will fester and increase. By understanding the complexities surrounding and the specific needs of LGBT people, government and private organizations on federal, state, and local levels, as well as community members, friends, and families, can work to help those LGBT people in need, and perhaps even work toward eradicating the problem.

Sociologist Alan Johnson (2008) wrote that if you want to solve social problems and create positive change, you need to first recognize the problem as being social. Moving the discussion from blaming LGBT families for social problems to understanding how societies build heteronormativity into laws, policies, and practices is a good first step to understanding the social nature of problems plaguing LGBT families. Johnson also says that in order to create change, two separate but related actions need to occur. First, we need to change social systems. The suggestions I have offered above aim at doing just that. When we change and enforce laws, when we implement training programs, when social institutions change their policies, then we change social systems. Second, and equally important, Johnson tells us, we need to change how people participate in social systems. This means that we need to change the hearts and minds of people so that rather than feeling threatened by LGBT people and their families, they recognize the benefits that LGBT people and their families provide to society. Therefore, we need to educate people so that they do not simply base their opinions on myths and misguided beliefs. As my sister stated in the quote above, if people knew what many LGBT families are really like, they would not feel threatened by those families. In fact, people might actually rally to support LGBT families.

By understanding the research and data, and simply by interacting with a variety of LGBT people and seeing how they organize and run their families, people can begin to think critically about issues and base their opinions on real evidence and knowledge. I hope this book provides such evidence and knowledge, so people can begin to understand the lives and experiences of LGBT people, the value of LGBT families, and the laws, policies, and practices that often make the lives of LGBT families so very difficult. By changing laws, policies, and practices, we have the power to help LGBT people and their families live with the dignity, respect, and rights they deserve. Once we truly support LGBT families, we create a better quality of relationships within families. Rather than focusing on the structure of families, we should focus on the quality of relationships within those families. By doing so, we will find that families with quality relationships contribute to society in ways that help reduce social problems and strengthen the larger family landscape.

References

ABA Commission on Domestic Violence. (n.d.). *Civil protection orders for LGBT victims of domestic violence: Relevant case summaries.* Retrieved from http://www.americanbar.org/groups/domestic_violence.html

Adoption.org. (n.d.). Adoption in Australia. Retrieved July 14, 2013, from http://www.adoption.org/adopt/adoption-in-australia.php

Advocate.com. (2010, July 14). Thomas Beatie's third child due. *Advocate.com.* Retrieved July 12, 2013, from http://www.advocate.com/news/daily-news/2010/07/24/thomas-beaties-third-child-due

Agigian, A. (2004). *Baby steps: How lesbian alternative insemination is changing the world.* Middletown, CT: Wesleyan University Press. Retrieved from http://www.amazon.com/Baby-Steps-Alternative-Insemination-Changing/dp/0819566306

Ahrons, C. (2007). No easy answers: Why the popular view of divorce is wrong. In S. J. Ferguson (Ed.), *Shifting the center: Understanding contemporary families* (3rd ed., pp. 523–534). Boston, MA: McGraw-Hill Higher Education.

Allen, J. (1983). The annihilation of women. In J. Trebilcot (Ed.), *Mothering: Essays in feminist theory* (pp. 315–330). Totowa, NJ: Rowman & Littlefield.

Allen, K. R., & Demo, D. H. (1995). Families of lesbians and gay men. *Journal of Marriage and Family, 57*(1), 111–127.

Almeling, R. (2007). Selling genes, selling gender: Egg agencies, sperm banks, and the medical market in genetic material. *American Sociological Review, 72*(3), 319–340. doi:10.1177/000312240707200301

American Psychiatric Association. (2013). Gender dysphoria. Arlington, VA: Author. Retrieved from http://www.psychiatry.org/

American Psychological Association (APA). (2008). *Answers to your questions: For a better understanding of sexual orientation and homosexuality.* Washington, DC: Author. Retrieved from www.apa.org/topics/sorientation.pdf

American Psychological Association (APA). (2011). *Answers to your questions about transgender people, gender identity, and gender expression.* Washington, DC: Author. Retrieved from http://www.apa.org/topics/sexuality/transgender.pdf

American Psychological Association (APA). (2013). Guidelines for Psychological Practice with Lesbian, Gay, and Bisexual Clients. Retrieved July 10, 2013, from http://www.apa.org/pi/lgbt/resources/guidelines.aspx

American Society for Reproductive Medicine. (2011). Assisted reproductive technologies. Birmingham, AL: Author. Retrieved from http://www.asrm.org/uploadedFiles/ASRM_Content/Resources/Patient_Resources/Fact_Sheets_and_Info_Booklets/ART.pdf

Andersen, M. L., & Witham, D. H. (2011). *Thinking about women: Sociological perspectives on sex and gender* (9th ed.). Boston, MA: Allyn & Bacon.

Anthony, D. J. (2012). Caught in the middle: Transsexual marriage and the disconnect between sex and legal sex. *Texas Journal of Women & the Law, 21*(2), 153–186.

Anti-bullying Bill of Rights Act. Anti-bullying Bill of Rights Act, March 2012 Amendment (2012). Retrieved from http://www.njleg.state.nj.us/2012/Bills/PL12/1_.PDF

Appell, A. R. (2012). Legal issues in lesbian and gay adoption. In D. M. Brodzinsky & A. Pertman (Eds.), *Adoption by lesbians and gay men: A new dimension in family diversity* (pp. 36–61). New York, NY: Oxford University Press.

Ard, K. L., & Makadon, H. J. (2011). Addressing intimate partner violence in lesbian, gay, bisexual, and transgender patients. *Journal of General Internal Medicine, 26*(8), 630–633. doi:10.1007/s11606-011-1697-6

Ausbrooks, A. R., & Russell, A. (2011). Gay and lesbian family building: A strengths perspective of transracial adoption. *Journal of GLBT Family Studies, 7*(3), 201–216. doi:10.1080/1550428X.2011.564936

Baca Zinn, M., Eitzen, D. S., & Wells, B. (2011). *Diversity in families* (9th ed.). Boston, MA: Allyn & Bacon.

Badgett, M. V. L. (2011). Separated and not equal: Binational same-sex couples. *Signs, 36*(4), 793–798.

Baker, M. (2001). Unconditional love. In P. W. Freeman & S. L. Windmeyer (Eds.), *Secret sisters: Stories of being lesbian and bisexual in a college sorority* (pp. 151–159). Los Angeles, CA: Alyson Books. Retrieved from http://www.amazon.com/Secret-Sisters-Stories-Bisexual-Sorority/dp/1555835880

Balsam, K. F., Rothblum, E. D., & Beauchaine, T. P. (2005). Victimization over the life span: A comparison of lesbian, gay, bisexual, and heterosexual siblings. *Journal of Consulting and Clinical Psychology, 73*, 477–487.

Balsam, K. F., & Szymanski, D. M. (2005). Relationship quality and domestic violence in women's same-sex relationships: The role of minority stress. *Psychology of Women Quarterly, 29*(3), 258–269. doi:10.1111/j.1471-6402.2005.00220.x

Barret, R. L., & Robinson, B. E. (2000). *Gay fathers: Encouraging the hearts of gay dads and their families* (New & Rev.). San Francisco, CA: Jossey-Bass. Retrieved from http://www.barnesandnoble.com/w/gay-fathers-robert-l-barret/111176533 5?ean=9780787950750

Barrett, B. J., & St. Pierre, M. (2013). Intimate partner violence reported by lesbian-, gay-, and bisexual-identified individuals living in Canada: An exploration of within-group variations. *Journal of Gay & Lesbian Social Services, 25*(1), 1–23. doi:10.1080/10538720.2013.751887

Beatie, T. (2008, March 13). Labor of love: Is society ready for this pregnant husband? *Advocate.com*. Retrieved July 12, 2013, from http://www.advocate.com/news/2008/03/14/labor-love?page=0,0

Benestad, E. (2009). Addressing the disturbed, like ripples in the water: Intervention with the social networks of children who transe. *Sexual and Relationship Therapy, 24*(2), 207–216.

Bennett, M., & Battle, J. (2001). "We can see them, but we can't hear them": LGBT members of African American families. In M. Berenstein & R. Reimann (Eds.), *Queer families, Queer politics: Challenging culture and the state* (pp. 53–67). New York, NY: Columbia University Press.

Benson, A. L., Silverstein, L. B., & Auerbach, C. F. (2005). From the margins to the center: Gay fathers reconstruct the fathering role. *Journal of GLBT Family Studies, 1*(3), 1–29. doi:10.1300/J461v01n03

Bergman, K., Rubio, R. J., Green, R.-J., & Padrón, E. (2010). Gay men who become fathers via surrogacy: The transition to parenthood. *Journal of GLBT Family Studies, 6*(2), 111–141. doi:10.1080/15504281003704942

Berkowitz, D. (2013). Gay men and surrogacy. In A. E. Goldberg & K. R. Allen (Eds.), *LGBT-parent families: Innovations in research and implications for practice* (pp. 71–85). New York, NY: Springer.

Berkowitz, D., & Marsiglio, W. (2007). Gay men: Negotiating procreative, father, and family identities. *Journal of Marriage and Family, 69*(2), 366–381. doi:10.1111/j.1741-3737.2007.00371.x

Bernstein, J., & Stephenson, L. (1995). Dykes, donors & dry ice: Alternative insemination. In K. Arnup (Ed.), *Lesbian parenting: Living with pride & prejudice* (pp. 3–15). Charlottetown, Prince Edward Island, Canada: Gynergy Books.

Biblarz, T. J., & Savci, E. (2010). Lesbian, gay, bisexual, and transgender families. *Journal of Marriage and Family, 72*(3), 480–497. doi:10.1111/j.1741-3737.2010.00714.x

Biblarz, T. J., & Stacey, J. (2010). How does the gender of parents matter? *Journal of Marriage and Family, 72*(1), 3–22. doi:10.1111/j.1741-3737.2009.00678.x

Black, D., Gates, G., Sanders, S., & Taylor, L. (2000, May). Demographics of the gay and lesbian population in the United States: Evidence from available systematic data sources. *Demography, 37*(2), 139–154.

Blankenhorn, D. (1991). American family dilemmas. In D. Blankenhorn, S. Bayme, & J. B. Elshtain (Eds.), *Rebuilding the nest: A new commitment to the American family* (pp. 3–25). Milwaukee, WI: Family Service America. Retrieved from http://www.amazon.com/Rebuilding-Nest-Commitment-American-Family/dp/0873042425

Blankenhorn, D. (1996). *Fatherless America: Confronting our most urgent social problem.* New York, NY: Harper Perennial.

Bockting, W. O. (2009). Transforming the paradigm of transgender health: A field in transition. *Sexual & Relationship Therapy, 24*(2), 103–107. doi:10.1080/14681990903037660

Boggis, T. (2001). Affording our families: Class issues in family formation. In M. Bernstein & R. Reimann (Eds.), *Queer families, queer politics* (pp. 175–181). New York, NY: Columbia University Press.

Bonilla-Silva, E. (2009). *Racism without racists: Color-blind racism and the persistence of racial inequality in America* (p. 318). Lanham, MD: Rowman & Littlefield.

Retrieved from http://www.amazon.com/Racism-without-Racists-Color-Blind-Persistence/dp/1442202181

Bos, H. (2010). Planned gay father families in kinship arrangements. *The Australian and New Zealand Journal of Family Therapy*, 31(4), 356–371.

Bos, H., & Gartrell, N. (2010). Adolescents of the USA National Longitudinal Lesbian Family Study: Can family characteristics counteract the negative effects of stigmatization? *Family Process*, 49(4), 559–572. doi:10.1111/j.1545-5300.2010.01340.x

Boyer, C. A. (2007). The impact of adoption issues on gay and lesbian adoptive parents. In R. A. Javier, A. L. Baden, F. A. Biafora, & A. Camacho-Gingerich (Eds.), *The handbook of adoption* (pp. 228–241). Thousand Oaks, CA: Sage.

Boykin, K. (1997). *One more river to cross: Black & gay in America*. New York, NY: Anchor Books. Retrieved from http://www.amazon.com/One-More-River-Cross-America/dp/0385479832

Bozett, F. W. (1987). *Gay and lesbian parents*. Westport, CT: Praeger. Retrieved from http://www.amazon.com/Gay-Lesbian-Parents-Frederick-Bozett/dp/0275923703

Breshears, D. (2011). Understanding communication between lesbian parents and their children regarding outsider discourse about family identity. *Journal of GLBT Family Studies*, 7(3), 264–284. doi:10.1080/1550428X.2011.564946

Brewer, P. R. (2008). The shifting foundations of public opinion about gay rights. *The Journal of Politics*, 65(04), 1208–1220. doi:10.1111/1468-2508.t01-1-00133

Brodzinsky, D. M. (2012). Adoptions by lesbians and gay men: A national survey of adoption agency policies and practices. In D. M. Brodzinsky & A. Pertman (Eds.), *Adoption by lesbians and gay men: A new dimension in family diversity* (pp. 62–84). New York, NY: Oxford University Press.

Brown, M. L., & Rounsley, C. A. (1996). *True selves: Understanding transsexualism—For families, friends, coworkers, and helping professionals*. San Francisco, CA: Jossey-Bass. Retrieved from http://www.amazon.com/True-Selves-Understanding-Transsexualism-For-Professionals/dp/0787967025

Brown, N. (2011). Holding tensions of victimization and perpetration. In J. L. Ristock (Ed.), *Intimate partner violence in LGBTQ lives* (pp. 153–168). New York, NY: Routledge.

Brown, S., Smalling, S., Groza, V., & Ryan, S. (2009). The experiences of gay men and lesbians in becoming and being adoptive parents. *Adoption Quarterly*, 12(3–4), 229–246. doi:10.1080/10926750903313294

Browning, F. (2004). Why marry? In A. Sullivan (Ed.), *Same-sex marriage: Pro and con a reader* (pp. 132–134). New York, NY: Vintage Books.

Burleson, W. (2005). *Bi America: Myths, truths, and struggles of an invisible community*. New York, NY: Harrington Park Press. Retrieved from http://www.amazon.com/Bi-America-Struggles-Invisible-Community/dp/1560234792

Burnett, J. A. (2005). Use of assisted reproductive technologies in gay and lesbian couples: What counselors need to know. *Journal of LGBT Issues in Counseling*, 1(1), 115–125. doi:10.1300/J462v01n01_08

Butler, J. (1993). Imitation and gender subordination. In H. Abelove, M. A. Barale, & D. M. Halperin (Eds.), *The lesbian and gay studies reader* (pp. 307–320). New York, NY: Routledge.

Buxton, A. P. (2006). A family matter: When a spouse comes out as gay, lesbian, or bisexual. In J. J. Bigner (Ed.), *Introduction to GLBT family studies* (pp. 67–87). New York, NY: The Haworth Press. Retrieved from http://www.amazon.com/Introduction-Family-Studies-Haworth-Series/dp/0789024977

Byard, E., Kosciw, J., & Barkiewicz, M. (2013). Schools and LGBT-parent families: Creating change through programming and advocacy. In A. E. Goldberg & K. R. Allen (Eds.), *LGBT-parent families: Innovations in research and implications for practice* (pp. 275–290). New York, NY: Springer.

Cahill, S. (2004). *Same-sex marriage in the United States: Focus on the facts* (Post 2004 election ed.). Lanham, MD: Lexington Books.

Cahill, S., & Tobias, D. S. (2007). *Policy issues affecting lesbian, gay, bisexual, and transgender families*. Ann Arbor: University of Michigan Press. Retrieved from http://www.amazon.com/Affecting-Lesbian-Bisexual-Transgender-Families/dp/0472030612

Calvo, K., & Trujillo, G. (2011). Fighting for love rights: Claims and strategies of the LGBT movement in Spain. *Sexualities, 14*(5), 562–579.

Cantor, M. H., Brennan, M., & Shippy, R. A. (2004). *Caregiving among older lesbian, gay, bisexual, and transgender New Yorkers*. New York, NY. Retrieved from http://www.thetaskforce.org/downloads/reports/reports/CaregivingAmongOlderLGBT.pdf

Cantú, L. (2009). *The sexuality of migration*. (N. A. Naples & S. Vidal-Ortiz, Eds.). New York: New York University Press.

Card, C. (1996). Against marriage and motherhood. *Hypatia, 11*(3), 1–23.

Card, C. (2007). Gay divorce: Thoughts on the legal regulation of marriage. *Hypatia, 22*(1), 24–38. doi:10.1353/hyp.2006.0059

Carrington, C. (1999). *No place like home: Relationships and family life among lesbians and gay men*. Chicago, IL: University Of Chicago Press. Retrieved from http://www.amazon.com/No-Place-Like-Home-Relationships/dp/0226094863

Carvalho, A. F., Lewis, R. J., Derlega, V. J., Winstead, B. A., & Viggiano, C. (2011). Internalized sexual minority stressors and same-sex intimate partner violence. *Journal of Family Violence, 26*(7), 501–509. doi:10.1007/s10896-011-9384-2

Chabot, J. M. (1998). *Transition to parenthood: Lesbian couples' experiences with donor insemination*. Unpublished doctoral dissertation, Michigan State University, Ann Arbor.

Chabot, J. M., & Ames, B. D. (2004). "It wasn't 'let's get pregnant and go do it'": Decision making in lesbian couples planning motherhood via donor insemination. *Family Relations, 53*(4), 348–356. doi:10.1111/j.0197-6664.2004.00041.x

Chamie, J., & Mirkin, B. (2011). Same-sex marriage: A new social phenomenon. *Population and Development Review, 37*(3), 529–551. Retrieved from http://www.ncbi.nlm.nih.gov/pubmed/22167814

Chauncey, G. (2004). *Why marriage?: The history shaping today's debate over gay equality*. New York, NY: Basic Books.

Cherlin, A. J. (2003). Should the government promote gay marriage? *Contexts, 2*(4), 22–29. doi:10.1525/.2003.2.4.22

Cherlin, A. J. (2004). The deinstitutionalization of American marriage. *Journal of Marriage and Family*, 66(4), 848–861. Retrieved from http://doi.wiley.com/10.1111/j.0022-2445.2004.00058.x

Cherlin, A. J. (2010). One thousand and forty nine reasons why it's hard to know when a fact is a fact. In B. J. Risman (Ed.), *Families as they really are* (pp. 10–14). New York, NY: W. W. Norton.

Child Welfare Information Gateway. (2011). *How many children were adopted in 2007 and 2008?* Washington, DC. Retrieved from https://www.childwelfare.gov/pubs/adopted0708.pdf

Chonody, J. M., Smith, K. S., & Litle, M. A. (2012). Legislating unequal treatment: An exploration of public policy on same-sex marriage. *Journal of GLBT Family Studies*, 8(3), 270–286. doi:10.1080/1550428X.2012.677238

Chung, G., Oswald, R. F., & Wiley, A. (2006). Good daughters good daughters: Three different ways of being Korean American queer women. *Journal of GLBT Family Studies*, 2(2), 101–124. doi:10.1300/J461v02n02_05

Cianciotto, J. (2005). *Hispanic and Latino same-sex couple households in the United States*. Washington, DC. Retrieved from http://www.thetaskforce.org/downloads/reports/reports/HispanicLatinoHouseholdsUS.pdf

Claasen, C. (2005). *Whistling women: A study of the lives of older lesbians*. Binghamton, NY: Haworth Press.

Clifford, D., Hertz, F., & Doskow, E. (2007). *A legal guide for lesbian and gay couples*. Berkeley, CA: Nolo. Retrieved from http://books.google.com/books/about/A_Legal_Guide_for_Lesbian_and_Gay_Couple.html?id=eiSFx_Fm-FcC&pgis=1

Cloud, J. (2005). The battle over gay teens. *Time Magazine*. Retrieved from http://content.time.com/time/magazine/article/0,9171,1112856,00.html

CNN. (2014, February 25). Uganda's President Museveni signs controversial anti-gay bill into law. *CNN.com*. Retrieved from http://www.cnn.com/2014/02/24/world/africa/uganda-anti-gay-bill

Cohen-Kettenis, P., Delemarre-van de Waal, H., & Gooren, L. (2008). The treatment of adolescent transsexuals: Changing insights. *Journal of Sexual Medicine*, 5, 1892–1897. doi:10.1111/j.1743-6109.2008.00870.x

Coker, T. R., Austin, S. B., & Schuster, M. A. (2010). The health and health care of lesbian, gay, and bisexual adolescents. *Annual Review of Public Health*, 31, 457–477. doi:10.1146/annurev.publhealth.012809.103636

Collins, P. H. (1990). *Black feminist thought: Knowledge, consciousness, and the politics of empowerment*. Cambridge, MA: Unwin Hyman. Retrieved from http://www.amazon.com/Black-Feminist-Thought-Consciousness-Empowerment/dp/0415964725

Coltrane, S. (1989). Household labor and the routine production of gender. *Social Problems*, 36(5), 473–490.

Coltrane, S. (2007). Fathering: Paradoxes, contradictions, and dilemmas. In S. J. Ferguson (Ed.), *Shifting the center: Understanding contemporary families* (3rd ed., pp. 416–431). Boston, MA: McGraw-Hill Higher Education.

Comstock, G. D. (1991). *Violence against lesbians and gay men*. New York, NY: Columbia University Press.

Congressional Budget Office. (2013). *Dual-eligible beneficiaries of medicare and medicaid: Characteristics, health care spending, and evolving policies*. Washington,

D.C. Retrieved from http://www.cbo.gov/sites/default/files/cbofiles/attachments/ 44308_DualEligibles.pdf

Connell, R. W. (1987). *Gender and power: Society, the person, and sexual politics* (1st ed.). Palo Alto, CA: Stanford University Press. Retrieved from http://www .amazon.com/Gender-Power-Society-Person-Politics/dp/0804714304

Connolly, C. M. (2006). Process of change: The intersection of the GLBT individual and his or her family of origin. In J. J. Bigner (Ed.), *An introduction to GLBT family studies* (pp. 5–22). Binghamton, NY: Haworth Press.

Cook-Daniels, L. (2008). Birthing new life. In M. Boenke (Ed.), *Trans forming families: Real stories about transgendered loved ones* (pp. 136–140). Washington, DC: PFLAG Transgender Network.

Coontz, S. (1993). *The way we never were: American families and the nostalgia trap.* New York, NY: Basic Books. Retrieved from http://books.google.com/books/ about/The_Way_We_Never_Were.html?id=DTqj0OPRSkUC&pgis=1

Coontz, S. (2005). *Marriage, a history.* New York, NY: Viking.

Coontz, S. (2007). Historical perspectives on family diversity. In S. J. Ferguson (Ed.), *Shifting the center: Understanding contemporary families* (3rd ed., pp. 63–80). Boston, MA: McGraw-Hill Higher Education.

Cott, N. F. (2002). *Public vows: The history of marriage and the nation.* Cambridge, MA: Harvard University Press.

Crozier, P. (2012). Parental rights after relationship dissolution. In J. L. Levi & E. E. Monnin-Browder (Eds.), *Transgender family law: A guide to effective advocacy* (pp. 105–130). Bloomington, IN: AuthorHouse.

Current-Juretschko, L., & Bigner, J. J. (2005). An exploratory investigation of gay stepfathers' perceptions of their role. *Journal of GLBT Family Studies, 1*(4), 1–20. doi:10.1300/J461v01n04_01

D'Amico, E., & Julien, D. (2012). Disclosure of sexual orientation and gay, lesbian, and bisexual youths' adjustment: Associations with past and current parental acceptance and rejection. *Journal of GLBT Family Studies, 8*(3), 215–242. doi:10.1080/1550428X.2012.677232

D'Augelli, A. R. (2002). Mental health problems among lesbian, gay, and bisexual youths ages 14 to 21. *Clinical Child Psychology and Psychiatry, 7,* 439–462.

D'Augelli, A. R., Grossman, A. H., Starks, M. T., & Sinclair, K. O. (2010). Factors associated with parents' knowledge of gay, lesbian, and bisexual youths' sexual orientation. *Journal of GLBT Family Studies, 6*(2), 178–198. doi:10.1080/15504281003705410

D'Emilio, J. (1983). *Sexual politics, sexual communities: The making of a homosexual minority in the United States, 1940–1970.* Chicago, IL: University of Chicago Press.

D'Emilio, J. (1998). *Sexual politics, sexual communities* (2nd ed.). Chicago, IL: University Of Chicago Press. Retrieved from http://www.amazon.com/Sexual-Politics-Communities-Second-Edition/dp/0226142671

D'Emilio, J. (2007). Will the courts set us free? Reflections on the campaign for same-sex marriage. In C. A. Rimmerman & C. Wilcox (Eds.), *The politics of same-sex marriage* (pp. 39–64). Chicago, IL: University Of Chicago Press.

Dang, A., & Frazer, S. (2005). Found—85,000 Black gay households. *The Gay and Lesbian Review Worldwide, 12*(1), 29–30.

Dang, A., & Vianney, C. (2007). *Living in the margins: A national survey of lesbian, gay, bisexual and transgender Asian and Pacific Islander Americans.* Washington, DC. Retrieved from http://www.thetaskforce.org/downloads/reports/reports/API_ExecutiveSummaryEnglish.pdf

De Sutter, P. (2001). DEBATE—Continued gender reassignment and assisted reproduction: Present and future options to transsexual people. *Human Reproduction,* 16(4), 612–614.

De Sutter, P. (2009). Reproductive options for transpeople: Recommendations for revision of the WPATH's standards of care. *International Journal of Transgenderism,* 11, 183–185. doi:10.1080/15532730903383765

De Sutter, P., Kira, K., Verschoor, A., & Hotimsky, A. (2002). The desire to have children and the preservation of fertility in transsexual women: A survey. *International Journal of Transgenderism,* 6(3), 1–12.

De Vries, A. L. C., Steensma, T. D., Doreleijers, T. A., & Cohen-Kettenis, P. T. (2011). Puberty suppression in adolescents with gender identity disorder: A prospective follow-up study. *The Journal of Sexual Medicine,* 8(8), 1–8. doi:10.1111/j.1743-6109.2010.01943.x

Demo, D. H. (1992). Parent-child relations: Assessing recent changes. *Journal of Marriage and Family,* 54(1), 104–117.

Dill, B. T. (1994). Fictive kin, paper sons, and compadrazgo: Women of color and the struggle for family survival. In M. Baca Zinn & B. T. Dill (Eds.), *Women of color in the U.S.* (pp. 149–169). Philadelphia, PA: Temple University Press.

Dill, B. T., Baca Zinn, M., & Patton, S. (1998). Valuing families differently: Race, poverty and welfare reform. *Sage Race Relations,* 23(3), 5–30.

Doherty, W. J. (2006). Forward. In J. J. Bigner (Ed.), *Haworth Series in GLBT Family Studies (GLBTFS): An introduction to GLBT family studies* (pp. xvii–xxiii). New York, NY: Haworth Press.

Donoghue, E. (2009). Go on, you choose: The ethics of getting pregnant by nagging. In R. Epstein (Ed.), *Who's your daddy?: And other writings on queer parenting* (pp. 47–52). Toronto, Canada: Sumach Press.

Donovan, C., & Hester, M. (2011). Exploring emotion work in domestically abusive relationships. In J. L. Ristock (Ed.), *Intimate partner violence in LGBTQ lives* (pp. 81–101). New York, NY: Routledge.

Donovan, C., & Wilson, A. (2008). Imagination and integrity: Decision-making among lesbian couples to use medically provided donor insemination. *Culture, Health & Sexuality,* 10(7), 649–665.

Douglas, E. M., & Hines, D. A. (2011). The helpseeking experiences of men who sustain intimate partner violence: An overlooked population and implications for practice. *Journal of Family Violence,* 26(6), 473–485. doi:10.1007/s10896-011-9382-4

Downing, J. B. (2013). Transgender-parent families. In A. E. Goldberg & K. R. Allen (Eds.), *LGBT-parent families: Innovations in research and implications for practice* (pp. 105–115). New York, NY: Springer.

Downing, J. B., & Goldberg, A. E. (2011). Lesbian mothers' constructions of the division of paid and unpaid labor. *Feminism & Psychology,* 21(1), 100–120. doi:10.1177/0959353510375869

Downing, J., Richardson, H., Kinkler, L., & Goldberg, A. (2009). Making the decision: Factors influencing gay men's choice of an adoption path. *Adoption Quarterly*, *12*(3–4), 247–271. doi:10.1080/10926750903313310

Downs, A. C., & James, S. E. (2006). Gay, lesbian, and bisexual foster parents: Strengths and challenges for the child welfare system. *Child Welfare*, *85*(2), 281–298. doi:0009-4021/2006/030281-18

Dudley, M. C., & Nolan, A. (2013). *United States v. Windsor. Legal Information Institute*. Retrieved November 27, 2013, from http://www.law.cornell.edu/supct/cert/12-307

Duke, A., & Davidson, M. M. (2009). Same-sex intimate partner violence: Lesbian, gay, and bisexual affirmative outreach and advocacy. *Journal of Aggression, Maltreatment & Trauma*, *18*(8), 795–816. doi:10.1080/10926770903291787

Dunne, G. A. (2000). Opting into motherhood: Lesbians blurring the boundaries and transforming the meaning of parenthood and kinship. *Gender & Society*, *4*(1), 11–35. doi:10.1177/089124300014001003

Durish, P. (2011). Documenting the Same-Sex Abuse Project, Toronto, Canada. In J. L. Ristock (Ed.), *Intimate partner violence in LGBTQ lives* (pp. 232–257). New York, NY: Routledge.

Dworkin, A. S. (2000). Bisexual histories in San Francisco in the 1970s and early 1980s. *Journal of Bisexuality*, *1*(1), 87–119. doi:10.1300/J159v01n0107

Eady, A., Ross, L. E., Epstein, R., & Anderson, S. (2009). To bi or not to bi: Bisexuality and disclosure in the adoption system. In R. Epstein (Ed.), *Who's your daddy?: And other writings on queer parenting* (pp. 124–132). Toronto, Canada: Sumach Press.

Eckholm, E. (2012, November 27). Gay "conversion therapy" faces tests in courts. *NYTimes.com*. Retrieved from http://www.nytimes.com/2012/11/28/us/gay-conversion-therapy-faces-tests-in-courts.html?pagewanted=all

Eckstut, M. E. (2008). Assisted reproductive technologies. *The Georgetown Journal of Gender and the Law*, *IX*(III), 1153–1182.

Eitzen, D. S., Baca Zinn, M., & Smith, K. E. (2011). *Social problems, census update* (12th ed.). Upper Saddle River, NJ: Pearson. Retrieved from http://www.amazon.com/Social-Problems-Census-Update-Edition/dp/020517907X

Eitzen, D. S., Baca Zinn, M., & Smith, K. E. (2012). *In Conflict and Order: Understanding Society* (12th ed.). Upper Saddle River: Prentice Hall.

Eitzen, D. S., Baca Zinn, M., & Smith, K. E. (2013). *Social problems* (13th ed.). Upper Saddle River, NJ: Pearson.

Ellison, C. G., Acevedo, G. A., & Ramos-Wada, A. I. (2011). Religion and attitudes toward same-sex marriage among U.S. Latinos. *Social Science Quarterly*, *92*(1), 35–56. Retrieved from http://www.ncbi.nlm.nih.gov/pubmed/21523946

Epstein, R. (2009). Introduction. In R. Epstein (Ed.), *Who's your daddy?: And other writings on queer parenting* (pp. 13–32). Toronto, Canada: Sumach Press. Retrieved from http://www.amazon.com/Whos-Your-Daddy-Writings-Parenting/dp/1894549783

Epstein, S. (1987). Gay politics, ethnic identity: The limits of social constructionism. *Socialist Review*, *17*, 9–54.

Epstein, S. (1994). A queer encounter: Sociology and the study of sexuality. *Sociology Theory, 12*(2), 188–202.

Erhardt, V. (2006). *Head over heels: Wives who stay with cross-dressers and trans-sexuals.* New York, NY: Haworth Press. Retrieved from http://www.amazon .com/Head-Over-Heels-Cross-Dressers-Transsexuals/dp/0789030950

Erich, S., Hall, S. K., Kanenberg, H., & Case, K. (2009). Early and late stage adolescence: Adopted adolescents' attachment to their heterosexual and lesbian/gay parents. *Adoption Quarterly, 12*(3–4), 152–170. doi:10.1080/10926750903330462

Erich, S., Leung, P., & Kindle, P. (2005). A comparative analysis of adoptive family functioning with gay, lesbian, and heterosexual parents and their children. *Journal of GLBT Family Studies, 1*(4), 43–60. doi:10.1300/J461v01n04_03

Estrada, R., & Marksamer, J. (2006). The legal rights of LGBT youth in state custody: What child welfare and juvenile justice professionals need to know. *Child Welfare, 85*(2), 171–194. doi:0009-4021/2006/030171-24

Ettelbrick, P. (2004). Since when is marriage a path to liberation. In A. Sullivan (Ed.), *Same-sex marriage: Pro and con a reader* (pp. 122–127). New York, NY: Vintage Books.

Faderman, L. (1991). *Odd girls and twilight lovers: A history of lesbian life in twentieth-century America.* New York, NY: Penguin Books. Retrieved from http://www.amazon.com/Odd-Girls-Twilight-Lovers-Twentieth-Century/ dp/0140171223

Farr, R. H., & Patterson, C. J. (2013). Coparenting among lesbian, gay, and heterosexual couples: Associations with adopted children's outcomes. *Child Development.* doi:10.1111/cdev.12046

Fatah, T., & Tapal, N. (2005). Canada's same-sex marriage law should not be opposed in the name of religion. In K. Burns (Ed.), *At issue opposing viewpoints: Gay marriage* (pp. 67–71). Farmington Hills, MI: Greenhaven Press.

Fausto-Sterling, A. (1993, March/April). The five sexes: Why male and female are not enough. *The Sciences,* pp. 20–25.

Fausto-Sterling, A. (2000). The five sexes, revisited. *The Sciences, 40*(4), 18–23. Retrieved from http://www.ncbi.nlm.nih.gov/pubmed/12569934

Feinberg, L. (1998). *Trans liberation: Beyond pink or blue.* Boston, MA: Beacon Press. Retrieved from http://www.amazon.com/Trans-Liberation-Beyond-Pink-Blue/ dp/0807079502

Feldman, M. B., Diaz, R. M., Ream, G. L., & El-Bassel, N. (2007). Intimate partner violence and HIV sexual risk behavior among Latino gay and bisexual men. *Journal of LGBT Health Research, 3*(2), 9–19. doi:10.1300/J463v03n02_02

Finneran, C., Chard, A., Sineath, C., Sullivan, P., & Stephenson, R. (2012). Intimate partner violence and social pressure among gay men in six countries. *The Western Journal of Emergency Medicine, 13*(3), 260–271. doi:10.5811/westjem.2012.3.11779

Firestone, S. (1970). *The dialectic of sex: A case for feminist revolution.* New York, NY: William Morrow.

Frank, N. (2012, June 13). Mark Regnerus' study on gay parenting is hopelessly flawed. *Los Angeles Times.* Retrieved July 12, 2013, from http://articles.latimes .com/2012/jun/13/opinion/la-oe-frank-same-sex-regnerus-family-20120613

Freedner, N., Freed, L. H., Yang, Y. W., & Austin, S. B. (2002). Dating violence among gay, lesbian, and bisexual adolescents: Results from a community survey. *The Journal of Adolescent Health, 31*(6), 469–474. Retrieved from http://www.ncbi .nlm.nih.gov/pubmed/12457580

Friedman, M. S., Marshal, M. P., Guadamuz, T. E., Wei, C., Wong, C. F., Saewyc, E., & Stall, R. (2011). A meta-analysis of disparities in childhood sexual abuse, parental physical abuse, and peer victimization among sexual minority and sexual nonminority individuals. *American Journal of Public Health, 101*(8), 1481–1494. doi:10.2105/AJPH.2009.190009

Fruhauf, C. A., Orel, N. A., & Jenkins, D. A. (2009). The coming-out process of gay grandfathers: Perceptions of their adult children's influence. *Journal of GLBT Family Studies, 5*(1–2), 99–118. doi:10.1080/15504280802595402

Gaboury, J. (2005). A personal perspective: Saying "I don't." *SIECUS, 33*(1), 29–33.

Gallagher, M. (2005). Same-sex marriage would harm children. In K. Burns (Ed.), *Gay marriage* (pp. 45–53). Farmington Hills, MI: Greenhaven Press.

Gardiner, J. (2010). Same-sex marriage: A worldwide trend? *Current Trends in the Regulations of Same-Sex Relationships, 28*(1), 92–107.

Gartrell, N., Bos, H., Peyser, H., Deck, A., & Rodas, C. (2011). Family characteristics, custody arrangements, and adolescent psychological well-being after lesbian mothers break up. *Family Relations, 60*(5), 572–585. doi:10.1111/j.1741-3729.2011.00667.x

Gartrell, N., Peyser, H., & Bos, H. (2012). Planned lesbian families: A review of the U.S. National Longitudinal Lesbian Family Study. In D. M. Brodzinsky & A. Pertman (Eds.), *Adoption by lesbians and gay men: A new dimension in family diversity* (pp. 112–129). New York, NY: Oxford University Press.

Gartrell, N., Rodas, C., Deck, A., Peyser, H., & Banks, A. (2006). The USA National Lesbian Family Study: Interviews with mothers of ten-year-olds. *Feminism & Psychology, 16,* 175–192.

Gates, G. J., Badgett, M. V. L., Macomber, J. E., & Chambers, K. (2007). *Adoption and foster care by gay and lesbian parents in the United States.* Los Angeles, CA. Retrieved from http://williamsinstitute.law.ucla.edu/wp-content/uploads/Gates-Badgett-Macomber-Chambers-Final-Adoption-Report-Mar-2007.pdf

Gates, G. J., & Ost, J. (2004). Where do gay and lesbian couples live? In *The gay and lesbian atlas* (pp. 1–11). Washington, DC: Urban Institute. Retrieved from http://www.urban.org/UploadedPDF/900695_GL_FactSheet.pdf

Gerson, K. (1985). *Hard choices: How women decide about work, career and motherhood.* Berkeley: University of California Press. Retrieved from http://www.amazon .com/Hard-Choices-Motherhood-California-Political/dp/0520057457

Gerstmann, E. (2004). *Same-sex marriage and the Constitution.* New York, NY: Cambridge University Press.

Ghavami, N., & Johnson, K. L. (2011). Comparing sexual and ethnic minority perspectives on same-sex marriage. *Journal of Social Issues, 67*(2), 394–412. doi:10.1111/j.1540-4560.2011.01704.x

Gianino, M. (2008). Adaptation and transformation: The transition to adoptive parenthood for gay male couples. *Journal of GLBT Family Studies, 4*(2), 205–243. doi:10.1080/15504280802096872

Gianino, M., Goldberg, A., & Lewis, T. (2009). Family outings: Disclosure practices among adopted youth with gay and lesbian parents. *Adoption Quarterly, 12*(3–4), 205–228. doi:10.1080/10926750903313344

Gibson, B. (2010). Care of the child with the desire to change genders—Part II: Female-to-male transition. *Pediatric Nursing, 36*(2), 112–117. Retrieved from http://www.ncbi.nlm.nih.gov/pubmed/21913598

Gibson, B., & Catlin, A. J. (2010a). Care of the child with the desire to change genders—Part I. *Pediatric Nursing, 36*(1), 53–59. Retrieved from http://www.ncbi.nlm.nih.gov/pubmed/21913596

Gibson, B., & Catlin, A. J. (2010b). Care of the child with the desire to change genders—Part III: Male-to-female transition. *Pediatric Nursing, 36*(5), 268–272. Retrieved from http://www.ncbi.nlm.nih.gov/pubmed/21913598

Gilmartin, B. G. (1987). *Shyness and love: Causes, consequences, and treatment.* New York, NY: University Press of America. Retrieved from http://www.amazon.com/Shyness-Love-Causes-Consequences-Treatment/dp/0819161020

Gimenez, M. E. (1983). Feminism, pronatalism, and motherhood. In J. Trebilcot (Ed.), *Mothering: Essays in feminist theory* (pp. 287–314). Totowa, NJ: Rowman & Littlefield.

Gimenez, M. E. (1991). The mode of reproduction in transition: A Marxist-feminist analysis of the effects of reproductive technologies. *Gender & Society, 5*(3), 334–350. doi:10.1177/089124391005003005

Glenn, E. N. (Ed.). (1994). *Social constructions of mothering: A thematic overview.* New York, NY: Routledge.

Glover, M., McKree, A., & Dyall, L. (2009). Assisted human reproduction: Issues for Takatapui (New Zealand indigenous non-heterosexuals). *Journal of GLBT Family Studies, 5*(4), 295–311.

Goldberg, A. E. (2006). The transition to parenthood for lesbian couples. *Journal of GLBT Family Studies, 2*(1), 13–42. doi:10.1300/J461v02n01

Goldberg, A. E. (2010). *Lesbian and gay parents and their children: Research on the family life cycle.* Washington, DC: American Psychological Association (APA). Retrieved from http://www.amazon.com/Lesbian-Gay-Parents-Their-Children/dp/1433805367

Goldberg, A. E. (2012). *Gay dads: Transitions to adoptive fatherhood.* New York: New York University Press. Retrieved from http://www.amazon.com/Gay-Dads-Transitions-Fatherhood-Qualitative/dp/0814732240

Goldberg, A. E., Downing, J. B., & Sauck, C. C. (2007). Choices, challenges, and tensions: Perspectives of lesbian prospective adoptive parents. *Adoption Quarterly, 10*(2), 33–64. doi:10.1300/J145v10n02_02

Goldberg, A. E., & Gianino, M. (2012). Lesbian and gay adoptive parent families: Assessment, clinical issues, and intervention. In D. Brodzinsky & A. Pertman (Eds.), *Adoption by lesbians and gay men: A new dimension in family diversity* (pp. 204–232). New York, NY: Oxford University Press.

Goldstein, J. R., & Kenney, C. T. (2001). Marriage delayed or marriage forgone? New cohort forecasts of first marriage for U.S. women. *American Sociological Review*, 66(4), 506–519. doi:10.2307/3088920

Golombok, S. (2007). Foreword: Research on gay and lesbian parenting: An historical perspective across 30 years. *Journal of GLBT Family Studies*, 3(2–3), xxi–xxvii. doi:10.1300/J461v03n02_a

Grant, J. M., Mottet, L. A., & Tanis, J. (2011). *Injustice at every turn: A report of the National Transgender Discrimination Survey*. Retrieved from http://www.thetask force.org/reports_and_research/ntds

Green, M. (2012, February 24). A brief history of the gay marriage struggle in California: *The Lowdown* [Blog post]. *KQUED News: The lowdown decoding the news.* Retrieved July 11, 2013, from http://blogs.kqed.org/lowdown/2012/02/24/interactive-a-brief-history-of-the-struggle-for-and-against-gay-marriage-in-califor nia-golden-state/

Greenberg, K. (2012). Still hidden in the closet: Trans women and domestic violence. *Berkeley Journal of Gender, Law & Justice*, 28, 198–251.

Greene, B. (2009). The use and abuse of religious beliefs in dividing and conquering between socially marginalized groups: The same-sex marriage debate. *The American Psychologist*, 64(8), 698–709. doi:10.1037/0003-066X.64.8.698

Grossman, A. H., Anthony, R. D., Nickolas, P., & D'Augelli, A. R. D. (2006). Male-to-female transgender youth. *Journal of GLBT Family Studies*, 2(1), 71–92. doi:10.1300/J461v02n01

Grossman, A. H., & D'Augelli, A. R. (2006). Transgender youth: Invisible and vulner-able. *Current Issues in Lesbian, Gay, Bisexual, and Transgender Health*, 51(1), 111–128. doi:10.1300/J082v51n01

GuyBow, IGLHRC, & SASOD. (2012). *Human rights violations of lesbian, bisexual, and transgender (LBT) people in Guyana: A shadow report* (pp. 1–13). New York, NY. Retrieved from http://www2.ohchr.org/english/bodies/cedaw/docs/ngos/GuyanaLGBTSubmission_for_the_session.pdf

Haas, A. P., Eliason, M., Mays, V. M., Mathy, R. M., Cochran, S. D., D'Augelli, A. R., . . . Clayton, P. J. (2011). Suicide and suicide risk in lesbian, gay, bisexual, and transgender populations: Review and recommendations. *Journal of Homosexuality*, 58(1), 10–51. doi:10.1080/00918369.2011.534038

Hardesty, J. L., Oswald, R. F., Khaw, L., & Fonseca, C. (2011). Lesbian/bisexual mothers and intimate partner violence: Help seeking in the context of social and legal vulnerability. *Violence Against Women*, 17(1), 28–46. doi:10.1177/107 7801209347636

Hattery, A., & Smith, E. (2012). Violence in same-sex couple families. In A. Hattery & E. Smith (Eds.), *The social dynamics of family violence* (pp. 291–307). Boulder, CO: Westview Press.

Heath, M. (2012). *One marriage under God: The campaign to promote marriage in America*. New York: New York University Press. Retrieved from http://www .amazon.com/One-Marriage-Under-God-Intersections/dp/0814737137

Heaton, J. (2010). The right to same-sex marriage in South Africa. *Law in Context*, 28(1), 108–122. Retrieved from http://search.informit.com.au/documentSummary;dn=896787254834267;res=IELHSS

Henehan, D., Rothblum, E. D., Solomon, S. E., & Balsam, K. F. (2007). Social and demographic characteristics of gay, lesbian, and heterosexual adults with and without children. *Journal of GLBT Family Studies*, 3(2–3), 35–79. doi:10.1300/J461v03n02_03

Henshaw, S. K. (1998). Unintended pregnancy in the United States. *Family Planning Perspectives*, 30(1), 24–29 & 46. Retrieved from http://www.guttmacher.org/pubs/journals/3002498.pdf

Hequembourg, A. L. (2007). *Lesbian motherhood: Stories of becoming*. New York, NY: Harrington Park Press.

Hequembourg, A. L., & Brallier, S. A. (2009). An exploration of sexual minority stress across the lines of gender and sexual identity. *Journal of Homosexuality*, 56(3), 273–298. doi:10.1080/00918360902728517

Herek, G. M., Norton, A. T., Allen, T. J., & Sims, C. L. (2010). Demographic, psychological, and social characteristics of self-identified lesbian, gay, and bisexual adults in a US probability sample. *Sexuality Research & Social Policy*, 7(3), 176–200. doi:10.1007/s13178-010-0017-y

Herman, G. (2012). Legal effects of same-sex marriage and divorce. *American Journal of Family Law*, 26(1), 5–7.

Highleyman, L. A. (2001). *A brief history of the bisexual movement*. Boston, MA: Bisexual Resource Center. Retrieved July 10, 2013, from http://combine.org.ohio-state.edu/resources/A Brief History of the Bisexual Movement.pdf

Hill, I. (1987). *The bisexual spouse*. McLean, VA: Barlina Books.

Hill, N., Woodson, K. M., Ferguson, A. D., & Parks, C. W. (2012). Intimate partner abuse among African American lesbians: Prevalence, risk factors, theory, and resilience. *Journal of Family Violence*, 27, 401–413.

Hill, S. A. (2012). *Families: A social class perspective*. Thousand Oaks, CA: Pine Forge Press. Retrieved from http://www.sagepub.com/books/Book236108?siteId=sage-uk&prodTypes=any&q=shirley+hill&fs=1

Hines, S. (2006). Intimate transitions: Transgender practices of partnering and parenting. *Sociology*, 40(2), 353–371. doi:10.1177/0038038506062037

Hollingsworth et al. v. Perry et al. (2013). Supreme Court of the United States. Retrieved from http://www.supremecourt.gov/opinions/12pdf/12-144_8ok0.pdf

Homma, Y., Chen, W., Poon, C. S., & Saewyc, E. M. (2012). Substance use and sexual orientation among East and Southeast Asian adolescents in Canada. *Journal of Child & Adolescent Substance Abuse*, 21(1), 32–50. doi:10.1080/1067828X.2012.636687

Hondagneu-Sotelo, P. (1994). *Gendered transitions: Mexican experiences of immigration*. Berkeley: University of California Press.

Hua, C. (2001). *A society without fathers or husbands: The Na of China* (A. Hustvedt, Trans.). Cambridge, MA: Zone Books.

Human Rights Campaign (HRC). (n.d.). Marriage center. *Human Rights Campaign.* Retrieved July 12, 2013, from http://www.hrc.org/campaigns/marriage-center# .UKZ6N4fefG8

Human Rights Campaign (HRC). (2009). *Answers to questions about marriage equality.* Washington, DC: Human Rights Campaign Foundation.

Human Rights Campaign (HRC). (2012). *Statewide marriage prohibitions.* Retrieved May 10, 2012, from http://www.hrc.org/files/assets/resources/us_marriage_prohibition.pdf

Human Rights Campaign (HRC). (2013). *Parenting laws: Joint adoption.* Washington, DC. Retrieved from http://www.hrc.org/files/assets/resources/parenting_joint-adoption_062013.pdf

Human Rights Campaign (HRC). (2014a). *Corporate equality index 2014.* Washington, DC. Retrieved from http://www.hrc.org/campaigns/corporate-equality-index

Human Rights Campaign. (2014b). Marriage center human rights campaign. *Marriage Center/Marriage Prohibition.* Retrieved March 18, 2014, from http://www.hrc.org/campaigns/marriage-center

Human Rights Campaign (HRC). (2014c). *Parenting laws: Joint adoption.* Retrieved March 27, 2014, from http://s3.amazonaws.com/hrc-assets//files/assets/resources/parenting_joint-adoption_082013.pdf#__utma=149406063.87664255.1392313 532.1395807150.1395898698.8&__utmb=149406063.7.9.1395898746708 &__utmc=149406063&__utmx=-&__utmz=149406063.1395807150.7.3.utmc sr=google|utmccn=(organic)|utmcmd=organic|utmctr=(not provided)&__utmv=-&__utmk=259440010

Human Rights Campaign (HRC). (2014d). *Parenting laws: Second parent or stepparent adoption.* Retrieved March 27, 2014, from http://s3.amazonaws.com/hrc-assets//files/assets/resources/parenting_second-parent-adoption_2-2014.pdf

Hunter, N. D., Joslin, C. G., & McGowan, S. M. (2004). *The rights of lesbians, gay men, bisexuals, and transgender people.* New York: New York University Press. Retrieved from http://www.abebooks.com/servlet/BookDetailsPL?bi=992878339 5&searchurl=an=hunter+nan+d+joslin+courtney+g+mcgowan+sharon+m&bsi= 0&ds=30

Hybarger, C. K. (2000). *Conjugal power: A study of gay, lesbian, and heterosexual couples.* Doctoral dissertation, United States International University.

Internal Revenue Service. (2013). Treasury and IRS announce that all legal same-sex marriages will be recognized for federal tax purposes: Ruling provides certainty, benefits and protections under federal tax law for same-sex married couples. *Internal Revenue Service Announcement IR-2013-72.* Retrieved November 27, 2013, from http://www.irs.gov/uac/Newsroom/Treasury-and-IRS-Announce-That-All-Legal-Same-Sex-Marriages-Will-Be-Recognized-For-Federal-Tax-Purposes;-Ruling-Provides-Certainty,-Benefits-and-Protections-Under-Federal-Tax-Law-for-Same-Sex-Married-Couples

Island, D., & Letellier, P. (1991). *Men who beat the men who love them: Battered gay men and domestic violence.* New York, NY: Routledge.

Israel, G. E. (2008). Translove. *Journal of GLBT Family Studies*, *1*(1), 53–67. doi:10.1300/J461v01n01_05

Jacobs, J., & Freundlich, M. (2006). Achieving permanency for LGBTQ youth. *Child Welfare*, *85*(2), 299–316. Retrieved from http://www.ncbi.nlm.nih.gov/pubmed/16846117

Jennings, K. (2003). *Always my child: A parent's guide to understanding your gay, lesbian, bisexual, transgendered, or questioning son or daughter*. New York, NY: Fireside. Retrieved from http://www.amazon.com/Always-Child-Understanding-Transgendered-Questioning/dp/0743226496

Johnson, A. G. (2008). *The forest and the trees: Sociology as life, practice, and promise* (2nd ed.). Philadelphia, PA: Temple University Press.

Johnson, G. (2003). Vermont civil unions: A success story. In L. D. Wardle, M. Strasser, W. C. Duncan, & D. O. Coolidge (Eds.), *Marriage and same-sex unions: A debate* (pp. 283–293). Westport, CT: Praeger.

Johnson, M. P. (1995, May). Patriarchal terrorism and common couple violence: Two forms of violence against women. *Journal of Marriage and Family*, *57*, 283–294.

Johnson, S., & O'Connor, E. (2002). *The gay baby boom: The psychology of gay parenthood*. New York: New York University Press. Retrieved from http://www.amazon.com/The-Gay-Baby-Boom-Psychology/dp/0814742610

Jones, M. (2005). Adolescent gender identity and the courts. *International Journal of Children's Rights*, *13*, 121–148. Retrieved from http://heinonline.org/HOL/Page?handle=hein.journals/intjchrb13&id=127&div=&collection=journals

Kendell, K. (1998). Lesbian couples creating families. In J. J. Cabaj & D. W. Purcell (Eds.), *On the road to same-sex marriage: A supportive guide to psychological, political, and legal issues* (pp. 41–57). San Francisco, CA: Jossey-Bass.

Kennedy, E. L., & Davis, M. D. (1993). *Boots of leather, slippers of gold: The history of a lesbian community*. New York, NY: Routledge. Retrieved from http://www.amazon.com/Boots-Leather-Slippers-Gold-Community/dp/B00DT600IY

Kerbo, H. K. (2009). *Social stratification and inequality* (7th ed.). New York, NY: McGraw-Hill.

Kidd, J. D., & Witten, T. M. (2008, June). Transgender and transsexual identities: The next strange fruit—Hate crimes, violence and genocide against the global trans-communities. *Journal of Hate Studies*, *6*, 31–63.

Kimmel, M. (1994). Masculinity as homophobia: Fear, shame, and silence in the construction of gender identity. In H. Brod & M. Kaufman (Eds.), *Research on men and masculinities series: Theorizing masculinities* (pp. 119–142). Thousand Oaks, CA: Sage. doi:10.4135/9781452243627.n7

Kimmel, M. (2012). *The gendered society* (5th ed.). New York, NY: Oxford University Press. Retrieved from http://www.oup.com/us/catalog/he/subject/WomensStudies GenderStudies/Topics/GenderInequality/?&ci=9780199927463

Kinsey, A. C., Pomeroy, W. B., & Martin, C. E. (1948). *Sexual behavior in the human male*. Philadelphia, PA: W. B. Saunders. Retrieved from http://www.amazon.com/Sexual-Behavior-Human-Alfred-Kinsey/dp/B000IWRZPS

Kinsey, A. C., Pomeroy, W. B., Martin, C. E., & Gebhard, P. H. (1953). *Sexual behavior in the human female*. Philadelphia, PA: Elsevier Health Sciences. Retrieved from http://www.amazon.com/Sexual-Behavior-Human-Female-Introduction/dp/025333411X

Kirk, C., & Rosin, H. (2012). Gay marriage around the world: Pew forum on religion & public life. *Slate*. Retrieved July 12, 2013, from http://www.pewforum.org/Gay-Marriage-and-Homosexuality/Gay-Marriage-Around-the-World.aspx

Kosciw, J. G., Greytak, E. A., Bartkiewicz, M. J., Boesen, M. J., & Palmer, N. A. (2011). *The 2011 National School Climate Survey: The experiences of lesbian, gay, bisexual and transgender youth in our nation's schools*. New York, NY. Retrieved from http://www.glsen.org/nscs

Krivickas, K. M., & Lofquist, D. (2011). Demographics of same-sex couple households with children. Retrieved from http://www.census.gov/hhes/samesex/files/Krivickas-Lofquist PAA 2011.pdf

Kurdek, L. A. (2007). The allocation of household labor by partners in gay and lesbian couples. *Journal of Family Issues, 28*(1), 132–148. doi:10.1177/0192513X06292019

Kurtzleben, D. (2011). Divorce rates lower in states with same-sex marriage. *US News and World Report*. Retrieved July 11, 2013, from http://www.usnews.com/news/articles/2011/07/06/divorce-rates-lower-in-states-with-same-sex-marriage

Kurz, D. (1989). Social science perspectives on wife abuse: Current debates and future directions. *Gender & Society, 3*(4), 489–505. doi:10.1177/089124389003004007

Lambda Legal. (2013). *Garden State Equality, et al. v. Dow, et al.* Retrieved from http://www.lambdalegal.org/in-court/cases/garden-state-equality-v-dow

Lasker, J. N. (1998). The users of donor insemination. In K. Daniels & E. Haimes (Eds.), *Donor insemination: International social science perspectives* (pp. 7–32). New York, NY: Cambridge University Press.

Lees, L. (2008). Transparenting. In M. Boenke (Ed.), *Trans forming families: Real stories about transgendered loved ones* (3rd ed., pp. 141–143). Washington, DC: PFLAG Transgender Network.

Lev, A. I. (2004). *Transgender emergence: Therapeutic guidelines for working with gender-variant people and their families*. New York, NY: Routledge. Retrieved from http://www.amazon.com/Transgender-Emergence-Therapeutic-Guidelines-Gender-Variant/dp/078902117X

Lev, A. I. (2006). Gay dads: Choosing surrogacy. *Lesbian & Gay Psychology Review, 7*(1), 72–76.

Lev, A. I., & Sennott, S. L. (2013). Clinical work with LGBTQ parents and prospective parents. In A. E. Goldberg & K. R. Allen (Eds.), *LGBT-parent families: Innovations in research and implications for practice* (pp. 241–259). New York, NY: Springer.

Levi, J. L. (2012). Divorce and relationship dissolution. In J. L. Levi & E. E. Monnin-Browder (Eds.), *Transgender family law: A guide to effective advocacy* (pp. 86–104). Bloomington, IN: AuthorHouse.

Levine, J. (2005). Why gays should oppose same-sex marriage. In K. Burns (Ed.), *At issue opposing viewpoints: Gay marriage* (pp. 76–81). Farmington Hills, MI: Greenhaven Press.

Lewin, E. (1993). *Lesbian mothers: Accounts of gender in American culture*. Ithaca, NY: Cornell University Press. Retrieved from http://www.amazon.com/Lesbian-Mothers-Accounts-Anthropology-Contemporary/dp/080148099X

Lewin, E. (2004, November). Does marriage have a future? *Journal of Marriage and Family, 66*, 1000–1006. doi:10.1111/.0022-2445.2004.00071.X

Limbaugh, D. (2005). Religion will be undermined by the Massachusetts same-sex marriage law. In K. Burns (Ed.), *At issue opposing viewpoints: Gay marriage* (pp. 72–75). Farmington Hills, MI: Greenhaven Press.

Liu, R. T., & Mustanski, B. (2012). Suicidal ideation and self-harm in lesbian, gay, bisexual, and transgender youth. *American Journal of Preventive Medicine, 42*(3), 221–228. doi:10.1016/j.amepre.2011.10.023

Luscombe, B. (2012). Polygamy's rising profile has encouraged plural families to fight for recognition. *Time Magazine*, pp. 43–46.

Lynch, J. M., & Murray, K. (2000). For the love of the children: The coming-out process of lesbian and gay parents and stepparents. *Journal of Homosexuality, 39*(1), 1–24.

Magpantay, G. D. (2006). The ambivalence of queer Asian Pacific Americans toward same sex marriage. *Amerasia Journal, 32*(1), 109–117.

Majka-Rostek, D. (2011). Same-sex couples in Poland: Challenges of family life. *Journal of GLBT Family Studies, 7*(3), 285–296.

Mallon, G. P. (2004). *Gay men choosing parenthood*. New York, NY: Columbia University Press. Retrieved from http://www.amazon.com/Gay-Choosing-Parenthood-Gerald-Mallon/dp/0231117973

Mallon, G. P. (2011). The home study assessment process for gay, lesbian, bisexual, and transgender prospective foster and adoptive families. *Journal of GLBT Family Studies, 7*(1-2), 9–29. doi:10.1080/1550428X.2011.537229

Mallon, G. P., & DeCrescenzo, T. (2006). Transgender children and youth: A child welfare practice perspective. *Child Welfare, 85*(2), 215–241. Retrieved from http://www.ncbi.nlm.nih.gov/pubmed/16846113

Marks, L. (2012). "We see what we seek": A rejoinder to the responses of Amato, Eggebeen, and Osborne. *Social Science Research, 41*(4), 784–785. doi:10.1016/j.ssresearch.2012.05.001

Marshal, M. P., Friedman, M. S., Stall, R., King, K. M., Miles, J., Gold, M. A., . . . Morse, J. Q. (2008). Sexual orientation and adolescent substance use: A meta-analysis and methodological review. *Addiction, 103*, 546–556.

Marzullo, M. A., & Lbman, A. J. (2009). *Hate crimes and violence against lesbian, gay, bisexual and transgender people*. Washington, DC. Retrieved from http://www.hrc.org/files/assets/resources/Hatecrimesandviolenceagainstlgbtpeople_2009.pdf

Matthews, J. D., & Cramer, E. P. (2006, March/April). Envisaging the adoption process to strengthen gay- and lesbian-headed families: Recommendations for adoption professionals. *Child Welfare, 85*, 317–341.

Mello, M. (2004). *Legalizing gay marriage*. Philadelphia, PA: Temple University Press.

Mendoza, J. (2011). The impact of minority stress on gay male partner abuse. In J. L. Ristock (Ed.), *Intimate partner violence in LGBTQ lives* (pp. 169–181). New York, NY: Routledge.

Messinger, A. M. (2011). Invisible victims: Same-sex IPV in the National Violence Against Women Survey. *Journal of Interpersonal Violence*, 26(11), 2228–2243. doi:10.1177/0886260510383023

MetLife Mature Market Institute (MetLife). (2010). Out and aging: The MetLife study of lesbian, gay, bisexual, and transgender baby boomers. *Journal of GLBT Family Studies*, 6(1), 40–57. doi:10.1080/15504280903472949

Meyer, I. H. (1995). Minority stress and mental health in gay men. *Journal of Health and Social Behavior*, 36(1), 38–56. Retrieved from http://cpmcnet.columbia.edu/dept/healthandsociety/events/ms/year4/pdf/sh_Meyer IH.pdf

Mezey, N. J. (2008a). *New choices, new families: How lesbians decide about motherhood*. Baltimore, MD: The Johns Hopkins University Press.

Mezey, N. J. (2008b). The privilege of coming out: Race, class, and lesbians' mothering decisions. *International Journal of Sociology of the Family*, 34(2), 257–276.

Mezey, N. J. (2013). How lesbians and gay men decide to become parents or remain childfree. In A. E. Goldberg & K. R. Allen (Eds.), *LGBT-parent families: Innovations in research and implications for practice* (pp. 59–69). New York, NY: Springer.

Mezey, N. J., & Boudreaux, C. (2005). *Is marriage the best way to "Do family"? Historical and current questions*. Paper presented at the 2005 Society for the Study of Social Problems meetings, Phildelphia, PA.

Mezey, N. J., Post, L. A., & Maxwell, C. D. (2002). Redefining intimate partner violence: Women's experiences with physical violence and non-physical abuse by age. *International Journal of Sociology and Social Policy*, 22(7/8), 122–154. doi:10.1108/01443330210790120

Millbank, J. (2003). From here to maternity: A review of the research on lesbian and gay families. *Australian Journal of Social Issues*, 38(4), 541–600.

Minter, S. P., & Wald, D. H. (2012a). Custody disputes involving transgender children. In J. L. Levi & E. E. Monnin-Browder (Eds.), *Transgender family law: A guide to effective advocacy* (pp. 131–145). Toronto, Canada.

Minter, S. P., & Wald, D. H. (2012b). Protecting parental rights. In J. L. Levi & E. E. Monnin-Browder (Eds.), *Transgender family law: A guide to effective advocacy* (pp. 63–85). Bloomington, IN: AuthorHouse.

Mintz, S., & Kellogg, S. (1988). *Domestic revolutions: A social history of American family life*. New York, NY: Free Press.

Mohr, R. D. (1994). *A more perfect union: Why straight America must stand up for gay rights*. Boston, MA: Beacon Press.

Moore, M. R. (2011). *Invisible families: Gay identities, relationships, and motherhood among Black women*. Berkeley: University of California Press.

Moore, M. R., & Brainer, A. (2013). Race and ethnicity in the lives of sexual minority parents and their children. In A. E. Goldberg & K. R. Allen (Eds.), *LGBT-parent families: Innovations in research and implications for practice* (pp. 133–148). New York, NY: Springer.

Moraga, C. L. (1997). *Waiting in the wings: Portrait of a queer motherhood*. Ann Arbor, MI: Firebrand Books. Retrieved from http://www.amazon.com/Waiting-Wings-Portrait-Queer-Motherhood/dp/1563410923

Moraga, C., & Anzaldúa, G. (1984). *This bridge called my back: Writings by radical women of color.* New York, NY: Kitchen Table/Women of Color Press. Retrieved from http://www.amazon.com/This-Bridge-Called-My-Back/dp/091317503X

Morales, E. S. (1990). Ethnic minority families and minority gays and lesbians. In F. W. Bozzett & M. B. Sussman (Eds.), *Homosexuality and family relations* (pp. 217–240). New York, NY: Harrington Park Press. Retrieved from http://www.amazon.com/Homosexuality-Family-Relations-Marvin-Sussman/dp/0866569472

Morris, J. F., Balsam, K. F., & Rothblum, E. D. (2002). Lesbian and bisexual mothers and nonmothers: Demographics and the coming-out process. *Journal of Family Psychology, 16*(2), 144–156. doi:10.1037//0893-3200.16.2.144

Mujuzi, J. D. (2009). The absolute prohibition of same-sex marriages in Uganda. *International Journal of Law, Policy and the Family, 23*(3), 277–288. doi:10.1093/lawfam/ebp001

Murphy, J. S. (2001). Should lesbians count as infertile couples? Antilesbian discrimination in assisted reproduction. In M. Bernstein & R. Reimann (Eds.), *Queer families, queer politics* (pp. 182–200). New York, NY: Columbia University Press. Retrieved from http://www.amazon.com/Queer-Families-Politics-Mary-Bernstein/dp/0231116918

Murphy, T. F. (2010). The ethics of helping transgender men and women have children. *Perspectives in Biology and Medicine, 53*(1), 46–60. doi:10.1353/pbm.0.0138

Muzio, C. (1999). Lesbian coparenting: On being/being with the invisible (m)other. In J. Laird (Ed.), *Lesbians and lesbian families: Reflections on theory and practice* (pp. 197–211). New York, NY: Columbia University Press.

Natale, A. P., & Miller-Cribbs, J. E. (2012). Same-sex marriage policy: Advancing social, political, and economic justice. *Journal of GLBT Family Studies, 8*(2), 155–172. doi:10.1080/1550428X.2012.660786

National Coalition of Anti-Violence Programs (NCAVP). (2012). *2011 report on lesbian, gay, bisexual, transgender, queer, and HIV-affected intimate partner violence.* New York, NY. Retrieved from http://www.avp.org/storage/documents/Reports/2012_NCAVP_2011_IPV_Report.pdf

National Hispanic Christian Leadership Conference (NHCLC). (2013). NHCLC, leading Hispanic organization in a call for a constitutional amendment to define marriage between a man and a woman. Retrieved July 11, 2013, from http://www.nhclc.org/news/nhclc-leading-hispanic-organization-call-constitutional-amendment-define-marriage-between-man-a

National Institute of Justice. (2010). Measuring intimate partner (domestic) violence. Retrieved July 15, 2013, from http://www.nij.gov/topics/crime/intimate-partner-violence/measuring.htm

New Jersey Civil Union Review Commission. (2008). *The legal, medical, economic & social consequences of New Jersey's civil union law.* Retrieved from http://gay-marriage.procon.org/sourcefiles/NJ-Commission-Civil-Union-Law.pdf

Newport, F. (2008). Blacks as conservative as Republicans on some moral issues. *Gallup.* Retrieved July 11, 2013, from http://www.gallup.com/poll/112807/blacks-conservative-republicans-some-moral-issues.aspx

Nixon, C. A. (2011). Working-class lesbian parents' emotional engagement with their children's education: Intersections of class and sexuality. *Sexualities*, *14*(1), 79–99. doi:10.1177/1363460710390564

NOLO Law for All. (2005). A legal history of same-sex marriage battles in the United States. In K. Burns (Ed.), *Gay marriage* (pp. 14–19). Farmington Hills, MI: Greenhaven Press.

O'Flaherty, M., & Fisher, J. (2008). Sexual orientation, gender identity and international human rights law: Contextualising the Yogyakarta Principles. *Human Rights Law Review*, *8*(2). doi:10.1093/hrlr/ngn009

Olson, L. R., Harrison, J. T., & College, B. (2006). Religion and public opinion about same-sex marriage. *Social Science Quarterly*, *87*(2), 340–360.

Orel, N. A. (2005). Lesbian and bisexual women as grandparents: The centrality of sexual orientation on the grandparent-grandchild relationship. In D. Kimmel & T. Rose (Eds.), *Handbook of gay, lesbian, bisexual, and transgender aging* (pp. 248–274). Washington, DC: American Psychological Association (APA).

Orel, N. A., & Fruhauf, C. A. (2006). Lesbian and bisexual grandmothers' perceptions of the grandparent-grandchild relationship. *Journal of GLBT Family Studies*, *2*(1), 43–70. doi:10.1300/J461v02n01

Outgames Montréal 2006. (2006). Declaration of Montréal. *International Conference Internationale on LGBT Human Rights*. Retrieved July 10, 2013, from http://www.declarationofmontreal.org/declaration/DeclarationofMontreal.pdf

Pallotta-Chiarolli, M., Haydon, P., & Hunter, A. (2013). "These are our children": Polyamorous parenting. In A. E. Goldberg & K. R. Allen (Eds.), *LGBT-parent families: Innovations in research and implications for practice* (pp. 117–131). New York, NY: Springer.

Panozzo, D. (2010). *Gay male couples who decide to parent: Motivations, division of child care responsibilities, and impact on relationship and life satisfaction.* New York: New York University.

Pantalone, D. W., Lehavot, K., Simoni, J. M., & Walters, K. L. (2011). I ain't never been a kid: Early violence exposure and other pathways to partner violence for sexual minority men with HIV. In J. L. Ristock (Ed.), *Intimate partner violence in LGBTQ lives* (pp. 182–206). New York, NY: Routledge.

Parker, K., & Wang, W. (2013). Modern parenthood. *Pew social & demographic trends*. Retrieved July 12, 2013, from http://www.pewsocialtrends.org/files/2013/03/FINAL_modern_parenthood_03-2013.pdf

Parlett, K., & Weston-Scheuber, K.-M. (2004). Consent to treatment for transgender and intersex children. *Deakin Law Review*, *9*(2), 375–397. Retrieved from http://www.deakin.edu.au/buslaw/law/dlr/docs/vol9-iss2/vol9-2-7.pdf

Pascoe, C. J. (2012). *Dude, you're a fag: Masculinity and sexuality in high school* (2nd ed., p. 248). Berkeley: University of California Press. Retrieved from http://www.amazon.com/Dude-Youre-Fag-Masculinity-Sexuality/dp/0520271483

Pattavina, A., Hirschel, D., Buzawa, E., Faggiani, D., & Bentley, H. (2007). A comparison of the police response to heterosexual versus same-sex intimate partner violence. *Violence Against Women*, *13*(4), 374–394. doi:10.1177/1077801207299206

Patterson, C. J., Sutfin, E. L., & Fulcher, M. (2004). Division of labor among lesbian and heterosexual parenting couples: Correlates of specialized versus shared patterns. *Journal of Adult Development*, *11*(3), 179–189. doi:10.1023/B:JADE.00000356 26.90331.47

Payne, K. K., & Gibbs, L. (2011). *First marriage rate in the U.S., 2010 (FP-11-12)*. Bowling Green. Retrieved from http://ncfmr.bgsu.edu/pdf/family_profiles/file104173.pdf

Pertman, A., & Howard, J. (2012). Emerging diversity in family life: Adoption by gay and lesbian parents. In D. M. Brodzinsky & A. Pertman (Eds.), *Adoption by lesbians and gay men: A new dimension in family diversity* (pp. 20–35). New York, NY: Oxford University Press.

Peterman, L. M., & Dixon, C. G. (2003, Winter). Domestic violence between same-sex partners: Implications for counseling. *Journal of Counseling & Development*, *81*, 40–47.

Pew Research Center. (2009). *Majority continues to support civil unions*. Washington, DC. Retrieved from http://www.people-press.org/files/legacy-pdf/553.pdf

Pew Research Center. (2010). The decline of marriage and rise of new families. *Pew Research social & demographic trends*. Retrieved July 11, 2013, from http://www.pewsocialtrends.org/2010/11/18/the-decline-of-marriage-and-rise-of-new-families

Pew Research Center. (2012). Opinions on gay marriage unchanged after Obama Announcement. *Pew forum on religion & public life*. Retrieved July 11, 2013, from http://www.pewforum.org/Politics-and-Elections/2012-opinions-on-for-gay-marriage-unchanged-after-obamas-announcement.aspx

Pfeffer, C. A. (2010). "Women's work"? Women partners of transgender men doing housework and emotion work. *Journal of Marriage and Family*, *72*(1), 165–183. doi:10.1111/j.1741-3737.2009.00690.x

Poon, M. K.-L. (2011). Beyond good and evil: The social construction of violence in intimate gay relationships. In J. L. Ristock (Ed.), *Intimate partner violence in LGBTQ lives* (pp. 102–130). New York, NY: Routledge.

Popenoe, D. (1993, August). American family decline, 1960–1990: A review and appraisal. *Journal of Marriage and the Family*, *55*, 527–555.

Popenoe, D. (1999). *Life with father: Compelling new evidence that fatherhood and marriage are indispensable for the good of children and society*. Cambridge, MA: Harvard University Press.

Powell, B., Bolzendahl, C., Geist, C., & Steelman, L. C. (2010). *Counted out: Same-sex relations and Americans' definitions of family*. New York, NY: American Sociological Association/Russell Sage Foundation. Retrieved from http://www.amazon.com/Counted-Out-Relations-Americans-Definitions/dp/0871546884

PrideSource.com. (2013). From the mouths of babes. *PrideSource: Between the lines*. Retrieved from http://www.pridesource.com/article.html?article=60130

Quinn, M.-E. (2010). *Open minds open doors: Transforming domestic violence programs to include LGBTQ survivors*. Boston, MA. Retrieved from http://www.ncdsv.org/images/TheNetworkLaRed_OpenMindsOpenDoors_2010.pdf

Rabun, C., & Oswald, R. (2009). Upholding and expanding the normal family: Future fatherhood through the eyes of gay male emerging adults. *Fathering: A Journal of Theory, Research, and Practice about Men as Fathers, 7*, 269–285.

Ragg, D. M., Patrick, D., & Ziefert, M. (2006). Slamming the closet door: Working with gay and lesbian youth in care. *Child Welfare, 85*(2), 243–265. Retrieved from http://www.ncbi.nlm.nih.gov/pubmed/16846114

Rappard, A. M., & Karikari-apau, N. (2014). Nigeria bans same-sex marriage. *CNN .com*. Retrieved March 27, 2014, from http://www.cnn.com/2014/01/13/world/africa/nigeria-anti-gay-law

Rauch, J. (2004). *Gay marriage: Why it is good for gays, good for straights, and good for America* [Holt Paperbacks version]. Retrieved from http://www.amazon.com/Gay-Marriage-Good-Straights-America/dp/0805078150

Ray, N. (2006). *Lesbian, gay, bisexual and transgender youth: An epidemic of homelessness*. New York, NY. Retrieved from http://www.thetaskforce.org/downloads/HomelessYouth.pdf

Regnerus, M. (2012). How different are the adult children of parents who have same-sex relationships? Findings from the New Family Structures Study. *Social Science Research, 41*(4), 752–770. doi:10.1016/j.ssresearch.2012.03.009

Reimann, R. (2001). Lesbian mothers at work. In M. Bernstein & R. Reimann (Eds.), *Queer families, queer politics* (pp. 254–271). New York, NY: Columbia University Press.

Renzetti, C. M. (1992). *Violent betrayal: Partner abuse in lesbian relationships*. Newbury Park, CA: Sage.

Rhee, M. (2006). Towards community: Korean journal and Korean American cultural attitudes on same-sex marriage. *Amerasia Journal, 32*(1), 75–88.

Richman, K. D. (2009). *Courting change: Queer parents, judges, and the transformation of American family law*. New York: New York University Press.

Ristock, J. L. (2011). Introduction: Intimate partner violence in LGBTQ lives. In J. L. Ristock (Ed.), *Intimate partner violence in LGBTQ lives* (pp. 1–9). New York, NY: Routledge.

Ristock, J. (with N. Timbang). (2005, July). Relationship violence in lesbian/gay/bisexual/transgender/queer [LGBTQ]: Communities moving beyond a gender-based frame-work (pp. 1–19). Violence Against Women Online Resources. Retrieved from http://www.mincava.umn.edu/documents/lgbtqviolence/lgbtqviolence.pdf

Rizzo, S., & Sherman, T. (2013). N.J. Supreme Court refuses to block same-sex marriage; first wedding expected Monday. Retrieved from http://www.nj.com/news/index.ssf/2013/10/supreme_court_refuses_to_block_same-sex_marriage_first_wedding_expected_monday.html#incart_river

Robertson, J. A. (2005). Gay and lesbian access to assisted reproductive technology. *Case Western Reserve Law Review, 52*(2), 323–372.

Robertson, M. J., & Toro, P. A. (1998). *Homeless youth: Research, intervention, and policy*. Retrieved from https://goproject.org/wp-content/uploads/2012/06/Homeless-Youth.pdf

Robinson, D. F., & Soderstrom, S. (2011). Legal recognition of same-sex relationships. *The Georgetown Journal of Gender and the Law, 12*(3), 521–575.

Rodriguez Rust, P. C. (2000a). The biology, psychology, sociology, and sexuality of bisexuality. In P. C. Rodriguez Rust (Ed.), *Bisexuality in the United States: A social science reader* (pp. 403–470). New York, NY: Columbia University Press.

Rodriguez Rust, P. C. (2000b). Review of statistical findings about bisexual behavior, feelings, and identities. In P. C. Rodriguez Rust (Ed.), *Bisexuality in the United States: A social science reader* (pp. 129–184). New York, NY: Columbia University Press.

Rosario, M., Schrimshaw, E. W., & Hunter, J. (2006). A model of sexual risk behaviors among young gay and bisexual men: Longitudinal associations of mental health, substance abuse, sexual abuse, and the coming-out process. *AIDS Education and Prevention, 18*(5), 444–460. doi:10.1521/aeap.2006.18.5.444

Rosario, M., Schrimshaw, E. W., & Hunter, J. (2011). Different patterns of sexual identity development over time: Implications for the psychological adjustment of lesbian, gay, and bisexual youths. *Journal of Sex Research, 48*(1), 3–15. doi:10.1080/00224490903331067

Ross, L. E., & Dobinson, C. (2013). Where is the "B" in LGBT parenting? A call for research on bisexual parenting. In A. E. Goldberg & K. R. Allen (Eds.), *LGBT-parent families: Innovations in research and implications for practice* (pp. 87–103). New York, NY: Springer.

Ross, L. E., Siegel, A., Dobinson, C., Epstein, R., & Steele, L. S. (2012). "I don't want to turn totally invisible": Mental health, stressors, and supports among bisexual women during the perinatal period. *Journal of GLBT Family Studies, 8*(2), 137–154. doi:10.1080/1550428X.2012.660791

Ross, L. E., Steele, L. S., & Epstein, R. (2006). Service use and gaps in services for lesbian and bisexual women during donor insemination, pregnancy, and the postpartum period. *Journal of Obstetrics And Gynaecology Canada, 28*(6), 505–11. Retrieved from http://www.ncbi.nlm.nih.gov/pubmed/16857118

Roste, V. (2005). Christians should support gay marriage in Canada. In K. Burns (Ed.), *At issue opposing viewpoints: Gay marriage* (pp. 89–92). Farmington Hills, MI: Greenhaven Press.

Russell, S. T. (2011). Bisexuality and adolescence. *Journal of Bisexuality, 11*, 434–438. doi:10.1080/152997.2011.620470

Rust, P. C. (1995). *Bisexuality and the challenge to lesbian politics: Sex, loyalty, and revolution.* New York: New York University Press. Retrieved from http://www.amazon.com/Bisexuality-Challenge-Lesbian-Politics-Revolution/dp/0814774458

Rust, P. C. (2000). Two many and not enough. *Journal of Bisexuality, 1*(1), 31–68.

Ryan, C., Huebner, D., Diaz, R. M., & Sanchez, J. (2009). Family rejection as a predictor of negative health outcomes in White and Latino lesbian, gay, and bisexual young adults. *Pediatrics, 123*(1), 346–52. doi:10.1542/peds.2007-3524

Saad, L. (2012). U.S. acceptance of gay/lesbian relations is the new normal. *Gallup Politics.* Retrieved from http://www.gallup.com/poll/154634/acceptance-gay-lesbian-relations-new-normal.aspx

Saewyc, E. M. (2011). Research on adolescent sexual orientation: Development, health disparities, stigma, and resilience. *Journal of Research on Adolescence, 21*(1), 256–272. doi:10.1111/j.1532-7795.2010.00727.x

Saewyc, E. M., Homma, Y., Skay, C. L., Bearinger, L. H., Resnick, M. D., & Reis, E. (2009). Protective factors in the lives of bisexual adolescents in North America. *American Journal of Public Health, 99*(1), 110–117. doi:10.2105/AJPH .2007.123109

Sausa, L. A. (2008). Are you going to have children? In M. Boenke (Ed.), *Trans form- ing families: Real stories about transgendered loved ones.* Washington, DC: PFLAG Transgender Network.

Schacher, S. J., Auerbach, C. F., & Silverstein, L. B. (2005). Gay fathers expanding the possibilities for us all. *Journal of GLBT Family Studies, 1*(3), 31–52. doi:10.1300/ J461v01n03_02

Scholinski, D., & Adams, J. M. (1998). *The last time I wore a dress.* New York, NY: Riverhead Books. Retrieved from http://www.amazon.com/The-Last-Time-Wore-Dress/dp/1573226963

Schulman, M. (2013, January 10). Generation LGBTQIA. NYTimes.com. *The New York Times,* pp. E1, E8. New York. Retrieved from http://www.nytimes.com/ 2013/01/10/fashion/generation-lgbtqia.html?pagewanted=all&_r=0

Schwartz, J. (2012). Guide to the Supreme Court decision on Proposition 8. *NYTimes .com.* Retrieved July 11, 2013, from http://www.nytimes.com/interactive/ 2013/06/26/us/annotated-supreme-court-decision-on-proposition-8.html

Schwartz, P. (1994). *Peer marriage.* New York, NY: Free Press. Retrieved from http:// www.amazon.com/Peer-Marriage-Pepper-Schwartz/dp/0029317150

Scott, L. S. (2009). *Two is enough: A couple's guide to living childless by choice.* Berkeley, CA: Seal Press.

Sedgwick, E. K. (1993). Epistemology of the closet. In H. Abelove, M. A. Barale, & D. Halperin (Eds.), *The lesbian and gay studies reader* (pp. 45–61). New York, NY: Routledge.

Segal-Engelchin, D., Erera, P. I., & Cwickel, J. (2005). The hetero-gay family. *Journal of GLBT Family Studies, 1*(3), 85–104. doi:10.1300/J461v01n03_04

Seidman, S. (2009). *The social construction of sexuality* (2nd ed.). New York, NY: W. W. Norton. Retrieved from http://www.amazon.com/Construction-Sexuality-Edition-Contemporary-Societies/dp/0393934020

Shah, D. (2004). *Defense of marriage act: Update to prior report.* Washington, DC. Retrieved from http://www.gao.gov/new.items/d04353r.pdf

Shaw, S. Y., Lorway, R. R., Deering, K. N., Avery, L., Mohan, H. L., Bhattacharjee, P., . . . Blanchard, J. F. (2012). Factors associated with sexual violence against men who have sex with men and transgendered individuals in Karnataka, India. *PLoS ONE, 7*(3), 1–8. doi:10.1371/journal.pone.0031705

Sheff, E. (2004). *Queer poly families.* Unpublished manuscript.

Sheff, E. (2011). Polyamorous families, same-sex marriage, and the slippery slope. *Journal of Contemporary Ethnography, 40*(5), 487–520. doi:10.1177/089124 1611413578

Sherkat, D. (2013). Darren Sherkat interview and Regnerus Study. *Southern Poverty Law Center*. Retrieved July 12, 2013, from http://www.gaynz.com/blogs/redqueen/?p=3633

Sherkat, D. E., de Vries, K. M., & Creek, S. (2010). Race, religion, and opposition to same-sex marriage. *Social Science Quarterly*, *91*(1), 80–98. doi:10.1111/j.1540-6237.2010.00682.x

Shore, E. (2004). Ethnic communities speak out against gay marriage. *Alternet*. Retrieved July 11, 2013, from http://food.alternet.org/story/18901/ethnic_com munities_speak_out_against_gay_marriage

Skougard, E. D. (2011, October 31). The best interests of transgender children (Student note). *Utah Law Review*, pp. 1161–1201.

Smith, T. W. (2011). *Public attitudes toward homosexuality* (pp. 1–4). Chicago, IL. Retrieved from http://www.norc.org/PDFs/2011 GSS Reports/GSS_Public Attitudes Toward Homosexuality_Sept2011.pdf

Socarides, R. (2013). The twelfth state: Minnesota approves marriage equality. *The New Yorker*. Retrieved February 10, 2014, from http://www.newyorker.com/online/blogs/newsdesk/2013/05/the-twelfth-state-minnesota-approves-marriage-equality.html

Solodnikov, V., & Chkanikova, A. (2010). Children in same-sex marriages. *Russian Social Science Review*, *51*(3), 38–59.

Solomon, S. E., Rothblum, E. D., & Balsam, K. F. (2004). Pioneers in partnership: Lesbian and gay male couples in civil unions compared with those not in civil unions and married heterosexual siblings. *Journal of Family Psychology*, *18*(2), 275–286. doi:10.1037/0893-3200.18.2.275

Spector, S. (2009). Red rock baby candy: Infertile homosexual speaks! In R. Epstein (Ed.), *Who's your daddy?: And other writings on queer parenting* (pp. 73–80). Toronto, Canada: Sumach Press.

Stacey, J. (1996). *In the name of the family: Rethinking family values in the postmodern age*. Boston, MA: Beacon Press.

Stacey, J. (1998). Gay and lesbian families: Queer like us. In M. A. Mason, A. Skolnick, & S. D. Sugarman (Eds.), *All our families: New policies for a new century* (pp. 117–143). New York, NY: Oxford University Press. Retrieved from http://www.amazon.com/All-Our-Families-Policies-Century/dp/0195108310

Stacey, J. (2006). Gay parenthood and the decline of paternity as we knew it. *Sexualities*, *9*(1), 27–55. doi:10.1177/1363460706060687

Stacey, J., & Biblarz, T. J. (2001). (How) Does the sexual orientation of parents matter? *American Sociological Review*, *66*(2), 159–183. doi:10.2307/1345670

Stacey, J., & Meadow, T. (2009). New slants on the slippery slope: The politics of polygamy and gay family rights in South Africa and the United States. *Politics & Society*, *37*(2), 167–202. doi:10.1177/0032329209333924

Stein, A., & Plummer, K. (1994). I can't even think straight: "Queer" theory and the missing sexual revolution in sociology. *Sociology Theory*, *12*(2), 178–187.

Steinberger, M. D. (2009). *Federal estate tax disadvantages for same-sex couples*. Los Angeles, CA. Retrieved from http://williamsinstitute.law.ucla.edu/wp-content/uploads/Steinberger-Federal-Estate-Tax-Nov-2009.pdf

Strah, D., & Margolis, S. (2003). *Gay dads: A celebration of fatherhood.* New York, NY: Tarcher. Retrieved from http://www.amazon.com/Gay-Dads-A-Celebration-Fatherhood/dp/1585422312

Straus, M. A. (1973). A general systems theory approach to a theory of violence between family members. *Social Science Information, 12*(3), 105–125. doi:10.1177/053901847301200306

Strozdas, J. (2011). Trendlines: Court decisions, proposed legislation, and their likely impact on binational same-sex families. *Loyola of Los Angeles Law Review, 44*(1339), 1342–1397.

Stryker, S. (2008). *Transgender history.* Berkeley, CA: Seal Press. Retrieved from http://books.google.com/books/about/Transgender_History.html?id=kEfZ1knAguMC&pgis=1

Sullivan, M. (1996). Rozzie and Harriet?: Gender and family patterns of lesbian coparents. *Gender & Society,10*(6),747–767.doi:10.1177/089124396010006005

Sullivan, M. (2001). Alma mater: Family "outings" and the making of the modern other mother (MOM). In M. Bernstein & R. Reimann (Eds.), *Queer families, queer politics* (pp. 231–253). New York, NY: Columbia University Press.

Sullivan, M. (2004). *The family of woman: Lesbian mothers, their children, and the undoing of gender.* Berkeley: University of California Press. Retrieved from http://www.amazon.com/The-Family-Woman-Lesbian-Children/dp/0520239644

Tasker, F. (2005). Lesbian mothers, gay fathers, and their children: A review. *Developmental and Behavioral Pediatrics, 26*(3), 224–240. doi:0196-206X/05/2603-0224

Tasker, F. (2013). Lesbian and gay parenting post-heterosexual divorce and separation. In A. E. Goldberg & K. R. Allen (Eds.), *LGBT-parent families: Innovations in research and implications for practice* (pp. 3–19). New York, NY: Springer.

Tasker, F., & Patterson, C. J. (2007). Research on gay and lesbian parenting. *Journal of GLBT Family Studies, 3*(2–3), 9–34. doi:10.1300/J461v03n02_02

Téllez Santaya, P. O., & Walters, A. S. (2011). Intimate partner violence within gay male couples: Dimensionalizing partner violence among Cuban gay men. *Sexuality & Culture, 15*(2), 153–178. doi:10.1007/s12119-011-9087-0

The Select Surrogate. (n.d.). Surrogacy laws by state. Retrieved July 12, 2013, from http://www.selectsurrogate.com/surrogacy-laws-by-state.html

The United States v. Windsor Opinion of the Court: 570 U. S. (2013). The United States Supreme Court. Retrieved from http://www.supremecourt.gov/opinions/12pdf/12-307_6j37.pdf

The White House. (n.d.). *Factsheet: The Violence Against Women Act.* Washington, DC. Retrieved from http://www.whitehouse.gov/sites/default/files/docs/vawa_factsheet.pdf

Thompson, J. M. (2002). *Mommy queerest: Contemporary rhetorics of lesbian maternal identity.* Amherst: University of Massachusetts Press. Retrieved from http://www.amazon.com/Mommy-Queerest-Contemporary-Rhetorics-Maternal/dp/1558493557

Tjaden, P., & Thoennes, N. (2000). *Extent, nature, and consequences of intimate partner violence: Findings from the National Violence Against Women Survey.* Washington, DC.

Tong, L. (1998). Comparing mixed-race and same-sex marriage. In R. P. Cabaj & D. W. Purcell (Eds.), *On the road to same-sex marriage: A supportive guide to psychological, political, and legal issues* (pp. 109–128). San Francisco, CA: Jossey-Bass.

Tornello, S. L., & Patterson, C. J. (2012). Gay fathers in mixed-orientation relationships: Experiences of those who stay in their marriages and of those who leave. *Journal of GLBT Family Studies, 8*(1), 85–98. doi:10.1080/15504 28X.2012.641373

Turell, S. C. (2000). A descriptive analysis of same-sex relationship violence for a diverse sample. *Journal of Family Violence, 15*(3), 281–293. doi:10.1023/A: 1007505619577

Umberson, D. (2013, June 26). Texas professors respond to new research on gay parenting. *Huffingtonpost.com.* Retrieved July 12, 2013, from http://www.huffing tonpost.com/debra-umberson/texas-professors-gay-research_b_1628988.html

UN High Commissioner for Human Rights (UN High Commissioner). (2011). *Discriminatory laws and practices and acts of violence against individuals based on their sexual orientation and gender identity.* New York, NY. Retrieved from http://www.ohchr.org/Documents/Issues/Discrimination/A.HRC.19.41_ English.pdf

UN High Commissioner for Human Rights (UN High Commissioner). (2012). *Born free and equal: Sexual orientation and gender identity in international human rights law.* Retrieved from http://www.ohchr.org/Documents/Publications/ BornFreeAndEqualLowRes.pdf

United Nations, UN News Centre. (2013, May 17). Countries must repeal laws that discriminate against LGBT individuals—UN officials. Retrieved July 12, 2013, from http://www.un.org/apps/news/story.asp?NewsID=44931#.Ud9_1vksnng

U.S. Department of Health and Human Services Administration for Children & Families. (2012). Adopting children of color. Retrieved from http://www.child welfare.gov/adoption/adoptive/minority_groups.cfm

U.S. Department of State, Bureau of Democracy, Human Rights, and Labor. (2011). *2010 country reports on human rights practices: Uganda.* Retrieved from http:// www.state.gov/j/drl/rls/hrrpt/2010/index.htm

U.S. Department of State, Bureau of Democracy, Human Rights, and Labor. (2013). *2012 country reports on human rights practices: India.* Retrieved from http:// www.state.gov/documents/organization/204611.pdf

Vaughn, R. B. (2011). Advising "non-traditional" families in multi-jurisdictional surrogacy arrangements. *American Journal of Family Law, 25*(3), 105–114.

Waite, L., & Gallagher, M. (2001). *The case for marriage: Why married people are happier, healthier and better off financially.* New York, NY: Random House. Retrieved from http://www.randomhouse.com/book/184776/the-case-for-mar riage-by-linda-waite-and-maggie-gallagher

Ware, S. M. (2009). Boldly going where few men have gone before: One trans man's experience. In R. Epstein (Ed.), *Who's your daddy? And other writings on queer parenting* (pp. 65–72). Toronto, Canada: Sumach Press.

Weeks, J., Heaphy, B., & Donovan, C. (2001). *Same sex intimacies: Families of choice and other life experiments* (Vol. 4). New York, NY: Routledge. Retrieved from http://books.google.com/books/about/Same_Sex_Intimacies.html?id=-PqjfGvHv94C&pgis=1

Weinberg, M. S., Williams, C. J., & Pryor, D. W. (1995). *Dual attraction: Understanding bisexuality*. New York, NY: Oxford University Press. Retrieved from http://www.amazon.com/Dual-Attraction-Understanding-Martin-Weinberg/dp/0195098412

Weston, K. (1991). *Families we choose: Lesbians, gays, kinship*. New York, NY: Columbia University Press.

Whalen, D. M., Bigner, J. J., & Barber, C. E. (2000). The grandmother role as experienced by lesbian women. *Journal of Women & Aging, 12*(3–4), 39–57. doi:10.1300/J074v12n03_04

Whitehead, B. D. (1993). Dan Quayle was right. *The Atlantic, 271*(4), 47–84.

Whittle, S. (2006). Foreword. In S. Stryker & S. Whittle (Eds.), *The transgender studies reader* (1st ed., pp. xi–xv). New York, NY: Routledge.

Wierckx, K., Van Caenegem, E., Pennings, G., Elaut, E., Dedecker, D., Van de Peer, F., . . . T'Sjoen, G. (2012). Reproductive wish in transsexual men. *Human Reproduction, 27*(2), 483–487. doi:10.1093/humrep/der406

Wildman, S. (2010, January 20). Children speak for same-sex marriage. *The New York Times*. Retrieved from http://www.nytimes.com/2010/01/21/fashion/21kids.html?pagewanted=all

Wilson, J. Q. (1993, April 1). The family-values debate. *Commentary*. Retrieved July 11, 2013, from http://www.commentarymagazine.com/article/the-family-values-debate/

Winkenhofer, C. D. (2008). From the mouths of babes: The truth. In *Trans forming families: Real stories about transgendered loved ones* (pp. 144–145). Washington, DC: PLAG Transgender Network.

Wittenberg, E., Joshi, M., Thomas, K. A., & McCloskey, L. A. (2007). Measuring the effect of intimate partner violence on health-related quality of life: A qualitative focus group study. *Health and Quality of Life Outcomes, 5*, 67–73. doi:10.1186/1477-7525-5-67

Wolfson, E. (2004). *Why marriage matters: America, equality, and gay people's right to marry*. New York, NY: Simon & Schuster Paperbacks.

World Professional Association for Transgender Health (WPATH). (2012). *Standards of care for the health of transsexual, transgender, and gender nonconforming people* (7th ed.). Minneapolis, MN: Author. Retrieved from http://www.wpath.org/publications_standards.cfm

Wright, J. M. (1998). *Lesbian step families: An ethnography of love*. New York, NY: Harrington Park Press. Retrieved from http://www.amazon.com/Lesbian-Step-Families-Ethnography-Innovations/dp/0789004364

Wright, J. M. (2001). "Aside from one little, tiny detail, we are so incredibly normal": Perspectives of children in lesbian step families. In M. Bernstein & R. Reimann (Eds.), *Queer families, queer politics* (pp. 272–290). New York, NY: Columbia University Press.

Yager, C., Brennan, D., Steele, L. S., Epstein, R., & Ross, L. E. (2010). Challenges and mental health experiences of lesbian and bisexual women who are trying to conceive. *Health & Social Work, 35*(3), 191–200. Retrieved from http://www.ncbi.nlm.nih.gov/pubmed/20853646

Yalom, M. (2002). *The history of a wife.* New York, NY: Perennial.

Yan, A., Peng, C., Lee, A., Rickles, J., & Abbott, L. (2004). *Asian Pacific American same-sex households: A census report on New York, San Francisco and Los Angeles.* Retrieved from http://www.aafny.org/cic/report/GLReport.pdf

Yep, G. A., Lovaas, K. E., & Elia, J. P. (2003). A critical appraisal of assimilationist and radical ideologies underlying same-sex marriage in LGBT communities in the United States. *Journal of Homosexuality, 45*(1), 45–64.

Zita, J. (1992). Male lesbians and the postmodern body. *Hypatia, 7*(4), 106–127.

Index

Figures and tables are indicated by f or t following the page number.